4-1

7/21

Alice Dunleavy

Denver

Colo,

A very fine book of a famous

Man:—

JOHN HENRY NEWMAN

JOHN HENRY NEWMAN
From a drawing in the possession of H. E. Wilberforce, Esq.

JOHN HENRY NEWMAN

BY JOHN MOODY

SHEED AND WARD · 1945 · NEW YORK

NIHIL OBSTAT
Arthur J. Scanlan, S.T.D.
Censor Librorum

IMPRIMATUR
✠ *Francis J. Spellman, D.D.*
Archbishop, New York

New York, June 14, 1945

TO MY SON

ERNEST ADDISON MOODY

We wish to make grateful acknowledgment
to the following publishers for permission
to quote from these books:

BURNS, OATES & WASHBOURNE, LTD.

Dominic Barberi in England, by Urban Young

Henry Edward Manning, by Shane Leslie

The Life and Times of Archbishop Ullathorne, by Cuthbert Butler

HOUGHTON MIFFLIN COMPANY

Cardinal Newman, by Richard Holt Hutton

LONGMANS, GREEN & CO., INC.

Cardinal Newman, by J. Lewis May

The Life of John Henry Cardinal Newman, by Wilfrid Ward

THE MACMILLAN COMPANY

A New History of the Book of Common Prayer, by W. H. Frere

The Oxford Movement, by R. W. Church

William George Ward and the Catholic Revival, by Wilfrid Ward

William George Ward and the Oxford Movement,
by Wilfrid Ward

CHARLES SCRIBNER'S SONS

Cardinal Newman, by William Barry

FOREWORD

THE YEAR 1945 marks the first centenary of John Henry Newman's reception into the Catholic Church. It was on October 9, 1845 that Father Dominic Barberi, the Italian Passionist, received him at the Littlemore retreat; and the next morning, at the first Mass ever offered in the little oratory, he received his First Communion. He was then in his forty-fifth year.

Since his death over half a century ago, numerous biographies of Cardinal Newman have appeared. There have also been published more than fifty critical and expository works and anthologies of his writings and many monographs and magazine articles relating to him and his career both as an Anglican and as a Catholic. But of this great mass of "Newmania," little is available to present-day readers. Most of it has long been out-of-print. This is also true of his own writings; there have been few recent reprints. But there is still a steady demand, at least among the studious, for books by him and about him. This, then, is one reason for another book about Newman and his times.

There is a more compelling reason why a new "life" of this great figure should prove timely. American Catholics hold Cardinal Newman in high esteem, loving his meditations and prayers and frequently quoting from his writings; but all too few are familiar with his background and life-story. Still fewer have a clear understanding of the famous Oxford Movement in the Anglican Church of a century ago, through which Newman, after a tragic struggle, reached the Catholic Church of the Ages. As for his Catholic career of nearly forty-five years, Americans, Catholic or other, seem to have little understanding of that.

The one complete biography of Newman is the definitive life by Wilfrid Ward, first published in 1912. Wilfrid Ward's life work was the study of the Oxford Movement. He covered the period in four volumes: *William George Ward and the Oxford Movement, William George Ward and the Catholic Revival, The Life and Times of Cardinal Wiseman,* and his monumental *John Henry Cardinal Newman.* These are splendid source books. He had access to many hundreds of Newman's letters; he brings together quotations from contemporary comment on every phase of Newman's life from the newspapers of the time and also from men still living who had been intimate with the Cardinal. All subsequent writers on Newman or Wiseman must of necessity be in his debt for these researches. Yet his books cannot be called source books in the ordinary use of the term. Wilfrid Ward did not merely assemble masses of material; he selected and drew it out in a certain order, and thereby established the vision of Newman and of his period which must profoundly affect all subsequent work.

Since he wrote, there have been many briefer biographies, but scarcely any one of these treats Newman's entire career in properly balanced fashion; either the Catholic period overbalances the story, to the neglect of the Anglican years, or *vice versa.* No Anglican writer has fully and accurately described the Catholic years; few Catholic writers have correctly described the Protestant or Anglican years. Perhaps it is often assumed that the Anglican years are of little significance to the Catholic reader. But they *are* significant, if only for the reason that they trace Newman's very original journey to the Catholic Church.

Late in life, Cardinal Newman said to his niece, Anne Mozley, who was then gathering his Anglican letters with a view to their publication: "Many years ago, on two distinct occasions, I came to the conclusion that if a memoir of me was to be published, a Protestant editor should take the Protestant part." In this connection I might state that for many years of my own life (before I became a Catholic) I was a member of the Protestant Episcopal Church and spent lengthy periods in each of its important divisions, High, Low and Broad. This should help me to write with some understanding of Newman as a Protestant and as an "Anglo-Catholic"—as well as of the Anglican Broad Church school. And being a Catholic for the past fifteen years, perhaps I now have some modest qualifications for writing of his Catholic career. As for my incidental comments on modern materialism and its effect on religion, it seems enough to say that I have lived and moved in the midst of its atmosphere for more than two-thirds of a century.

In this book I am attempting a popular readable narrative of Cardinal Newman and his times, giving equal attention to both his Anglican and his Catholic careers. I have tried to be interpretative, insofar as my capacity allows, introducing his Protestant background, with a somewhat detailed description of the Oxford Movement. The sources I have used are listed at the end of this book.

It will be noted that some chapters contain fairly frequent quotations from Newman's writings and from his correspondence. To allow him, wherever possible, to speak for himself, seems important. His letters, particularly, help us to an understanding of both his personality and his temperament. Moreover, by giving a little space to passages from his notable writings, there is conveyed to the reader some conception of his literary genius as well as of his deep spirituality.

JOHN MOODY

CONTENTS

JOHN HENRY NEWMAN

PART ONE

THE ANGLICAN YEARS

CHAPTER ONE

THE UNFOLDING MIND

1

JOHN HENRY NEWMAN'S LIFE all but spanned the nineteenth century. Born in London, February 21, 1801, he lived until August 11, 1890. Had he survived six months longer, he would have rounded out his ninetieth year. For the first half of his life, he was a member of the Anglican Church. During the second half, he was a Catholic.

He was the oldest son of John Newman and his wife, Jemima (Fourdrinier) Newman. The father was of a family of landed proprietors in Cambridgeshire and during John Henry's childhood and youth was a member of the banking firm of Ramsbottom, Newman and Company in the city of London. The mother was descended from a French Huguenot family which had emigrated to England at the time of the revocation of the Edict of Nantes in 1685. Both parents conformed to the Church of England, the mother being inclined towards the mild type of Calvinism which was then characteristic of many of the Low Church school.

John Henry was one of six children, three boys and three girls. He was baptized a few weeks after his birth in the old Church of St. Benet Fink, where the Royal Exchange now stands.

Neither his brothers nor his sisters (except Mary, the youngest) ever displayed any sympathetic interest in his gradual evolution, in later years, from his very Protestant upbringing to the "Anglo-Catholic" version of Christianity he reached in his twenty-ninth year. Nor did his mother, who lived on until he was thirty-five. She was a most devoted mother and very religious, but she always viewed her eldest son's religious evolution with puzzled misgiving, especially during her last years. It was surely fortunate for her peace of mind that she passed away well before there were any indications that John Henry would abandon the Anglican communion and enter the Catholic Church.

As for the father, his health undermined by business reverses after the year 1815, as a result of the economic collapse following the end of the Napoleonic wars (his banking firm was long in a precarious financial condition), he died rather suddenly in 1824. Evangelical in his upbringing, he was not particularly orthodox but tolerant of the teachings of all Protestant sects, being especially sympathetic toward the Quakers.

John Henry's two brothers were markedly different from him in temperament and tastes. Francis William, the youngest, who won a brilliant double first at Oxford, began by being quite religious and after his graduation went to Persia as a Protestant missionary—and for study also. But he seems to have lost faith in the Anglican Church very early. After his return from Persia in 1833, he fell under the influence of the Plymouth Brethren; then he joined the Baptists for a time, finally becoming a Unitarian. When he died he was said to be an agnostic. He was a good Greek and Latin scholar and made a new translation of the Iliad; later in life he was an instructor in Latin and Greek at University College, London. But he wasted his energies and had no real stability. He was often in financial straits and was frequently helped out by his brother John Henry.

The other brother, Charles Robert, was unstable and peculiar. Dropping all religious belief in his youth, he followed various fantasies throughout his long life. Very early he adopted the socialistic theories of Robert Owen, but soon, becoming disillusioned with Owen's ideas, tried to promote a plan of his own for the establishment of what he called "a new moral world." Of course it came to nothing. He, too, was often dependent financially on his brother John Henry.

Both brothers brooded over John Henry's abandonment of Calvinistic beliefs, even though they had no serious beliefs of their own. After the Cardinal's death in 1890, Francis wrote a spiteful little book attacking him. It was the work of a querulous old man in his dotage (he was over eighty when he published it). In it he admits that his brother John Henry "supported me not out of his substance, but when he knew not whence weekly and daily funds were to come"; yet he goes on to say, "I could not possibly have written freely of the late Cardinal to grieve him while he lived, but I see a new side of duty opened to me now that my words cannot pain him." The book clumsily attacks his brother's change to "Anglo-Catholicism" (about which he knew nothing) and launches into a savage attack on the Catholic Church. He attempts to refute his brother's beliefs, charging him with hypocrisy and untruth; yet he naïvely admits that he never read any of John Henry's Catholic writings! He lived for seven years after the Cardinal's death. The other brother had died in the 1880's.

The Newman family was long-lived, though the youngest sister, Mary, died early. The other two, Jemima and Harriet, married the Mozley brothers, both clergymen in the Anglican Church. They were both much influenced by their brother-in-law and worked with him in support of the Oxford Movement. But when he departed to the Catholic Church, they soon lapsed into an anomalous position between High Church and Broad Church. Jemima and Harriet were never bitter like the brothers; at times they seem to have been moderately tolerant. But, like the mother, they could not understand or clearly grasp the scope and significance of John Henry's religious pilgrimage. And of course, both were utterly horrified when, years later, he left the Church of England and entered the Catholic Church.

Such was the family in which John Henry Newman grew to man's estate and to ultimate maturity. In a sense he was the lost sheep, the wanderer from the hearthstone—a condition no doubt often duplicated in those days as well as in our own. It must have seemed harder then, when most English families held religious beliefs more seriously than do many in these indifferent days of the twentieth century.

If this growing boy early displayed a religious bent, it must have been largely inspired by the training of his mother, who tried to instill in the minds of all her children her own mild type of Calvinism. Her guidance led him very early to a great love for the King James version of the Bible; he is said to have read it from cover to cover before he was eight years old and even thus early knew whole chapters by heart. But he was also much influenced in boyhood by his father, who was a great lover of music and a devotee of Shakespeare. The father was definitely objective in temperament, had a horror of all speculative metaphysics and was an expert mathematician. He was possessed of an acute logical mind—a trait which was to be characteristic of his eldest son.

Until after John Henry had passed his seventh year, the family resided at Grey's Court, Ham, near Richmond, and here were spent the happiest days of his childhood. In a little book called *Family Adventures*, his sister Harriet describes him at the age of eleven as "a very philosophical young gentleman, very conservative and considerate"; he was fastidious and bored by society, and loved to read to the servants from serious books and explain their meaning. A prodigy indeed at eleven! When reminiscing in his old age he wrote of his boyhood home at Grey's Court: "I dreamed about it when a schoolboy as if it were paradise. It would be here where the angel faces appeared, 'loved long since and lost awhile.'" We oldsters can shed a sympathetic tear over that. Our own childhood years brought "angel faces" to most of us.

On the first of May, 1808, when he was well along in his eighth year, he was installed in a boarding school at Ealing, near London, which accommodated over two hundred boys under the care of Dr. George Nicholas of Wadham College, Oxford. Here he remained until after he was fifteen. He was a shy lad, romantic and imaginative, rather impulsive and headstrong but very affectionate, displaying mental alertness and versatility well beyond that of many gifted children. It was at Ealing that his bent for writing verse began to show itself; and here he did his first prose writing—trying to imitate Addison, and then Dr. Johnson, and finally Gibbon. He kept a copious journal, wrote plays and stories as well as verse; he says, "a sort of passion for scribbling possessed me." In referring to this period years later, in his *Apologia,* he says:

"I used to wish that the Arabian Nights were true. My imagination ran on unknown influences, on magical powers and talismans. I thought life might be a dream, or I an angel, and all this world a deception, my fellow angels, by a playful device, concealing themselves from me, and deceiving me with a semblance of a material world."

He remembered as a child staring at the lights which were kindled to celebrate the victory of Trafalgar. Indeed, he must have been greatly stirred by the unsettled times in which he grew up. When he first saw the light of day, England was at war with France, the first of the wars which, growing out of the French Revolution and the rise of Napoleon, ended with the Peace of Amiens only to be resumed two years later and to continue until the fall of Bonaparte in 1815. One wonders what may have been the feelings of this boy of fourteen when the news arrived that the Corsican had finally been overthrown.

During these eight years at the Ealing school, John Henry was not only developing his versatility in writing, but was becoming a voracious reader, displaying a strong penchant for the great dramatists like Shakespeare, and also for the historical romances of Sir Walter Scott. Evidently as yet he knew little or nothing of writers like John Milton or other seventeenth century Puritans. He never mentions Bunyan, for instance. And certainly he seems not to have been influenced by his father's interest in writers like Benjamin Franklin and Thomas Jefferson—nor any of the other sceptics that fascinated the old gentleman.

Nevertheless he does tell us of some slight wanderings into sceptical fields. He says, "When I was fourteen I read Paine's tracts against the Old Testament, and found pleasure in thinking of the objections which were contained in them. Also, I read some of Hume's Essays; and perhaps that on miracles. So at least I gave my father to understand; but perhaps it was a brag. Also, I recollect copying out some French verses, perhaps Voltaire's, in denial of the immortality of the soul, and saying to myself something like 'How dreadful, but how plausible!'"

2

In December 1816, shortly before his sixteenth birthday, John Henry set out with his father for Oxford. And here is one of the accidents of his life which had most far-reaching consequences— that Oxford rather than Cambridge was chosen. We are told that even when the post-chaise was at the door, Mr. Newman was still in doubt as to which university to choose. But on the urging of the curate at St. James's Church, Piccadilly, who just then happened by, Oxford was at the last moment chosen.

It was the father's intention to enter his son at Exeter, but there happened to be no room. He was matriculated at Trinity College, which, after all, according to Dr. Nicholas, was "most gentlemanlike." In the following June, young Newman went into residence there and, within less than a year, won a Trinity Scholarship. His first tutor was the well known Dr. Thomas Short, who, when meeting the happy father after the winning of the Scholarship, is said to have exclaimed, "Oh, Mr. Newman, what *have* you given us in your son!"

He was to be at the university for a long time; to take his degree at Trinity College in 1820; to acquire an Oriel Fellowship in 1822; to take Orders in the Anglican Church before he was twenty-four and to be offered a curacy at once; then to tutor for some years at Oriel and to become the Vicar of St. Mary's, the University church, in the year 1828, a post which he would hold for more than fifteen years.

When he matriculated at Oxford, he of course had no intimation of the sort of career that was in store for him. All he then had in mind, apparently, was to secure a good classical education, to be followed, perhaps, by his becoming a barrister (a course which seems to have been the choice of his father) ; and he may then have dreamed of a public career—some day to become a power in the House of Commons, like William Pitt, perhaps, or Edmund Burke.

But to qualify such dreams, if they ever occurred, something important happened to him shortly after his arrival at Oxford. He tells us that until he had passed his fourteenth year he was not very religious—although he always possessed a profound consciousness of the reality of God. While he wished to be virtuous, he did not like the idea of being thought religious. But just as he went into residence at Oxford, he came under the influence of the Reverend Walter Mayers, one of the classical teachers at Pembroke College. Mr. Mayers was a very pious Low Churchman, and Newman says he received from him "deep religious impressions, at the time Calvinistic in character, which were to me the beginning of a new life." He ever after regarded this experience as his "first conversion."

"Above and beyond the conversations and sermons of the excellent man, long dead," he said in his *Apologia*, many years later, "who was the human means of this beginning of divine faith in me, was the effect of the books which he put into my hands, all of the school of Calvin. . . . I believed that the inward conversion of which I was conscious (and of which I am still more certain than that I have hands and feet), would last into the next life, and that I was elected to eternal glory. I have no consciousness that this belief had any tendency whatever to lead me to be careless about pleasing God. I retained it till the age of twenty-one, when it gradually faded away; but I believe that it had some influence on my opinions, in the direction of those childish imaginations which I have already mentioned, viz., in isolating me from the objects which surrounded me, in confirming me in my mistrust of the reality of material phenomena, and making me rest in the thought of two and two only absolute and luminously self-evident beings, myself and my Creator; for while I considered myself predestined to salvation, my mind did not dwell upon others, as fancying them simply passed over, not predestined to eternal death. I only thought of the mercy to myself."

Here we have a picture of a very serious, pious youth, preoccupied with the heinousness of sin and no doubt watching his step in his daily doings in true puritanical fashion. It is perhaps hard for the present-day college boy, whether sophisticated or not, to visualize the serious young Calvinist of a century or more ago. The pious are not so gloomy today.

But perhaps John Henry was not all gloomy. His imagination was too vital for that. He had a sense of humor as well as a keen, objective sensitiveness to the brighter side of life. Yet it is quite evident that, from seventeen on, theological questions continuously gripped his mind at Oxford. He read many sermons and studied much religious literature, no doubt under the guidance of his mentor, Mr. Mayers, frequently expressing views which label him as an ardent disciple of John Calvin. Before he was eighteen he was composing sermons for his own edification and guidance, dissecting questions like predestination and efficacious grace. Some of the texts of these youthful sermons preached to himself remind one of the outpourings from certain Protestant pulpits of a century or more ago: "These shall go into everlasting punishment" or, "Man is like to vanity, his days are as a shadow," and so on.

Had he continued on this course until maturity, he might have had a life career as a sensational and supremely self-satisfied evangelist mission preacher—or else ultimately have reverted into complete scepticism—probably the latter, for his mind was too acute for him to adhere permanently to a mere emotional religion. But his Calvinism began to break up before it was firmly "set." Well before he was twenty-one he became interested in a man who made a very deep impression upon him—Dr. Thomas Scott, Rector of Aston Sandford, a distinguished writer on religious subjects. To Dr. Scott, he says, "I almost owe my soul". Dr. Scott cured him of "the detestable doctrine of predestination," which had been all but gripping him. It was a complete cure.

He made a thorough study of Scott's essays. He says they implanted deep in his mind for the first time a zealous faith in the doctrine of the Holy Trinity. This led him to an intimate study of the Athanasian Creed. Dr. Scott also fixed permanently in his mind the need of *holiness* rather than peace as the guide of life; and "growth the only evidence of life." Here were seeds which would fructify many years later and mark his entire career; we find evidences of this in his doctrine of "development" and in his great work on faith and reason. It was also in these early days that he studied Joseph Milner's Church History, which gave him his first acquaintance with St. Augustine, St. Ambrose and the early Church Fathers.

But it was also about this time that he read Newton on the Prophecies, and in consequence he "became most firmly convinced that the Pope was the Anti-Christ predicted by Daniel, St. Paul and St. John." In referring to this in the *Apologia* he says: "My imagination was stained by the effects of this doctrine up to the year 1843; it had been obliterated from my reason and judgment at an earlier date, but the thought remained upon me as a sort of false conscience. Hence came that conflict of mind, which so many have felt besides myself. . . ."

His inherent Protestant bias against Catholicism was then deep-seated and strong, even though he had entered a transition period leading away from the theology earlier imbibed from Mr. Mayers. Perhaps this change was partly unconscious, for a letter to his mother in reply to one in which she has evidently shown distress over his religious broodings throws some light on his mentality at this particular time.

"As to my opinions, and the sentiments I expressed in my last letter, they remain fixed in my mind, and are repeated deliberately and confidently. If it were any new set of opinions I had lately adopted, they might be said to arise from nervousness or over-study, or ill health; but no, my opinions have been exactly the same for these five years. The only thing is, opportunities have occurred for my mentioning them more than before; but believe me, these sentiments are neither new nor lightly founded. If they made me melancholy, morose, austere, distant, reserved, sullen, then indeed they might with justice be the subject of anxiety; but if, as I think is the case, I am always cheerful, if at home I am ready and eager to join in any merriment, if I am not clouded with sadness, if my meditations make me neither absent in mind nor deficient in action, then my principles may be gazed at and puzzle the gazer, but they cannot be accused of any bad practical effects."

This is a serious mood, well and solemnly put. But he was not usually so seriously solemn as that. His imagination was vivid, his temperament bright and sparkling. His great love was his violin, on which he was a notable performer. In the field of sports he seems to have been a cypher, but his study hours were by no means confined to religious subjects; they were largely devoted to the classical and secular. While mastering Latin and Greek, he was falling in love with Cicero; and in philosophy, Francis Bacon and John Locke (both heterodox enough!) were his main guides. In the study of history at this time, Gibbon stands out for him as the great master of ancient and medieval lore.

Indeed, exhaustion due to overwork and intense application in his studies resulted in his doing poorly in the B.A. examinations. He secured only second-class honours. This was a keen disappointment which seems never to have been wholly alleviated in his mind by any later success. But it was only about a year after this that he atoned for this failure in the Schools (certainly in the minds of his friends) by winning the Oriel Fellowship—then regarded as a great triumph.

One man who had a marked influence on him in these early years was Dr. Hawkins, then a tutor and later the Provost of Oriel. Dr. Hawkins taught him how to reason logically, and it was through him that he discovered the doctrine of Tradition— and that the Church was the true interpreter of Scripture. Indeed, the influence of Dr. Hawkins did much to cleanse his thought of what remained of its Calvinistic coloring, as well as to enable him to grasp fully the doctrine of Baptismal Regeneration. Dr. Hawkins, however, was far from being a High Churchman. He was really a conservative Low Churchman—not of the evangelical school.

Judging by young Newman's activities and expressed views when he gained his Oriel Fellowship in 1822, he was an ardent Low Churchman who had dropped the last of his Calvinistic aberrations. Long before this time, he had reached the conviction that he was destined to lead a life of celibacy—a conviction which, after a few temporary doubts, had become permanent in his mind by the time he was twenty-eight.

Such was his state when, after debating the matter for long, he definitely decided on the Anglican ministry as his life vocation. I do not say that he chose the "priesthood"; for when he made his decision it is quite obvious that he had no notion of an "Apostolic priesthood." He tells us that he was far advanced in his preparations for ordination when the Reverend William James, then a Fellow of Oriel, "taught me the doctrine of Apostolic Succession, in the course of a walk, I think, round Christ Church meadow. I recollect being somewhat impatient of the subject at the time."

Whether his decision to enter the Anglican ministry pleased his father (as it no doubt did his mother and sisters) is not clear. But it is known that the father had come to feel that a barrister's profession might be unsuitable for this talented son whose religious leanings were so pronounced. The old gentleman saw his son ordained, but he did not survive far beyond the day. He died in October of that year. In Newman's brief memoir of these early years, he quotes the following item from his journal:

"Performed the last sad rites to my dear father. When I die, shall I be followed to the grave by my children? My mother said the other day she hoped to see me married; but I think I shall either die within college walls, or as a missionary in a foreign land. No matter where, so that I die in Christ."

3

Ordained to the diaconate in June 1824, he was at once offered the curacy of St. Clement's, Oxford, an old church too small for a congregation which had doubled in twenty years. The infirm old rector needed a young curate to look after his large congregation—mostly poor, ignorant people—and to help promote the erection of a larger church. It was quite a task for a novice, but on the urging of Edward Bouverie Pusey he accepted it—not, however, until he had also consulted Mr. Mayers, who likewise urged him to accept it. Thus he was being guided, perhaps for the first time, by the potential High Churchman Dr. Pusey as well as by the seasoned Low Churchman Mr. Mayers. But Pusey was scarcely as yet in the High Church category; he had not been ordained, and his reputation was still to be made. A few lines regarding him will, however, fit into the narrative here.

Edward Bouverie Pusey was born at Pusey House, Berkshire, in 1800. The son of Philip Bouverie of Pusey, he assumed the name of the manor on his father's death. Educated at Eton and Christ Church College, Oxford, he became a Fellow of Oriel in 1824. He was a brilliant scholar and graduated with high honors. Shortly after his ordination in 1825, he married, and then left for Göttingen, Germany, where he studied oriental languages and patristic theology. Returning to Oxford in 1828, he was appointed by the Duke of Wellington, then Prime Minister, to the Chair of Regius Professor of Hebrew and also made Canon of Christ Church.

His youthful theological views are obscure, but he had become a close student of Church history, which seems to have led him to much admiration of the High Church movement of the seventeenth century. This development was gradual, however. Not for some years after 1828 did he display any interest in the High Church stirrings among the young men at Oxford. But after the movement began to take form in 1833, his interest awakened, though he maintained a detached attitude until 1835. In the latter year he contributed to the series of Tracts for the Times an important essay on the sacrament of Baptism; he then joined actively in the High Church revival.

During subsequent years, Dr. Pusey became a prolific writer of scholarly treatises, most of them lengthy and ponderous and of little popular appeal. As a preacher he was turgid and dull. But he was a lovable character, gentle and charitable, though his austerity prevented him from making many intimate friends. However, he was blessed with an optimistic, imaginative temperament, which was reflected in his strong belief that the Anglican

Church could in time be converted to the Catholic teachings of the "Church of Antiquity" (meaning the Church of the first half-dozen centuries). He later did much, by his writings and other activities, to promote the practice in the Anglican Church of auricular confession and was a strong advocate of the doctrine of the Real Presence in the Holy Eucharist—as interpreted by the High Church school of the seventeenth century.

It is sometimes assumed that John Keble, who, prior to 1824, was a tutor at Oriel, must have begun to influence Newman very early. But this is not so. John Keble then viewed Newman as a young Evangelical Low Churchman of sceptical tendencies and displayed no interest in him.

But Keble's judgment of Newman was at that time not wholly accurate. It is indeed true that Newman then seemed to be taking the path that many Evangelicals ultimately choose—the path to a species of broad scepticism and loose thinking in relation to Christian dogma; for the Evangelical was then as now dominated more by emotion than reason, and his doctrinal anchor would drag easily. When John Keble was having doubts about Newman, the latter had come under the influence of Dr. Robert Whately, who, after leaving Oxford some years later, became the Anglican archbishop of Dublin. Whately was neither High nor Low Church, but one of a new school of "liberal" theologians—as was also Dr. Thomas Arnold of Rugby fame, the religious views of whose son Matthew Arnold, in later life, indicate the direction in which this new school was heading. Keble thought Whately's influence with Newman was leading the latter quite definitely astray.

As for Whately's actual influence on Newman, it is clearly stated in the *Apologia*. He says, "While I was still awkward and timid in 1822, he took me by the hand, and acted towards me the part of a gentle and encouraging instructor. He emphatically opened my mind, and taught me to think and to use my reason. After being first noticed by him in 1822, I became very intimate

with him in 1825, when I was his Vice-Principal at Alban Hall.
I gave up that office in 1826, when I became Tutor of my College, and his hold upon me gradually relaxed. . . . His mind
was too different from mine for us to remain long on one line.
. . What he did for me in point of religious opinion, was, first,
to teach me the existence of the Church as a substantive body
or corporation; next to fix in me those anti-Erastian views of
Church polity which were one of the most prominent features of
the Tractarian movement."

But perhaps more important was the recommendation by Dr.
Whately that he study Bishop Butler's *Analogy*, a masterly work
which, far from inducing sceptical views, places Christianity on
a philosophical basis, though Butler's theology was not flawless.
An Anglican prelate of the eighteenth century, he defended
revealed religion against deism and made much of the doctrine of
"probability" as the guide to faith. Newman's study of Butler's
masterpiece influenced his thinking for all the years. In his *Apologia* he says: ". . . if I may attempt to determine what I most
gained from it, it lay in two points . . . they are the underlying
principles of a great portion of my teaching. First, the very idea
of an analogy between the separate works of God leads to the
conclusion that the system which is of less importance is econom-
ically or sacramentally connected with the more momentous
system, and of this conclusion the theory, to which I was inclined
as a boy, viz., the unreality of material phenomena, is an ultimate resolution. . . . Secondly, Butler's doctrine of Probability
as the guide of life, led me, at least under the teaching to which
a few years later I was introduced, to the question of the logical
cogency of Faith, on which I have written so much. Thus to Butler I trace those two principles of my teaching, which have led to
a charge against me both of fancifulness and of scepticism."

While it did look on the surface as though the intimacy with
Whately was, as Keble thought, leading Newman astray, his
study of Butler was having the reverse effect. A definite break

with Whately soon followed. Whately was of course indignant when he found his star pupil throwing him overboard. But Newman's mind was far deeper and more penetrating than Whately's —as the subsequent history of both men was to demonstrate in time.

It is interesting to follow Newman's mental and spiritual progress from this time on. His experience at St. Clement's from 1824 to 1826 was invaluable to him. Parish work among the poor and his preaching, which was steadily improving with practice, were giving him stability and force as well an increase in his growing sense of the spiritual aspects of his calling. No longer the timid, hesitating student, self-control and aggressiveness were now his outstanding characteristics. At this time he said of the "two-bottle orthodox": "Those who make comfort the great subject of their preaching, seem to mistake the end of their ministry. *Holiness* is the great end. There must be a struggle and a toil here. Comfort is a cordial, but no one drinks cordials from morning till night." [1]

Newman had been ordained to the Anglican priesthood in May of 1825. Within a year thereafter he was passing out from the influence of Whately, and if John Keble was watching him then, he must have felt that Whately's pupil was improving. No devotee of the Whately philosophy would have produced a sermon like "The Lapse of Time"—a little masterpiece of its kind —delivered in 1827. Newman may have been giving side glances at John Keble's teaching even thus early.

Who was this John Keble, the future great friend and guide of the rising young preacher? He was the son of a Gloucestershire clergyman who sent his two sons to Oxford, where John, the elder (born in 1792) proved an unusually brilliant scholar. After ordination to the ministry, he was a tutor of Oriel College for a number of years. He was, like his father, a deeply convinced High

---

[1] Those clergymen designated as "two-bottle orthodox" were the self-indulgent pastors whose religious zeal was manifested mainly by drinking port wine to the health of Church and King on every possible public occasion.

Churchman when that appellation, taken in its genuine sense, was anything but common or popular in England. He was a strong defender of the so-called "Catholic" interpretation of the Anglican Book of Common Prayer; and he was of course a bitter opponent of the religious views of both Dr. Whately and Dr. Thomas Arnold. On the other hand, he was a great admirer of the sixteenth century Richard Hooker, author of the famous controversial work *Laws of Ecclesiastical Polity,* who was still regarded by some High Churchmen as strictly orthodox because he defended certain Anglican formularies against the Puritans of his day. Hooker was particularly revered by High Churchmen as a defender of the Catholic doctrine of the Holy Eucharist.[1] Keble was, in fact, one of the few outstanding champions of the seventeenth century "Catholicising movement" in the English Church, which had come to naught in the eighteenth century. At the same time, the traditional anti-Popery attitude, also characteristic of his father, ran strong in his veins—fully as strong as in Newman's.

John Keble had left Oxford at the end of 1823, feeling that his true vocation was to follow his father as a country pastor. He cared not for emoluments of any kind, nor for the excitement or responsibilities of leadership. Poetically inclined, very imaginative, and steeped in the best Greek and Latin literature and early Church history, he found the writing of religious verse his most congenial avocation. The well known volume *The Christian Year,* which became a classic of its kind, was written by him during the early years of his curacy in his father's parish at Halford—where he continued until after his marriage in 1835, when he became

---

[1] Yet Richard Hooker's defence of this doctrine was strikingly vague and confusing. He said: "Why do we vainly trouble ourselves with so fierce contentions whether by Consubstantiation or Transubstantiation the Sacrament itself be first possessed with Christ, or no? A thing which in no way can further or hinder us, however it stand, because our participation of Christ in this Sacrament dependeth on the cooperation of His omnipotent power which maketh it His body and blood to us." Keble, who sincerely believed in the Real Presence, was never able to explain it any more clearly than that. But then, neither do the Anglican formularies!

rector of Hursley parish, in which he remained until his death in 1866.

Long after he became a Catholic, Newman commented on *The Christian Year* as follows: "When the general tone of religious literature was so nerveless and impotent, Keble struck an original note and woke up in the hearts of thousands a new music, the music of a school long unknown in England. Nor can I pretend to analyze, in my own instance, the effect of religious teaching so deep, so pure, so beautiful. I have never till now tried to do so; yet I think I am not wrong in saying, that the two main intellectual truths which it brought home to me, were the same two which I had learned from Butler, though recast in the creative mind of my new master. The first of these was what may be called, in a large sense of the word, the Sacramental System. . . . the second intellectual principle which I gained from Mr. Keble . . . the firmness of assent which we give to religious doctrine, not to the probabilities which introduced it. . . . It is faith and love which give to probability a force which it has not in itself. . . . Thus the argument from Probability, in the matter of religion, became an argument from Personality, which in fact is one form of the argument from Authority. . . . I did not at all dispute this view of the matter, for I made use of it myself; but I was dissatisfied, because it did not go to the root of the difficulty."

Although living thus quietly in the country, John Keble by no means limited his interests to parish work or to the writing of verse. He had long viewed with alarm the antichristian tendencies both within his Church and outside it, which were spreading throughout the country. He was also much distressed by the effects of Erastianism,[1] which he viewed as a calamity for the Church.

---

[1] The term "Erastianism" is derived from the name of Thomas Erastus, who was a follower of Zwingli, the Swiss reformer, and before Luther came to the same view, was a pronounced advocate of the subservience of the Church to the State. After Zwingli's death, Erastus developed his theory further, basing

He saw increasing power coming into the hands of men who were utterly indifferent to the character of religious teaching. Yet as a country parson with few friends who saw eye to eye with him on such matters, it seemed unlikely that he would be able to make his influence felt outside his own limited circle.

But what at first seemed a minor incident cleared the way. When Keble had left Oxford at the close of 1823, one of his younger pupils was Richard Hurrell Froude, an elder brother of James Anthony Froude, who in later life wrote history and wandered far from his youthful pro-Catholic views. Now Keble had liked Hurrell Froude at Oxford and had later kept in touch with him; and when Froude was about to finish his University studies, Keble invited him to spend the Long Vacation at Halford, where he could study at leisure for his degree. At the same time he invited two others, Robert Wilberforce and Isaac Williams, also Oxford students.

Hurrell Froude was, as Newman has said, "an Englishman to the backbone"; but he was unique. Although a strong Tory, he never hesitated to express radical or rebellious views if the occasion seemed to demand it. Deeply religious and a strong believer in traditional Christianity, he was an independent thinker who went to the bottom of things, both human and divine. One of these things was the Anglican Church, which he criticised forcefully and boldly. "His judgments of the [sixteenth century] Reformers, startling as they were at the time," commented Dean Church, "are not so very different, as to the facts of the case, from what most people now agree in. Whatever allowances may be made for the difficulties of the time—and however well they may have done parts of their work, such as the translations and adaptations of the Prayer Book—it is safe to say that the divines

---

it on the old Jewish law. Hence the policy of State control over religion came to be called Erastianism. But the term is really a misnomer; for long before Erastus appeared on the scene, King Henry VIII adopted the principle in England, while his daughter Elizabeth established it as a permanent system for that country. It still exists in England.

of the Reformation never can again, with their confessed Calvinism, their shifting opinions, their extravagant deference to the foreign oracles of Geneva and Zurich, and their subservience to bad men in power, be the heroes and saints of Churchmen." [1]

But in Hurrell Froude's day, these reformers *were* honored as heroes and saints—to the great indignation of this unique English Tory.

While Froude cherished a strong bias in favor of High Church principles, he was not very seriously interested in the history of the "Church of Antiquity"—the subject of all subjects that young High Anglicans were then concentrating on—but was more interested in the medieval Church and the events that preceded the Protestant Reformation of the sixteenth century. And he was more inclined to be tolerant towards the Catholic Church than were those still affected by the traditional British distrust of the Papacy.

Froude shocked many by his views, which he always expressed with blunt frankness. He was bitterly resentful of the status of the Anglican Church at that time, with its multitude of Protestant bishops, heretical schools of thought, and Evangelical leanings. He was devoted to the Anglican Prayer Book and could not understand why so many failed to see that it was not Protestant but Catholic, being a direct outgrowth, he insisted, of the Latin service books of the pre-Reformation Church. And with all the confusion he saw in his own Church, he longed for some definite authority to endorse and strengthen his own convictions.

This was his mood when he visited John Keble for the Long Vacation. And evidently he found his craving for "authority" answered in Keble himself, for the latter's charming personality, with his purity and keenness of mind, disposed Froude to accept without much reserve this master's teaching. Perhaps this was also true of Robert Wilberforce and Isaac Williams. In any event, in

---

[1] R. W. Church, *The Oxford Movement.*

these young men John Keble gained enthusiastic disciples before they returned to Oxford.

Not long after, Hurrell Froude was elected a Fellow of Oriel, and in time he became a tutor of the college. He thus came in contact with Newman, who was now "moving out of the shadow of Liberalism." They soon became fast friends; which had far-reaching consequences, as we shall see.

4

At the close of 1826, Newman resigned his curacy at St. Clement's and returned to the University as a tutor of Oriel. The next year he was made the Public Examiner of Classics. And finally, in 1828, on the retirement of Dr. Hawkins, he became Vicar of St. Mary's, the University church. Almost immediately his Sunday afternoon sermons began to attract attention.

Down to this time there seems to have been little outward indication of his departing very far from Low Churchmanship, even though Hurrell Froude must have influenced him to some extent. It was characteristic of Low Churchmen at this time, if they changed at all, to wander into a species of Arminianism.[1] They seldom were drawn towards Catholicism, even of a diluted kind. But, it will be recalled, Newman had years before been an ardent student of Milner's Church history, which had led him to study St. Chrysostom and other early Fathers. And while still at St.

[1] *Arminianism* was a modified type of Calvinism adopted by one section of the Netherlands Calvinists in the seventeenth century. It is so called from the leader of the sect, Jacobus Arminius, who was a professor at Leyden. His followers were called the "Remonstrants," as were the five propositions he proclaimed against the teachings of John Calvin. These rejected the doctrines of predestination, election, the teaching that Christ died for the elect only, and that grace benefits only the elect. Ultimately Arminianism diluted most of its positive teachings and became one of the precursors of the widely held modern view that "one religion is as good as another."

Clement's he had devoted his leisure moments to writing a short life of Apollonius of Tyana and an essay on Scripture miracles. From this he was led, in 1827 or 1828, to write an elaborate defence of infant Baptism, based mainly on patristic evidences, a work which shows how well he had now grasped the orthodox doctrine of Baptismal Regeneration. It was a distinct contradiction of the indifferent Protestant view of Baptism as a mere rite or symbol which has no supernatural effect on the soul. And now he was devoting himself to a still more intense study of the early Church Fathers.

"This was the period," he says, "when I came out of my shell. From that time my tongue was, as it were, loosened." His intimacy with Hurrell Froude was undoubtedly now beginning to tell; for we soon see a great change and a more definite veering in the direction of the High Church position.

In the *Apologia* he says that there were two or three years of "drifting" but that in the year 1829 he was "rudely awakened by two great blows, illness and bereavement; and then came the increasing intimacy with Hurrell Froude." The bereavement, which affected him very deeply and awakened him further to the spiritual aspects of his calling, was the sudden death of his sister Mary. She had always shown greater sympathy for his religious changes than had the other sisters, and her loss utterly crushed him. Even in old age, we find him still thinking of her most tenderly.

His systematic study of Church history and the early Fathers —especially the Alexandrian school—preoccupied him from now on. The more he studied, the farther he got away from his former Protestant viewpoint. He no longer spoke with respect of the sixteenth century reformers, but began to show increasing interest in and respect for the seventeenth century Caroline divines.[1] He

---

[1] "Caroline divines" were those Anglican prelates and scholars of the seventeenth century, beginning with Archbishop Laud and Bishop Launcelot Andrewes, who lived prior to and during the reign of Charles I; and also

was now becoming more vividly aware that the divinely revealed truths of Christianity, as interpreted by the early Church Fathers and Church Councils, had been largely forgotten by the Established Church during the long domination of the Low Churchmen. The High Church view was that these great revealed truths should once more be brought to life and defended as the fundamental doctrines of the Anglican Church, which (he now had come to feel, for the first time) was really not a Protestant Church at all, but the true Church Catholic in England—that is to say, a true branch of the historic Catholic Church.

In our day there is an active, aggressive group calling itself "Anglo-Catholic," which firmly holds this view of the Church of England and of the American Episcopal Church; but in the 1820's this idea was decidedly novel. John Keble held it, with a few others; scarcely one of the English bishops held it. To the question, What is the Church of Christ? there were a multitude of answers. It is an invisible and mystical body, said the Low Churchmen; it is the Parliamentary creation of the Reformation, said the Erastians; it is "the Establishment," said the politicians and a great majority of the laity; it is the aggregate of separate congregations, said the Dissenters. The Catholic answer, that it is the Church in communion with the Pope, was of course cried down everywhere.

But to get a definite opinion regarding the Anglican Church itself was equally difficult. Keble and his friends said they were fighting for a Church of England as conceived by the High Anglican divines of the seventeenth century. Yet while Richard Hooker, so admired by Keble, had said that the Church of England was "the nation of England," Dr. Thomas Arnold, whose ideas of the purposes of the Church were the reverse of Keble's, said the same thing! And Dr. Whately, who said that the Church

the High Churchmen of Charles II's time who followed them; as well as a number who lived on through the days of James II and the Revolution of 1688 and after, even into the early years of the eighteenth century.

of England was a divine religious society, unique in its origin and
existence (as did Keble), contradicted Keble all along the line
regarding the purposes for which it had been created.

It will be seen, therefore, that for Newman to work his way
through this labyrinthine tangle to solid ground was no mean
undertaking. But through Hurrell Froude he was now being
brought closer to John Keble. It was the view of John Keble he
was expressing, as well as his own, when in the spring of 1829, in
a letter to his mother discussing the Anglican Church, he deplored the growing Liberal opinion of the day and expressed views
which were surely strange to her Calvinistic mind.

"We live in a novel era, one in which there is an advance
towards universal education. Men have hitherto depended on
others, and especially on the clergy, for religious truth; now each
man attempts to judge for himself. Now, without meaning of
course that Christianity is in itself opposed to free inquiry, still
I think it *in fact* at the present time opposed to the particular
form which that liberty of thought has now assumed. Christianity
is of faith, modesty, lowliness, subordination; but the spirit at
work against it is one of latitudinarianism, indifferentism, and
schism, a spirit which tends to overthrow doctrine, as if the fruit
of bigotry and discipline—as if the instrument of priestcraft. All
parties seem to acknowledge that the stream of opinion is setting
against the Church. . . . It is no reply to say that the majesty of
truth will triumph, for man's nature is corrupt; also, even should
it triumph, still this will only be ultimately, and the meanwhile
may last for centuries. Yet I do still think that there is a promise
of preservation to the Church, and in its Sacraments there are
such means of Heavenly Grace, that I do not doubt that it (the
Church) will live on even in the most irreligious and sceptical
times."

That brief but well-put statement sums up the anti-Liberal
view, not of the great Protestant majority in the Established
Church, but of the school of High Churchmen, soon to be called

"Anglo-Catholics," who would shortly start a movement in the Church of England which would be greeted, first by ridicule, but ultimately by consternation among the bishops. These bishops, accredited by the Crown and Parliament, naturally viewed the Church as an established creature of the State. Doctrine and discipline, as always in the past, were to be determined, in the last analysis, by the government of England, which cared little or nothing for the principles that Keble and his small group were trying to bring to the front. At this particular time this "liberal" view was the popular one; not the view of Keble, Froude, Newman and their following.[1]

Was there really any chance, in the face of such opposition, to popularize the ideas of Keble and his friends? Aside from the small group at Oxford, the field seemed quite bare; and John Keble himself was only a country pastor far from Oxford. But under the surface, things were stirring. The energetic Froude, with Isaac Williams, Henry and Robert Wilberforce and other young men, was busily proselytising; Newman was as busily writing; and his sermons, which were becoming more Catholic in tone, were beginning to attract much comment. The yeast was working.

Incidentally, his sermons were beginning to cause uneasiness among many of his Protestant friends; even within his own family. A letter from his sister Harriet reads: "We have read your two sermons. They are *very* High Church. I don't think I am near so High as that!"

Within a short time after Newman was installed as the Vicar of St. Mary's, he began writing his *Arians of the Fourth Century,*

---

[1] The term "liberal" has many connotations. In our day it is used, in a broad sense, to denote all sorts of "progressive" or loose political or economic views, generally of a democratic or even socialistic or communistic character—as well as "free-thinking" in the domain of religious beliefs. But as used in Newman's time and by him, it was more specifically the designation of those who were indifferent or opposed to orthodox Christianity and believers in the doctrines of the rising schools of secular and materialistic philosophy. This Liberal view is elaborated to some extent in the next chapter.

his first attempt at an extended historical study—although he had already written some briefer studies. The *Arians* was to be a prelude to a complete history of the early Church Councils. He never fully carried out this plan, though later he wrote voluminously of St. Athanasius. The Alexandrian Fathers were of lifelong interest to him.[1]

His Arian researches had a marked effect on his mind. The Church of the fourth century seemed to him to be in a strikingly similar position to that of the Anglican Church of the nineteenth century. As an Anglican drawn to the High Church view, he had of course been much disturbed by the fact that the English Sees were filled with very Protestant bishops. But the Catholic Sees in the fourth century were largely filled with Arian bishops. This fact profoundly impressed him. As the Catholic Church in the fourth century had in time weathered the Arian intrusions, could not the modern Anglican Church also in time weather the intrusions of Protestantism and still preserve its integrity as an Apostolic Church? It may well be that he conjured up the hope (as has been suggested by some writers) that a new Athanasius or Basil would arise to set things right in England as did these militant Catholics in their own day. Indeed, his still youthful imagination may have made him dream that this might be his own future role!

5

The *Arians* was finished in 1832, but did not appear in print until 1833. It was such an arduous task that it utterly exhausted

---

[1] "Arianism" was a widespread heresy propagated by one Arius early in the fourth century. It denied the Divinity of Christ and the doctrine of the Holy Trinity and was the main source for many other heresies. Arius, who lived from A.D. 250 to 336, introduced the heresy at Alexandria, and it spread rapidly, bringing on a distressing period for the Church. It was bitterly fought by St. Athanasius and was condemned at the Council of Nicaea in 325, when Arius himself was banished.

him; a long rest was an urgent necessity. Two years had been
given to the work, with all his other duties. Then came the news
that Froude was planning a trip with his father to the Mediterranean, primarily for Hurrell's health, which was very bad at the
time. They invited Newman to accompany them, an invitation
which he gladly accepted. They started in the early part of December 1832, sailing from England on the ship *Hermes,* bound
for Malta.

For Newman it was a thrilling experience, being his first sea
voyage. The trip through the Mediterranean blended well with
his recent studies of early Church history. He says, "I thought of
St. Paul's shipwreck at Malta; of Cyprian's and Athanasius'
journeys to Rome; of the Phoenicians, of Tyre, of the Punic
wars, and of the glorious churches, now annihilated." He wrote
many interesting letters on the journey, most of them to his
mother and sisters, to John Keble and other close friends. And
throughout the voyage he wrote verses, many of them bearing on
the ancient Church, her fortunes and misfortunes. The best of
these were later included in the *Lyra Apostolica.*

They visited Gibraltar, Malta, Corfu, Palermo, Messina and
Naples, and finally reached Rome, which, of course, made the
most lasting impression. They visited all the famous churches
and holy places, beginning with St. Peter's. Newman was profoundly impressed, despite his deep conviction that Rome "embraced awful perversions of the truth." Yet as a whole it fascinated him; many of his letters indicate this. In one letter he
writes:

"And now what can I say of Rome, but that it is the first of
cities, and that all I ever saw are as dust (even dear Oxford in-
clusive) compared with its majesty and glory. Is it possible that
so serene and lofty a place is the cage of unclean creatures? I will
not believe it until I have evidence of it. In St. Peter's yesterday,
in St. John Lateran today, I have felt quite abased, chiefly by
their enormous size, added to the extreme accuracy and grace of

their proportions, which makes one feel little and contemptible. . . ."

His enthusiasm was profound and lasting, despite his confused
feelings regarding the Church which Rome housed. In a letter to
his sister Harriet, he shows his mixed feelings:

"Rome grows more wonderful every day. The first thought one
has of the place is awful—that you see the great enemy of God—
the Fourth Monarchy, the Beast dreadful and terrible. . . . It is
strange to be standing in the city of the Apostles, and among the
tombs of martyrs and saints. . . . The Roman clergy are said to
be a decorous, orderly body, and certainly most things are very
different from Naples. There are no trumpery ornaments and
absurd inscriptions on the streets, profaning the most sacred subjects, and the look of the priests is superior. . . . But the chor-
isters at St. Peter's are as irreverent as those at St. Paul's."

A heavy correspondence with Keble, with his friend Henry
Bowden and others (they were keeping him in touch with events
in England), and letters to Thomas Mozley, Frederick Rogers and
Albany Christie, all indicate his confused judgment of ecclesiastical Rome. One to Christie contains the following amusingly
contradictory passage:

"Well then again, after this, you have to view Rome as a place
of religion; and here what mingled feelings come upon one—
you are in the place of martyrdom and burial of Apostles and
saints; you have about you the buildings and sights they saw,
and you are in the city to which England owes the blessing of the
Gospel. But then, on the other hand, the superstitions, or rather
what is far worse, the solemn reception of them as an essential
part of Christianity. But then again, the extreme beauty and
costliness of the churches; and then, on the contrary, the knowledge that the most famous was built (in part) by the sale of indulgences. Really, this is a cruel place. . . . There is more to be
seen and thought of daily. It is a mine of all sorts of excellences."

With but one exception, they made no important Catholic contacts in Rome, none with Italians. Nor did they seek an audience with the Pope—which might easily have been arranged. They really saw little of the Catholic Church except externals, their prejudices being too deep-seated to permit them to get closer to the center of Catholicity; like the average Englishman, they touched the Roman scene with carefully gloved fingers. Hurrell Froude's father, who was a well known Anglican Archdeacon, no doubt set the tempo.

However, they made use of a letter of introduction to Monsignor Nicholas Wiseman, a young priest who was then President of the English College (for seminarians) and by him were introduced to a few English and Irish ecclesiastics. Monsignor Wiseman extended a cordial welcome, and an acquaintanceship was then formed which would have important consequences for Newman in later years. For Monsignor Wiseman would return to England, becoming President of Oscott College and also a bishop, later to be made the Cardinal Archbishop of Westminster.

But at this time the cordiality of the young Monsignor accomplished very little. The anti-Roman feeling was strong with his visitors, and especially so with Newman. The latter, at least, if not young Froude, was ill at ease with him. When Wiseman expressed the hope that they would soon make a second visit to Rome, Newman shook his head and with great solemnity replied, in a somewhat belligerent tone, "*We* have a work to do in England!"

Perhaps the following passage in a letter he wrote home best indicates his attitude at the end of the Roman visit.

"As to the *Roman* Catholic system, I have ever detested it so much that I cannot detest it more by seeing it; but to the Catholic system I am more attached than ever, and quite love the little monks (seminarists) of Rome; they look so innocent and bright, poor boys; and we have fallen in, more or less, with a number of interesting Irish and English priests. I regret that we could form no intimate acquaintance with them. . . . I fear that there are many grave and far-spreading scandals among the Italian priest-hood, and there is mummery in abundance; yet there is a deep substratum of true Christianity."

Both in Rome and on the return voyage he wrote more verses. One of these embraces the following lines:

> *O that thy creed were sound!*
> *For thou dost soothe the heart, thou Church of Rome,*
> *By thy unwearied watch and varied round*
> *Of service, in thy Saviour's holy home.*
> *I cannot walk the city's sultry streets,*
> *But the wide porch invites to still retreats,*
> *Where passion's thirst is calmed, and care's*
> *unthankful gloom . . .*

Several weeks more were spent by him alone in Sicily. The Froudes had decided to go directly home. While in Castro Giovanni in Sicily he had a severe attack of fever and nearly died, being three weeks in bed, very lonely and depressed. But towards the end of May he was able to get to Palermo, where, after a dreary period of waiting, he finally embarked for Marseilles. A memorandum describing his sickness, which he wrote much later, contains the following typically Newman introspective lines:

"As I lay in bed the first day, many thoughts came over me. I felt God was fighting against me—at least I knew why—it was my self-will. I felt that the Froudes had been against my coming. . . . Yet I felt and kept saying to myself, 'I have not sinned against light', and at one time I had a most consoling, overpowering thought of God's electing love, and seemed to feel I was His. But I believe all my feelings, painful and pleasant, were heightened by somewhat of delirium, though they still are from God in the way of Providence. Next day the self-reproaching feelings increased. I seemed to see more and more my utter hollowness. I began to think of all my professed principles, and felt they were mere intellectual deductions from one or two admitted truths. I compared myself with Keble, and felt that I was merely developing his, not my convictions. I know I had *very* clear thoughts about this then, and I believe in the main true ones. Indeed, this is how I look on myself: very much, (as the illustration goes) as a pane of glass, which transmits heat, being cold itself. I have a vivid perception of the consequences of certain admitted principles, have a considerable intellectual capacity of drawing them out, have the refinement to admire them, and a rhetorical or histrionic power to represent them; and, having no great (that is, no vivid) love of this world, whether riches, honors, or anything else, and some firmness and natural dignity of character, take the profession of them upon me, as I might sing a tune which I liked—loving the Truth, but not possessing it, for I believe myself at heart to be nearly hollow, i.e. with little love, little self-denial. I believe I have some faith, that is all."

Some commentators have called that his morbid strain. But it is really his inherent humility expressed rather too heavily. Newman was ever fearful of spoiling himself through pride, and this made him dwell perhaps too strongly at times on the consciousness of his human frailty. We note the same tendency in other crises of his life.

He was aching to get home, and to calm his impatience explored all the churches in Palermo, although he attended no services. He says, "I knew nothing of the Presence of the Blessed Sacrament there." Which indicates how superficial had been his judgment of the Catholic Church during his stay in the Eternal City. But as he convalesced in Palermo he began to recover his strength, threw off his moods of depression, and the feeling revived that God was to lead him to some great work. He kept repeating to himself the thought he had expressed so solemnly to Monsignor Wiseman, "We have a work to do in England."

He finally got away from Palermo on an orange-boat bound
for Marseilles. The boat was becalmed for an entire week in the
Straits of Bonifacio, during which he wrote the famous lines:

> Lead, kindly Light, amid the encircling gloom,
>   Lead Thou me on!
> The night is dark, and I am far from home—
>   Lead Thou me on!
> Keep Thou my feet; I do not ask to see
> The distant scene—one step enough for me.
>
> I was not ever thus, nor pray'd that Thou
>   Shouldst lead me on.
> I loved to choose and see my path; but now
>   Lead Thou me on!
> I loved the garish day, and spite of fears,
> Pride ruled my will; remember not past years.
>
> So long Thy power hath blessed me, sure it still
>   Will lead me on,
> O'er moor and fen, o'er crag and torrent, till
>   The night is gone;
> And with the morn those angel faces smile
> Which I have loved long since and lost awhile.

Although so widely known, these verses are inserted here as an
essential part of our Newman portrait. They are a concise reflection of himself; they mirror his whole career.

At length the orange-boat reached Marseilles, and he immediately started on his overland journey for England. After stop-
ping in Lyons for a few days rest, he pushed on through Paris
without spending more than a few hours to make connections,
and arrived in London quite exhausted, but with his health fully
restored. He went directly to his mother's home. As it happened,
only a few hours before, his brother Francis had arrived home
from Persia.

It was but a few days before July 14, 1833, an important date in the annals of the Anglican Church; for it was on Sunday, July 14, 1833, that John Keble preached at St. Mary's, Oxford, his famous sermon on "National Apostasy." "I have ever considered and kept the day," Newman has said, "as the start of the religious movement of 1833."

CHAPTER TWO

"NATIONAL APOSTASY"

1

WHAT WAS THE THEME of John Keble's sermon, which, Newman has declared, marked the beginning of the Oxford Movement?

To answer this question necessitates a brief outline of the trend of thought which had been conditioning society in general, and the Anglican Establishment in particular, for a very long period, the seeds of which had been sown in the seventeenth century by Thomas Hobbes, Francis Bacon and John Locke (not to except John Calvin and Martin Luther of the previous century). For underlying the era of Puritanism and the drift away from Christian dogma, the philosophy of utility (materialism) was taking deep root. It was the spread of this philosophy in the eighteenth century which expressed itself in the so-called Age of Enlightenment—so definitely reflected in the "latitudinarianism" then dominant in the Anglican Church, with the complete abandonment of the Christian orthodoxy which had characterized the Caroline divines.

Without tracing this evolution of thought in detail, suffice it to say that with this eclipse of Christian dogma, and its replacement with a species of deism, the stage was set for the extraordinary growth of scepticism among the educated classes in England; so much so, that by the time David Hume wrote, he was applauded in scholastic circles as the great prophet of the coming age of liberalism and free thought.

Coincident with this intellectual trend was the progress which was going on apace in the field of mechanical science. The Industrial Revolution was under way, with its far-reaching changes in the economic field. The rise of capitalism in the seventeenth century was followed by its great expansion in the eighteenth. The primitive methods of small-scale industry were being rapidly superseded by mechanical inventions and devices for producing goods on a large scale. This was having a profound effect on men's minds. Even in religious circles interest in the new wealth-producing processes was steadily displacing interest in the truths of religion—among both Anglicans and Dissenters.

This trend away from religion was of course made the easier by the attenuated type of Christianity characteristic of the latitudinarian divines. People were no longer being taught to keep their eyes on their immortal destiny, but rather on a future heaven on earth which was said to be in the making through scientific advance. The new "law of human progress" was taking the place of the moral law.

Many of these Liberals still recognized the existence of God— otherwise, how explain the fact of the universe and of life itself? But as for the Christian Creed as traditionally interpreted, or the reality of Revelation, these things were now often viewed as mere "pious beliefs for the ignorant," without objective reality. Such, in sum, was the type of scepticism carried to great lengths by David Hume and his school.

As this "Age of Enlightenment" had advanced, the writings of the French Physiocrats—Voltaire, Rousseau, Diderot, Condorcet and others, whose teachings culminated in the French Revolution —added fuel to the Liberal flame. Many sceptical writers of note arose in England, among them the Scotsman Adam Smith, who wrote exhaustively on morals as well as political economy; James Mill, an infidel disciple of Smith, and the famous Jeremy Bentham. As the latter had a marked influence on English thought in the whole nineteenth century, a few lines may here be devoted to him.

Jeremy Bentham was born in 1748 and lived until 1832. His parents were well-to-do, and he had the advantage of a good education at Oxford, followed by the study of law at Lincoln's Inn, where he was admitted to the bar in 1772. But physically he was very small—almost a dwarf—and a life of public activity was beyond him. With a profoundly serious temperament, he was really a mental prodigy, though totally without a saving sense of humor. Becoming a fanatical reformer, he lived a life of seclusion and devoted it to writing scores of books in which he attacked religion, morals, government and politics. His confidence in his own infallible wisdom was colossal.

Out of this profundity there grew in time the famous Benthamite philosophy of Utilitarianism. Its fundamental concept is that mankind is governed by two motives, to seek pleasure and to avoid pain; pleasure is the only good, pain the only evil. The Christian teaching that man is a child of God with an immortal destiny was, in his view, "nonsense on stilts." All moral and religious systems are in the same class and a waste of man's energies. Individual actions are to be judged entirely by their utility in promoting the interests of the doer.

As the justification of this philosophy of selfishness, Bentham laid emphasis on "enlightened self-interest." The more successful the individual is in serving this enlightened self-interest, the greater will be his contribution to the welfare of society as a whole, since the happiness of the individual necessarily reacts on his fellow men. And in the same way, whatever produces unhappiness in one's fellow men reacts on oneself. Giving this teaching a broader application, all legislation, in fact all social science, should be directed towards securing the greatest happiness for the community. When this philosophy is accepted and lived by the vast majority it will result in "the greatest good to the greatest number."

This effort to reconcile hedonism with altruism sounds absurd, but is basic in the Liberalism which dominated English thought in the nineteenth century. Out of it grew the English version of laissez faire, identified with such names as Thomas Robert Malthus, David Ricardo and John Stuart Mill—though these men developed the principle in some directions neglected by the humorless Bentham. But in a fundamental sense, Benthamism conditioned all Liberal theorizing in nineteenth century England, not only in the field of economics and politics, but largely in that of religion and morals as well.

2

So much for the background. Now the "National Apostasy" arraigned by Keble in his sermon had two main aspects: one religious, the other political and secular; but these aspects necessarily blended in view of the fact that the Anglican Church, an Erastian institution, was under the domination of the secular state and largely at the mercy of secular politics—as it had always been since the founding of the Establishment by the Elizabethan government in the sixteenth century.

These were the days of agitation over the famous Reform Bill and its aftermath. Parliament, which was now strongly dominated by the Whigs, was riding roughshod over traditional religion. It had begun by abolishing ten of the Anglican bishoprics in Ireland, on the plea that to maintain them in sections where the Protestant population was all but non-existent, was a waste of public funds.

As most of the Anglican bishops were Tories, they quite uni-

formly opposed the reform legislation of the Whig majority. But
the latter, of course, viewed the bishops as mere officials whose
office was kept in being by the State, and what authority over
the Church they might have, as derived wholly from the State.
Any alleged Apostolic authority was to them a mere myth. And
quite naturally so, for few of the bishops at that time claimed to
possess any Apostolic authority!

Now the Tory party (at last dislodged) had been in power
upwards of forty years. During this long ascendancy the nation
had been carried through the French revolutionary period and
the Napoleonic wars. The Whigs, so strong before the days of
George III, had become too weak to overthrow the Tories. This
was not so much due to poor leadership as it was to the "rotten
borough" system of voting, whereby the great Tory landlords
were always able to elect at least two-thirds of the members of
the House of Commons. While this system prevailed, there was
little hope of success for the Whigs in any general election.[1]

For many years the Whigs, with the Liberal wing steadily growing in strength, had been agitating for reform of the election laws,
to give the new industrial centers the right to vote. During the
war years this question was side-tracked, but it came to the fore
immediately after the peace. Then a serious industrial depression
followed, which lingered on for years, threw men out of work and
lowered the wage level. Unrest spread widely throughout the
country, and agitation for the removal of the high protective
duties on the importation of corn and other agricultural products
was rampant. The maintenance of this tariff was a cardinal principle of the Tory landlords. The Tories were therefore blamed for
the prevailing high cost of food as well as the low wages of the
workers in the industrial centers.

This acute situation offered the Whig opposition a great op-

---

[1] The Reform legislation of 1831 and 1832 radically changed the electoral
system, wiping out many of the "rotten boroughs," and extended the franchise
to the growing industrial districts, which had had no voice in government.

portunity. They agitated aggressively for a change in the Corn Laws as well as a reform of the "rotten borough" system—where it did not affect their own "rotten boroughs"! But their plans for reform appealed to the voters, and after the death of George IV, the Whigs were swept into power by a huge majority in a general election.

Naturally in such a landslide, many men were swept into office who favored changes more radical than repeal of the Corn Laws and electoral reforms. Many were followers of Jeremy Bentham's utilitarian philosophy, which tended to threaten the destruction of all moral and religious standards that stood in their way. And, as with radical movements in our own time, numerous people were drawn to the support of revolutionary schemes who had little conception of their deeper significance.

It is not to be assumed that all the Whig leaders and their supporters were experts on "Benthamism," or even suspected its inner significance; but many of them were tainted by general utilitarian, materialistic notions and consequently were utterly indifferent to the claims of a Christian Church that was supposed to be propagating, under its own spiritual authority, the teachings of Christ. These Liberal Whigs claimed to be offering, in their own way, "the greatest good to the greatest number," with their promises of justice and new hope for the masses—who had been suffering for long years under the rule of the Tories, with their appended religious Establishment. And they were quite prepared to toss the latter into the discard if it seemed necessary—or, at any rate, to trim its wings and claws.

The victorious Whigs did bring about some much-needed reforms, reforms of far-reaching constructive value, and they greatly widened the franchise. But, with their strong backing of public opinion, they felt free to attempt almost anything radical, even to the utter elimination of century-old institutions and other accumulated evils of the ages. One of these evils in the eyes of many was the Established Church with its bench of Tory bishops, all of them members of the House of Lords. In the view of these radicals, the Church should either be brought under closer Parliamentary supervision, and its doctrines scrutinized and revised in the interest of Liberal Whig opinion, or else eliminated altogether.

3

This was the state of things which John Keble cried out against in his Assize sermon. But he went far beyond all that. Not only did he declaim against the attacks on the Church by the Whigs, but also against the strong growing party within the Church which was in sympathy with the Liberal attitude of the Whigs, and whose own skirts were besmirched with Benthamism. The radical party in the Church included many who gave little or no weight to Christian dogma and ridiculed the claim of men like John Keble that the Anglican Church derived authority for its teaching, not from the secular state, but from the Apostles, as handed down through the Apostolic succession of its bishops.

There were, of course, some Churchmen of Liberal tendencies who did not go as far as the extremists. Perhaps typical of the less radical group were men like Dr. Thomas Arnold and Dr. Whately. Not that these two clerics agreed on all matters; they disagreed on many things. But both were in favor of "broadening the base" of what they viewed as a moribund institution which, in its present state, had all but outlived its usefulness. Dr. Arnold was advocating a merger of the Church with the Protestant Dissenter sects, a proposal which was creating horror among High Churchmen like Keble and even Low Churchmen of the earlier vintage. As many of the Dissenters were themselves inclined to Liberalism, to risk their domination in a united communion augured disaster for the traditional Anglican point of view.

At that time Dr. Arnold was openly saying: "The Church, as it now stands, no human power can save. Nothing, it seems to me, can save it but an union with the Dissenters; now they are leagued with the anti-Christian party, and no internal reforms can satisfy them." Dr. Whately differed with Dr. Arnold; not that he opposed the idea of absorbing the Dissenters, but he wished to make a clean sweep of government control, freeing the Church from the State. This was of course Keble's wish also— but for quite different reasons.

As matters turned out, Dr. Arnold's plan failed, as did Dr. Whately's. The Establishment did not absorb the Dissenters, nor was it severed from State control. But these and other developments of a disastrous nature did seem imminent—until John Keble's blast awoke the more conservative Churchmen to aggressive discussion and action.

There had been but little vitality displayed by the more conservative clergy or bishops for many a long year. Utter indifference to the trends of the times had long been characteristic of them. Far too long had they been living on the opium of contented security in a financially supported department of the State. They were in no sense prepared to shield their Church from the flood of indifferentism and heterodoxy that had long been pouring in and saturating its educated laity. The middle classes had not been so fully affected, but many of evangelical leanings, imbibing the emotional religion of Wesley and White-field, tended to abandon the Church and ally themselves with the Wesleyan sect or the Plymouth Brethren—or some other dissenting communion.

Dean Church, in his history of the Oxford Movement, in depicting the state of the Anglican Church at this time, says: "The Church, as it had been in the quiet days of the eighteenth century, was scarcely adapted to the needs of more stirring times. The idea of clerical life had certainly sunk, both in fact and in the popular estimate of it. The idea of the priest was not *quite* forgotten, but there was much to obscure it. The beauty of the

English Church at this time was its family life of simplicity and purity; its blot was quiet worldliness. . . . But the fortunes of a Church are not safe in the hands of a clergy, of which a great part take their obligations so easily. It was slumbering and sleeping when the visitation of days of change and trouble came upon it." [1]

That quite concisely describes the state of things in the Anglican Church in 1833, when the threats of the politicians and the plans of the Liberals of Benthamite leanings, and the attitude of milder reformers like Arnold and Whately, were threatening its disruption. As Keble saw the situation, the Church was in danger of having its foundations completely undermined by these modern movements, and he was sincerely alarmed. If the radicals in Parliament went to the lengths they threatened, the Church, as a Christian Church, would, in his view, be destroyed; or, should a middle course be followed, as Arnold and Whately advocated, the Church would only continue as the mere legalized home of a meaningless and watered-down Christianity which would ultimately mean total abandonment of belief in the teachings of Christ.

In his sermon, Keble asserted that hitherto Englishmen had taken it for granted that "England was a nation which for centuries had acknowledged, as an essential part of its theory of government, that she is also a part of Christ's Church, and bound, in all her legislation and policy, by the fundamental laws of that Church." [2] "But," he continued, "when a government and people so constituted, throw off the restraints which in many respects such a principle would impose upon them, nay, disavow the principle itself [this was nothing less than] direct disavowal of the

---

[1] Church, *The Oxford Movement*.

[2] This was Richard Hooker's theory as stated in his *Ecclesiastical Polity*. In actual practice, however, precisely the reverse of this prevailed. The Establishment, as part of the government, had always been bound in all its acts by the fundamental laws *of that government*.

sovereignty of God. If it be true anywhere that such enactments are forced on the legislature by public opinion, is *apostasy* too hard a word to describe the temper of such a nation?"

He ended by making a touching appeal to those Churchmen (small as might be their number) who still believed in the divine authority of the Church as a teaching body, to bestir themselves and fight these threatening calamities. He deplored the tendency of men to engross their whole minds in material matters and neglect their religion. "Public concerns," he asserted, "ecclesiastical or civil, will prove indeed ruinous to those who permit them to occupy all their care and thought, neglecting or undermining ordinary duties, more especially those of a devotional kind. . . . These cautions being duly observed, I do not see how any person can devote himself too entirely to the cause of the Apostolic Church in these realms."

The sermon was, in sum, a direct appeal for prompt and aggressive action by Anglicans of the type of the young Oxford group.

4

Before telling the story of the Oxford awakening, it may be well to explain briefly the character of the Protestantism in the Church of England which John Keble and his sympathizers were now to oppose, as well as the distinguishing characteristics of the "Anglo-Catholicism" they were now about to bring to the fore. There are, among both Catholics and Protestants of our day, many vague and erroneous notions regarding what the terms "Protestant" and "Anglo-Catholic" signify in the Anglican communion and what they signified in Newman's time.

To the modern mind the term "Protestant" applies to every Christian body except the Catholic Church. But the term has a more specific connotation in the Church of England and the American Episcopal Church. The latter carries the word Protestant in its official title, but this does not mean that *all* Episcopalians consider themselves Protestants. The Low Church Episcopalian says he is a Protestant and glories in the fact. The Broad Churchman, or Modernist, though classifying himself as a Protestant, often views the term as obsolete, preferring to use the word Liberal. But the High Church Episcopalian definitely repudiates the term and calls himself a Catholic. If he is very High (there are many degrees of High Churchmen) he calls himself an "Anglo-Catholic." The latter term first came into use in Newman's time, though not universally. In modern days, High Churchmen use it more freely, and in America it has been widely adopted by the High Church group, who try to ignore the official title of their Church, which is "Protestant Episcopal."

The traditional Protestant Anglican or Low Churchman of Newman's time sincerely believed the Apostles' Creed. He took his religion seriously as a reformed and purified Christianity and usually lived it seriously. But he had a horror of any Catholic "taint," considered the Pope Antichrist, and venerated Luther and Calvin as great reformers. For him, Christianity in its purity came to life with the Reformation in the sixteenth century; before that, it was a blur or an abomination—until one leaped back to Bible times. The Bible, as interpreted by private judgment, was his sole Rule of Faith. "Evangelicalism," so-called, inspired by the Wesleyan revival, was a growing characteristic of this school.

The Broad Churchmen of Newman's time were formulating their own "liberal" interpretations of the Christian Creed in attempts to harmonize it with the "enlightened" thought of the day. Dogma meant little to them.

While the Low Churchman of those days was apt to rest his case on the Reformation, the High Churchman, on the other hand, preferred to blot out the Reformation and rest his case on the "Church of Antiquity"—the first centuries of Christianity.

He was in substantial agreement with Archbishop Laud and the Anglican divines of the seventeenth century. This Laudian High Church movement had been obscured during the days of Oliver Cromwell; and although it revived after the return of Charles II in the 1660's, it was utterly crushed by the Whig Revolution of 1688. Archbishop Sandcroft, seven other bishops and more than four hundred of the lower clergy were in effect tossed out of the Church for refusing to recognize the Calvinist, William of Orange, as their divine right sovereign. These High Churchmen were known as "Non-jurors." Later, on the accession of the Lutheran, George I, the remaining remnant of High Churchmen also became "Non-jurors." After that the Latitudinarian or Liberal school would dominate the Anglican Church throughout the eighteenth century and well into the nineteenth.

But now, with the Oxford awakening of the 1830's, "Anglo-Catholicism" was to live once more. For this Oxford movement was not to be limited to an attack on the Benthamite Liberalism of the day; it was also to be a constructive movement, aiming to bring to light, and place in the ascendancy in the Anglican Church, those "forgotten truths" regarding the genesis and mission of Christianity which had long been buried under the Latitudinarian and Protestant evangelical dominations.

CHAPTER THREE

THE OXFORD AWAKENING

1

INSPIRED BY JOHN KEBLE'S SERMON, which (as explained in the last chapter) was a forcible attack on the tendencies of the times in both Church and State and a strong plea for a return to the ideals of primitive Christianity, the reforming spirit which Newman, Froude and their friends had long been endeavoring to promote now began to take objective form.

Extended discussions had already taken place among the younger men in the Oriel Common Room before Newman's return from abroad. Hurrell Froude, who had arrived home earlier, had had much to do with this. There were perhaps a dozen young enthusiasts who had gathered at these discussions, aside from which a number of parish rectors and curates outside Oxford, and more mature followers of Keble, were discussing plans for turning the latter's words into deeds.

The first tangible result of Keble's sermon seems to have been a small gathering at Hugh James Rose's parsonage at Hadleigh, Suffolk. Rose was editor of the *British Magazine*, a religious publication strongly favoring the High Church movement. At this meeting there was much discussion, but little action resulted. It devolved upon the younger Oxford group to start the ball really rolling.

But just what to do under the circumstances and how to go

about doing it was the moot question on which no agreement was reached. Sentiment was strong at first for the formation of an organized "party," with rules and regulations, officers and committees, a sort of "Church within the Church," which would set in motion a formal plan of action. Others thought that the bishops should be asked to assume the lead—a rather wild idea, in view of their well known attitude as Protestants! Still others pictured Keble as official leader of an organized body.

These ideas got nowhere, however—except that an appeal was later submitted to the Archbishop of Canterbury, who merely turned his face the other way. As for Keble acting as formal leader, he was not at Oxford, was not by nature an administrator, and quite naturally would not be drawn into abortive movements of any kind. Finally they turned to Newman and found that he was not thinking at all of a formal organization.

Newman's idea was not to form a party within the Church, thus creating a sort of schism, but to start agitation by individuals of like mind, with discussion, writing, preaching and correspondence. And in the event, this was the plan adopted, with Newman (who was blessed with better writing talent than any of the others at Oxford) beginning to write, "out of my own head," he says, "the Tracts for the Times." [1] They began to appear in September of that same year, at first in very brief form but quite frequently, over thirty Tracts appearing before that year was out. Later on they were extended into long discussions of doctrine or of contemporary criticism. In the larger form they appeared less frequently, until Tract Ninety in 1841 brought the series to a close.

---

[1] The issuance of the Tracts was by no means favored by the entire group. Many feared their effect on the bishops; for of course Newman gave them a "Catholic" tinge from the start. In view of this opposition, he was about to drop the idea, but Keble and Froude strongly supported him. Full unity never prevailed; this incident at the start was the first sign of the many serious discords between the Tractarians which were later to develop. Unfortunately, quarrelling was typical of the movement. This was partly due to the fact that, in connection with "Catholicity," there were both maximizers and minimizers contending for leadership.

It has often been said that Newman was a most impractical person, and many have compared him, to his disadvantage in this respect, with the eminently practical Cardinal Manning. Indeed, he was impractical, and no one knew this better than himself. In temperament and in his methods he was quite the reverse of Manning. Nevertheless, the course followed by the Tractarians [1] under Newman's inspiration proved to be a most effective method for popularizing and promoting their ideas. When Newman began to issue the Tracts he reasoned, as he later explained: "No great work was ever done by a system; whereas systems rise out of individual exertions. Luther was an individual. The very faults of an individual excite attention; he loses, but his cause (if good and he powerful-minded) gains. This is the way of things; we promote truth by a self-sacrifice." And so it was that while some of the group were trying to form organizations on secular lines, which soon came to grief, Newman went ahead with the Tracts.

These Tracts were anonymous, and they were first viewed with mild amusement by most of the bishops and ignored by all but a few of the clergy and laity. Newspapers paid no attention to them. But as time went on and Tract after Tract appeared in sequence, and they were circulated throughout the country without cost to the recipients, all carrying the refrain that there must be a "second reformation" in the Anglican Church to bring it back to the traditional standards of the seventeenth century (when the great Caroline divines were guiding its fortunes), the entire bench of bishops began to take notice of what was going on. And they certainly were startled when the following comment on the Episcopacy, written by Newman and intended to be complimentary, was pointed out to them: "Black event though it would be for the country, yet we could not wish them [the bishops] a

---

[1] The term "Tractarian" came early into use as a designation for the movement. Although "Oxford Movement" was its natural name (as having first arisen in Oxford University), the movement spread far beyond Oxford, and soon, owing to the constant issuing of the Tracts, the term "Tractarian Movement" became more common.

more blessed termination of their course than the spoiling of their goods and martyrdom." It was a bombshell. These dignified Protestant bishops had no ambition to be martyrs.

The Tracts were increasingly Catholic in tone as their issue went on. The very first one, advocating the theory of Apostolic Succession, did not unduly disturb the bishops, who for the most part viewed that theory as a purely academic matter of no practical importance.[1] But later Tracts, emphasizing the sacramental principle and condemning the Calvinistic leanings of certain of the bishops themselves, were not greeted so indifferently. The Tracts began to be criticised as "Romish." It was not long before these young reformers were being closely watched by their ecclesiastical superiors. Many bishops decided that something must be done to put a quietus on these rising "Romanizers." The University authorities began to feel the same way.

There was also, aside from purely doctrinal matters, another phase of the movement which the bishops deplored. The Tracts were attacking the Erastianism of the Church and advocating dis-establishment. To advocate dis-establishment, removing the governmental prop which gave the Church its strength and financial security, seemed far more heretical than anything else. What would become of the Church if forced to compete on even terms with the Nonconformists and Dissenters—not to mention the non-believers and pagans?

Nearly all the earlier Tracts were written by Newman. Yet, after all, it was not the Tracts alone that gave the movement its early impetus. It was Newman's sermons at St. Mary's that had most to do with starting the modern "Anglo-Catholic" movement

---

[1] Apostolic Succession is of course true of the Catholic Church. But, as has been said by a distinguished Protestant writer, "There is a great difference in the attitude of a Church which puts in such a claim at a time when a very considerable proportion of its clergy repudiate it, and when the claim sounds to the ears of most men strange and paradoxical." When reading this claim in the first Tract, the Anglican Bishop of London said: "Why, I thought the idea of Apostolic Succession had died with the Non-jurors." He was not far from right!

in the Church of England. The Tracts stated principles to be believed, but the sermons explained and elaborated on these principles in their moral and spiritual aspects. Although delivered before only small groups of people, their influence spread far and wide. Dean Church asserted that while the three men Newman, Keble and Froude were the triumvirate that started the movement, it was Newman who "made it go"—and he made it go with his sermons.

2

Newman had by this time made great strides as an effective preacher; his sermons of Tractarian days—particularly those published as *Parochial and Plain Sermons* and *Oxford University Discourses*—made his fame for all time. They brought the movement to the front in a unique way, and their effect was permanent. Canon William Barry, in his interesting study *Cardinal Newman*, written in 1904, eulogises his sermons in the following illuminating way:

"They can be read after all the years for their illustrations, their lucid English, their exquisite touches of pathos, their creative faculty, as real as Dante's but altogether different, by which they call up the dead or the past or the invisible to our shrinking presence. . . . We may also read the sermons as soliloquies on the events of the day. They cry out against the whole Liberal advance. They pierce with irony the religion of which Mozley declares that it makes young Evangelicals 'clever men of the world.' They lay on the dissecting table that peculiar English creation, Pharisaic and Philistine, which foreigners call hypocrisy, not knowing what else to make of it. Savonarola brought Florence to the 'burning of the vanities'; Newman would have introduced into the popular religion, ideas, 'first principles in Scripture,' con-

cerning poverty and self denial, which it loathed. True, he did
not dream, then nor afterwards, of converting the world; his
judgment of his followers, their grace, their refinement, courtesy,
even their natural affection, was Maccabean in its severity. But,
standing aloof, he sees the Dance of Death as in some Orcagna
fresco, and no prophet has flung over its many twinkling radi-
ances a gloom more intense."

Another striking comment on his preaching was made by Sir
Francis Doyle in his *Reminiscences:*

"That great man's extraordinary genius drew all those within
his sphere, like a magnet, to attach themselves to him and his
doctrines. . . . Whenever I was at Oxford, I used to go regularly
on Sunday afternoons to listen to his sermon at St. Mary's, and
I have never heard such preaching since. . . . He always began
as if he had determined to set forth his idea of truth in the plainest
and simplest language—language, as men say, 'intelligible to the
meanest understanding.' But his ardent zeal and fine poetical
imagination were not thus to be controlled. As I hung upon his
words, it seemed to me as if I could trace behind his will, and
pressing, so to speak, against it, a rush of thoughts, of feelings
which he kept struggling to hold back, but in the end they were
generally too strong for him, and poured themselves out in a
torrent of eloquence all the more impetuous for having been so
long repressed. The effect of these outbursts was irresistible, and
carried his hearers beyond themselves at once."

It was really a great moral movement that Newman was trying to promote, with the deep-seated hope, and with unceasing
prayer, that it would reach the nation's heart. His day-to-day
activities may be vividly pictured, as he labored heroically to carry
on this effort to awaken the minds of his auditors, of those who
listened to him and those who read him: living in his simple
rooms at Oriel; working overtime on his sermons; writing Tracts
and also many essays, and carrying on an immense personal correspondence; always advocating, in language of great beauty and

as lucid as he could make it, a return to the spirituality and teachings of the primitive Christian Church as reflected in the lives and
teachings of the great Fathers of the early centuries.

But these Fathers appealed not at all to the British Protestant
mind. They were viewed askance as monks, narrowly orthodox
and superstitious, and as celibates who were presumably immoral. Men like Macaulay and Carlyle pictured the Church
Fathers as ignorant and vile and declared their opinions worthless. Yet Newman was seriously trying to educate the English
public to the idea that their lives and writings were the true key
to Christian godliness and orthodoxy. One of his worthwhile
undertakings at this time were some sketches of the early saints
and martyrs, a series which he finally reissued in book form under
the title *Church of the Fathers*. But though profoundly interesting
and very readable, the book was spurned by the multitude.

Yet even the Liberals were recognizing the power of Newman's
work in the pulpit, if not that of his pen. Matthew Arnold and
James Anthony Froude were both to speak later in the highest
terms of his powers as a preacher. Principal Shairp of St. An-
drews, never in sympathy with Newman's Catholic views and
always a critic of the movement, wrote years later (in his *Essay on
John Keble*):

"The movement when at its height, extended its influence far
beyond the circle of those who directly adopted its views. It raised
the average morality in Oxford to a level which perhaps it had
never reached before. . . . If such was the general aspect of
Oxford society at that time, where was the center and soul from
which so mighty a power emanated? It lay, and had for some
years lain, mainly in one man, a man in many ways the most
remarkable that England has seen during this century—John
Henry Newman. The influence he had gained, without apparently
setting himself to seek it, was something altogether unlike anything else in our time. A mysterious veneration had by degrees
gathered round him, till now it was almost as though some Am-

brose or Augustine of older ages had reappeared. He himself tells how one day, when he was an undergraduate, a friend with whom he was walking on an Oxford street cried out eagerly, 'There's Keble,' and with what awe he looked at him. A few years and the same took place in regard to himself. In Oriel Lane light-hearted undergraduates would drop their voices and whisper, 'There's Newman,' as with head thrust forward and gaze fixed as though at some vision seen only by himself, with swift, noiseless step he glided by. Awe fell on them for a moment almost as if it had been some apparition that had passed. . . .

"What were the qualities that inspired these feelings? There was, of course, learning and refinement. There was genius, not indeed of a philosopher (*sic*), but of a subtle and original thinker, an unequalled edge of dialectic, and these all glorified by the imagination of a poet. Then there was the utter unworldliness, the setting aside of all things which men most prize, the timelessness of soul which was ready to essay the impossible. Men felt that here was—

> *'One of that small transfigured band*
> *Which the world cannot tame.' "*

A further comment from the same observer—on Newman's style of preaching—is worthy of quotation, despite its length:

"Both Dr. Pusey and Mr. Keble at that time (1836–8) were quite second in importance to Mr. Newman. The center from which his power went forth was the pulpit of St. Mary's, with those wonderful afternoon sermons. Sunday after Sunday, year after year, they went on, each continuing and deepening the impression produced by the last. What there was of High Church teaching was implied rather than enforced. The local, the temporary and the modern were ennobled by the presence of the Catholic truth belonging to all ages that pervaded the whole. His power showed itself chiefly in the new and unlooked for ways in which he touched into life old truths, moral and spiritual, which all

Christians acknowledge but most have ceased to feel—when he spoke of Unreal Words, of the Individuality of the Soul, of the Invisible World, of Ventures of Faith, of the Cross of Christ the Measure of the World. . . . As he spoke, how the old truth became new; how it came home with a meaning never felt before! He laid his finger, how gently, yet how powerfully, on some inner place in the hearer's heart, and told him things about himself he had never known till then. Subtlest truths, which it would have taken philosophers pages of circumlocution and big words to state, were dropped by the way in a sentence or two of the most transparent Saxon. What delicacy of style, yet what strength! How simple yet how suggestive! How homely, yet how refined! How penetrating, yet how tender-hearted!"

An example of Newman's preaching power may be shown by quoting a passage from a sermon in which he has been discussing the complacency of the Pharisee, with his secret sins, and then pointing out the only good—that which is to be found in the Unseen world:

"O how great a good it will be . . . if the time shall one day come, when we shall enter into His Tabernacle above, and hide ourselves under the shadow of His wings; if we shall be in the number of those blessed dead who die in the Lord, and rest from their labor. Here we are tossing upon the sea, and the wind is contrary. All through the day we are tried and tempted in various ways. . . . But in the Unseen world, where Christ has entered, all is peace. 'There is no more death, neither sorrow nor crying, neither any more pain; for the former things are passed away'. Nor any more sin; nor any more guilt; no more remorse; no more punishment; no more penitence; no more trial; no infirmity to depress us; no affection to mislead us; no passion to transport us; no prejudice to blind us; no sloth, no pride, no envy, no strife; but the Light of God's countenance, and a pure river of water of life, clear as crystal, proceeding out of the Throne.

That is our home; here we are but on pilgrimage, and Christ is calling us home."

There is never any bitterness in his discourses, even when he dwells on men's weaknesses. His indignation does at times seem to overwhelm him as he criticises the indifferentism and lukewarmness which seems everywhere to prevail, both within and outside the Church. But instead of sending his hearers away in a mood of despair, he dwells on the need of their obeying God's laws. Always he is urging his hearers to equip themselves for the trials of life, such as suffering, persecution, and even martyrdom if necessary, through *sanctity*—personal sanctity and holiness. He urges them to acquire "that inward witness to the truth lodged in our hearts," which can only be felt through holiness of spirit. In one of his sermons he says, "Let us turn from shadows of all kinds—shadows of sense, or shadows of argument and disputation, or shadows addressed to our imagination and tastes. Let us attempt, through God's grace, to advance and sanctify the inward man."

His influence on Oxford at this time is nowhere better indicated than by what Matthew Arnold wrote many years later in a famous passage: "The name of Cardinal Newman is a great name to the imagination still; his genius and style are still things of power. Forty years ago he was in the very prime of life; he was close at hand to us at Oxford; he was preaching in St. Mary's pulpit every Sunday; he seemed about to transform and to renew what was for us the most national and natural institution in the world, the Church of England. Who could resist the charm of that spiritual apparition, gliding in the dim afternoon light through the aisles of St. Mary's, rising in the pulpit, and then, in the most entrancing of voices, breaking the silence with words and thoughts which were a religious music—subtle, sweet and mournful?"

As for a vivid picture of Newman's personality in these years, that given by James Anthony Froude in his *Short Studies* is perhaps as accurate as any. He says, "When I entered at Oxford, John Henry Newman was beginning to be famous. The responsible authorities were watching him with anxiety; clever men were looking with interest and curiosity on the apparition among them of one of those persons of indisputable genius who was likely to make a mark upon his time. His appearance was striking. He was above the middle height, slight and spare. His head was large, his face remarkably like that of Julius Caesar. The forehead, the shape of the ears and nose were almost the same. . . . I have often thought of the resemblance, and believed that it extended to the temperament. . . . Both were formed by nature to command others, both had the faculty of attracting to themselves the passionate devotion of friends and followers."

3

That the progress of the movement during the first years was preponderantly due to Newman's particular talents as a preacher and a writer can scarcely be questioned. This is granted by all Tractarians who later expressed their views on paper or otherwise. Moreover, most of the critics of its activities directed their shafts against Newman—who was making the most noise—rather than against personalities like Keble, Froude or others. But very soon after the movement got well under way, new developments of importance took place. One of the most important was the full cooperation of Dr. Pusey, which began in 1835.

Dr. Pusey at once supplied prestige, for his contacts with Churchmen outside Oxford were extensive. Moreover, his dignified position and his general solidity of character were of immense help. The movement soon became closely associated with his name. Indeed, the critics of the Tractarian group promptly gave them the title of "Puseyites" as a nickname—with the notion, no doubt, that there was something funny about it. The words *Puseismus, Puséisme,* and *Puseista* penetrated Germany, France and Italy and were bandied about in England. But this name, first used in derision, stuck and became honored. The term "Puseyites" was before very long to overshadow the local Oxford term, "Newmanites," which had already been fastened on the Tractarians at the University.

The importance of the acquisition of Dr. Pusey as an active participant has been concisely explained by Newman in his *Apologia.* "Dr. Pusey," he says, "gave us at once a position and a name. Without him we should have had no chance of making any serious resistance to the Liberal aggression. But Dr. Pusey was a Professor and Canon of Christ Church; he had a vast influence in consequence of his deep religious seriousness, the munificence of his charities, his Professorship, his family connections, and his easy relations with the University authorities. There was henceforth a man who could be the goal and center of the zealous people in every part of the country who were adopting the new opinions; and not only so, but here was one who furnished the movement with a front to the world, and gained for it a recognition from other parties in the University."

Dr. Pusey was not a notable preacher like Newman—in fact, as a preacher he was tiresome—but he had other talents. It was he who planned the issuance of translations of the writings of the early Church Fathers, under the editorship of Keble, Newman and himself. He also wrote several of the important Tracts and cooperated in the writing of many of the later voluminous ones—which were, in some cases, great intellectual studies. But perhaps it was his characteristic optimism that was the most valuable thing he brought to the movement. He visioned great things for the future; he thought that ten years of effort, rightly directed, would work wonders in bringing the Church around to the High Anglican view. Despite the fact that, with all his prestige, he failed to secure any real support or sympathy from the bishops, it seems never to have occurred to him that long before ten years had gone by there might arise a war against the movement by these bishops, and that rifts would develop among the rank and file of his followers—not rifts in friendships, but in fundamental convictions regarding the Anglican Church.

It was not long after Pusey joined the movement that this gain was offset by a loss—a tragic loss for Newman. His close friend and collaborator Hurrell Froude died after a long illness—in March 1836. What his friendship had meant to Newman from the days when they first became intimate at Oriel has been indicated, to some extent, in earlier pages. Froude had been not only his beloved friend but his teacher. Although when Froude had become intimate with Newman he had brought him and Keble together, it is obvious that Froude's own influence on his friend was the more penetrating and lasting. Long years after, Newman was to pay to Froude's memory the following affectionate tribute:

"I speak of Hurrell Froude—in his intellectual aspect—as a man of high genius, brimful and overflowing with ideas and views, in him original, which were too many and strong even for his bodily strength, and which crowded and jostled against each other in their effort after distinct shape and expression. Dying prematurely as he did, and in the conflict and transitional state of opinion, his religious views never reached their ultimate conclusion. . . . He expressed openly his admiration of the Church of Rome, and his hatred of the Reformers. He had a high and severe idea of the intrinsic excellence of Virginity; and he considered the Blessed Virgin its great pattern. He delighted in thinking of the saints; he had a vivid appreciation of the idea of sanctity, its possibilities and its heights; and he was more than inclined to believe a large amount of miraculous interference as occurring in the early and middle ages. He embraced the principle of penance and mortification. He had a deep devotion to the Real Presence, in which he had a firm faith. He was powerfully drawn to the medieval Church but not to the primitive. . . . It is difficult to enumerate the precise additions to my own theological creed which I derived from a friend to whom I owe so much. He taught me to look with admiration towards the Church of Rome, and in the same degree to dislike the Reformation. He fixed deep in me the idea of devotion to the Blessed Virgin, and he led me gradually to believe in the Real Presence."

It is apparent that Hurrell Froude had more to do with implanting the seeds of Catholicity which later flowered in Newman than any other of the Tractarians, not excepting Pusey and Keble, whose Catholicity was to a far greater extent circumscribed by their inherent prejudices regarding things that Froude did not hesitate to accept. Had he not been cut off in his youth, it seems probable that Froude would have followed—or perhaps preceded—Newman into the Catholic Church.

The loss of Hurrell Froude was now to be quickly followed by another affliction for Newman, the death of his own mother, which occurred on May seventeenth of this same year. It was very sudden and quite tragic for him. Only three weeks before, his sister Jemima had married John Mozley, and the strain and excitement of the wedding seems to have brought about the mother's sudden collapse. She had been in poor health, however, for some years.

Newman was devoted to his mother, and in earlier years they had been very close. But she never sympathized with his later evolution into "Anglo-Catholic" views; probably she never understood them. This was scarcely made easier by the attitude of her other two sons, nor to any real extent by that of her daughters. That her sympathy was missed by John Henry is evidenced in many ways. But sympathy she could not give, and doubtless the strained relations which resulted were hard for both to bear. A rather pathetic passage in a letter to his sister Harriet illustrates the situation. He says, "What has been to me distressing in my work is that it has been one of the causes which kept me from being much with mother lately. But there was another cause. I mean of late years mother has misunderstood my religious views, and considered she differed from me; and she thought I was surrounded by admirers and had everything my own way; and, in consequence, I, who am conscious to myself I never thought anything more precious than her sympathy and praise, had none of it."

It was a comfort to him that he was present with his sister Harriet when their mother died. The funeral was held at St. Mary's, Oxford, and many of his friends were present, including Dr. Pusey, Williams, Copeland and other leading Tractarians. Isaac Williams told how he discovered Newman, long after the funeral, kneeling before the altar and lost in prayer.

4

Both exciting and amusing were certain of the reactions of different groups in the Church to the early activities of the movement. Dr. Arnold's party furiously attacked the young Tractarians as reactionaries whose minds were closed to the progressive tendencies of the times, and Dr. Arnold himself published an acrimonious article in the *Edinburgh Review*, calling them "The Oxford Malignants." Dr. Whately, suspecting that their secret object was to propagate infidelity, called them "Children of the Mist" and "Veiled Prophets" of a rapidly spreading pestilence. The Low Churchmen and Evangelicals saw the movement as a subtle attempt to Romanize the Anglican Church, and even thus early, rumors circulated that they were secretly in league with the Jesuits.

There was also considerable doubt and misgiving among some of the old-line "High and Dry" Churchmen—an old-fashioned group who professed High Church beliefs, associated with the "two-bottle orthodox," but did little to promote their beliefs. To them, the Tractarian venture *was too venturesome*, and they feared to encourage it unduly. "Depend upon it," one of them had said a few years before, "the day will come when these [Catholic] doctrines, now buried, will be brought out to the light of day; and then the effect will be quite fearful." And when the day did come, fearful were the feelings of just such men as these.

Yet in the face of widespread criticism, the movement was growing and its influence increasing; new men were constantly coming in, and while a few timid ones dropped out and differences of opinion as to policies arose within the ranks, a note of great sincerity marked all the activities. It was becoming recognized by both friends and foes as an "Anglo-Catholic" movement of no mean significance. Its progress was a surprise even to its founders. Newman commented on this progress long afterward in this frequently quoted passage:

"From beginnings so small, from elements of thought so fortuitous, with prospects so unpromising, the Anglo-Catholic party suddenly became a power in the National Church, and an object of alarm to her rulers and friends. Its originators would have found it difficult to say what they aimed at of a practical kind; rather, they put forth views and principles for their own sake, because they were true, as if they were obliged to say them; and, as they might be themselves surprised at the success which attended their propagation. And in fact, they could only say that those doctrines were in the air; that to assert was to prove, and that to explain was to persuade; and that the movement in which they were taking part was the birth of a crisis rather than of a place. In a very few years a school of opinion was formed, fixed in its principles, indefinite and progressive in their range; and it extended itself into every part of the country. If we enquire what the world thought of it, we have still more to raise our wonder; for not to mention the excitement it caused in England, the movement and its party names were known to the police of Italy and the back-woodmen of America. And so it proceeded, getting stronger and stronger every year, till it came into collision with the Nation, and that Church of the Nation, which it began by professing especially to serve."

But even this early (1838) there were signs of hesitation and confusion as new men with new points of view flocked into the movement. Notable among these new acquisitions, who made their influence felt very promptly, were William George Ward, Frederick Oakeley, and Frederick William Faber, all forceful men but with strong Catholicizing tendencies and with a leaning towards the Catholic Church quite as strong as (or perhaps stronger than) that which Hurrell Froude had begun to display. Almost at once they were classed as "Romanizers" by the more sober Tractarians; Pusey, Newman and Keble had their hands full to keep them in line.

The most aggressive of these new men was William George Ward. Eleven years younger than Newman, he had not been ordained until 1837. He had long displayed very broad and liberal views and was classed as one of the faithful followers of Dr. Arnold. Blessed with a good mind, he was a fine debater, and his capacity for defending his beliefs and exposing the fallacies of his opponents was very great. Yet he had his own prejudices, which he hugged tightly. For instance, without troubling to understand the Tractarian movement, he insisted that its aims were trivial and silly. He would have nothing to do with it.

Not that Ward was a hopeless sceptic; fundamentally he was a deeply religious man when ordained to the Anglican ministry, but the prevailing Liberalism of the times, both in politics and religion, had permeated his mind, and he was even receptive towards the popular Benthamite theories. He surely seemed to be a champion-in-the-bud of the rising Broad Church school.

Then a remarkable change came. Ward had often been urged to go to hear Newman preach at St. Mary's but had petulantly refused. "Why should I listen to such myths?" he asked. What he had heard about Newman's sermons disgusted him. Finally, one of his friends, taking him for a stroll Sunday afternoon, brought him to the porch of St. Mary's at precisely the time Newman was about to begin his sermon. "Now, Ward," said he, "Newman is at this moment going up into the pulpit. Why not hear him once; it can do you no harm. If you don't like his preaching you need not go again." Ward was persuaded and entered with his friend. And the sermon he heard changed his whole life.

Not that he immediately changed all his views, but he was started on a new line of thought, and his honest logical mind led him inevitably to the "Anglo-Catholic" position. His friend Bonamy Price, an admirer of Dr. Arnold and an advocate of the economic views of Bentham and James Mill, decided that Ward's change was a triumph of emotion over reason. Said he, "Ward after this joined Newman and his friends, the Newmanites as they were called. The powerful sermons remained masters of the field. Ward submitted his reason to the magic of those wonderful words; the principle that virtue was the greatest happiness to the greatest number was thrown to the winds . . . and with the submissiveness of a little child the great intellect abandoned a mass of strongly held convictions and at once embraced new and unexampled principles which changed the whole life of the man. The conversion was moral, spiritual, but in no sense intellectual."

How far from true this judgment was is demonstrated by the career of Ward from that time on. Though moral and spiritual, of course, his conversion was also definitely intellectual. It was what the Catholic Church calls a genuine way of conversion.

Like many a militant convert, Ward was not slow in going to extremes after he had started on his new line. Almost at once he saw flaws in the High Church position that he never would have detected when he was only in the Broad Church school. He soon placed himself with the group who were displaying an increasingly friendly attitude towards the full Catholic point of view, particularly with those who were losing faith in Dr. Pusey's optimistic hope that this very Protestant Establishment could be promptly converted to "Anglo-Catholic" principles. It was clearly his intent, and that of those who surrounded him, to change the course of the movement, turning it in a more definite direction towards the Catholic Church.

It was a distinctly radical change. The movement had arisen in 1833 as definitely anti-Papal as well as anti-Protestant and anti-Erastian. It was partly designed to head off any danger of High Churchmen becoming Catholics, by emphasizing the fundamentally Catholic character of the Anglican Church's own doctrines. But now things began to be reversed. According to the views of William George Ward and his friends, it was not the Catholic but the Anglican Church itself which was on trial. As Newman said: "A new school of thought was rising and sweeping the original party of the movement aside and taking its place; eager, resolute minds, who had heard much of Rome, and cut into the original movement at an angle, and set about turning it in a Roman direction. The Reformation was looked upon by them as a deadly sin, and restoration to the Papal obedience the ideal, though perhaps unattainable aim."

5

And now one of those disturbing incidents so characteristic of the doctrinal turmoils in the Anglican communions had come to the surface at Oxford still further to increase confusion in the ranks of the Tractarians. Dr. Hampden, Provost of Oriel College, a muddle-headed theologian who claimed to be strictly orthodox in his Anglican beliefs, suddenly took the position that the age-long custom of requiring matriculating students at Oxford to subscribe to the Thirty-Nine Articles of Religion should be abandoned; and he advocated this change in the rule for the express purpose of allowing Dissenters and non-believers of all kinds to enter the University.

Similar proposals had been advocated from time to time by the Liberals, and some Evangelicals had favored such proposals— but the strict Anglicans, never. These Articles were viewed as the great bulwark against the intrusion of heresy into the University. Protestant though these Articles were, High Churchmen considered it wiser to require students to sign them, thus pledging loyalty to the Anglican Church, than to allow young men to enter Oxford free to disseminate infidelity—or heretical religions, like "Roman" Catholicism!

In the meanwhile Dr. Hampden, in the Bampton lectures that year, had expressed heterodox views which astonished all parties in the University, whether High, Low or Broad. Caustic criticism of his views arose from many quarters. An earnest man but weak as a logician, he was very indignant at these adverse criticisms and at once wrote a defence of his expressed views. This defence, which he apparently thought orthodox, developed the astonishing theory that "all creeds and formularies, however incidentally useful, are in their nature the inventions of a mistaken and corrupt philosophy, and invasions of Christian liberty." This surprising opinion from an orthodox Oxford professor called forth the comment of R. W. Church that "if Dr. Hampden is right, there is neither Church nor doctrine worth contending for, except as men contend about the Newtonian or undulatory theory of light."

All parties in the University were nonplussed at Hampden's pronouncement, but the only party which seems to have exposed its fallacies was the Tractarian. The dull Dr. Hampden presented a copy of his defence to Newman, evidently expecting a complimentary acknowledgment. But Newman staggered the well-meaning professor by replying: "While I respect the tone of piety which your pamphlet displays, I dare not trust myself to put on paper my feelings about the principles contained in it; tending as they do, in my opinion, to make shipwreck of the Christian faith."

As a result of the agitation by the opponents of Dr. Hampden, the proposal for abandoning the requirement for subscription to the Articles by students at matriculation, on coming to vote, was defeated by a majority of at least five to one.

This looked like a great victory for the Tractarians, as they had been more instrumental in bringing about this vote than any of the others. But in the event, this victory signified nothing. Before that year was out, Lord Melbourne, the Prime Minister, appointed (with the approval of the Archbishop of Canterbury) the heretical Dr. Hampden as Regius Professor of Divinity to replace Dr. Burton, who had recently died. With what dismay the Tractarians greeted this event may well be imagined. It was the appointment, as Church said, "of a man who looked upon all creeds, and all the documents which embodied the traditional doctrine and collective thought of the Church, as invested by ignorance and prejudice with an authority which was without foundation, and which was misleading and mischievous."

Naturally this appointment by Lord Melbourne raised a mighty storm; High and Low Churchmen, and even some Liberals, stood together on the matter; a war of pamphlets ensued, while Dr. Hampden tried to defend himself by still more confusing arguments, making many contradictory statements regarding his beliefs. An attempt was made to have him removed. His activities *were* curtailed for a while, but in the long run this "persecution," as it was called by his friends, left him in full control of the situation—as well as a more bitter enemy of the Tractarians. He was later made a bishop—with what dire consequences for the Puseyites one can well imagine. But fortunately for Newman, by that time he had left this City of Confusion and was safely at peace in the Catholic Church.

In due course this incident passed, and for a while things seemed to be going along swimmingly for the Tractarians at Oxford. But now Newman, Pusey and Keble, working hopefully to defend the Church against the danger (as they saw it) of the growing menace of "Romanism"—which seemed to be permeating their own ranks—were to be confronted with a new dilemma devised by the strong Protestant party in the University, a dilemma which had its amusing as well as its tragic side.

A plan was formulated, with the eager approval of the University heads, to raise funds for the erection on University grounds of a memorial to the "three great martyrs" of the English Reformation, Thomas Cranmer, Hugh Latimer and Nicholas Ridley, the sixteenth century prelates who had done so much to promote Protestantism in England but had been put to death for persecuting Catholics prior to and during the reign of the Catholic Queen Mary in the 1550's.

The plan for the memorial was devised by Dr. Golightly, a vindictive enemy of Newman. He had a personal grudge resulting, apparently, from the fact that long before this, Newman had abruptly dismissed him from the curacy of St. Mary's. Golightly was Low Church and very antagonistic towards the Oxford Movement. He knew that the Tractarians viewed these Reformation divines as the chief villains in the sixteenth century religious upheavals. Here was an opportunity to hoist the Tractarians on their own petard. If they opposed this memorial campaign, they would show themselves in their true colors—as traitors to their own communion, the Anglican Church.

It was a bitter pill for the Tractarians to swallow when, after most of them had strenuously opposed the plan, the subscription for the memorial was a resounding success. It was a bitter pill too for Newman when he discovered that a number of the more lukewarm Puseyites had privately contributed to this fund to raise a memorial to the execrated reformers who had caused so much trouble for the more Catholic-minded during the religious struggles of the sixteenth century. There were evidently a good many stragglers in the Oxford Movement who still clung to strong

Protestant prejudices. Even his good friend Dr. Pusey, Newman was annoyed to learn, had been disposed to contribute something to the fund "in the interest of harmony."

In due course the memorial arose in Oxford, where it still can be seen and admired—or not—to this day. That the success of the venture inspired glee in Golightly and his friends, can well be imagined; but it also inspired sarcastic shafts from the irrepressible Ward—and inner pain to Newman and the more sober Puseyites.

With the reaching of the high point in the movement in the year 1838 and the early part of 1839, it was becoming most apparent that the authorities, not only of the Church but of the University, were seriously at work with plans for crushing or at least crippling and discrediting this novel Oxford awakening. They left no stone unturned in their attempts to besmirch it as an insidious "Romanizing" move, fraught with danger to the staid old Established Church. But very soon troubles were to arise within the ranks of the Tractarians themselves which would prove far more devastating than this stolid Protestant opposition.

CHAPTER FOUR

STORM AND STRESS

1

ONE OF THE DIFFICULTIES that confronted the Tractarians was the absence of a clearly defined Confession of Faith. Criticised by Protestants as heading towards "Romanism," by Catholics as essentially Protestant, and by Liberals as a hybrid development which did not know its own mind, the movement was urgently in need of a formal statement of its doctrinal position. "High Church" signified in the minds of most Englishmen a mere Tory tradition, while the term "Anglo-Catholic" was too new to do more than awaken suspicions of a definite leaning towards "Papalism."

Now Newman had been for some time delivering a series of lectures on the Prophetical Office of the Church, its relation, on the one hand, to popular Protestantism and, on the other, to Catholicism. Out of these lectures gradually developed his conception of a *via media,* or middle way, as the true position of Anglicanism. He strove to demonstrate that the Anglican Church was not fundamentally Protestant but essentially Catholic, occupying a middle ground between Protestantism and modern Catholicism but devoid of the errors, accretions and corruptions of both.

His *via media* ideas were enthusiastically welcomed by those Tractarians who resented being accused by Protestants and Liberals of flirting with Rome. *Via media* was only a negative term, but Newman strove to give it a positive meaning. "A via media," he says, "was but a receding from extremes; therefore it needed to be drawn out into a definite shape and character. Before it could have claims on our respect, it must first be shown to be one, intelligible and consistent. This was the first condition of any reasonable treatise on the *Via Media*. The second condition, and necessary too, was not in my power. I could only hope that it would one day be fulfilled. Even if the *Via Media* were ever so positive a religious system, it was not as yet objective and real; it had no original anywhere of which it was the representative. It was at present a paper religion. This I confess in my Introduction. I say, 'Protestantism and Popery are real religions . . . but the *Via Media*, viewed as an integral system, has scarcely had existence except on paper.' I grant the objection, though I endeavor to lessen it. 'It still remains to be tried, whether what is called Anglo-Catholicism, the religion of Andrewes, Laud, Hammond, Butler and Wilson, is capable of being professed, acted on, and maintained on a large sphere of action, or whether it be a mere modification or transition-state of either Romanism or popular Protestantism.' I trusted that some day it would prove to be a substantive religion."

He then proceeds to emphasize the points of agreement between Catholicism and Anglicanism in the following words: "In both systems the same Creeds are acknowledged. Besides other points in common, we both hold that certain doctrines are necessary to be believed for salvation; we both believe in the doctrines of the Trinity, Incarnation and Atonement; in original sin; in the necessity of regeneration; in the supernatural grace of the sacraments; in the Apostolical Succession; in the obligation of faith and obedience, and in the eternity of future punishment." He reasons that if the two Churches are one in such fundamentals, then the two Churches are really one—despite the fact that they disagree on many less fundamental matters. This being so, he asserts, the Anglican Church is surely a true "branch" of the Church Catholic. He draws this out in this passage:

"The Catholic Church in all lands had been one from the first for many centuries; then, various portions had followed their way to the injury, but not to the destruction, whether of truth or of charity. These portions or branches were mainly three:— the Greek, the Latin, and Anglican. Each of these inherited the undivided Church, and in the unity of that Church it had unity with the other branches. The three branches agreed together in *all but* their later accidental errors. Some branches had retained in detail, portions of Apostolical truth and usage, which the others had not; and these portions might be and should be appropriated again by the others which had let them slip. Thus the middle age belonged to the Anglican Church, and much more did the middle age of England. The Church of the twelfth century was the Church of the nineteenth. Dr. Howley sat in the seat of St. Thomas the Martyr; Oxford was a mediaeval University. Saving our engagements to Prayer Book and Articles, we might breathe and live and act and speak, as in the atmosphere and climate of Henry III's day, or the Confessor's, or of Alfred's. . . ."

This was practically the genesis of the "branch theory," now made so much of by High Anglicans. It had been suggested before but never outlined in this way. Newman says it grew on him over a period of years; that it was not necessarily the view of Dr. Pusey at that time. It was, perhaps, a surprise to most of the Tractarians. "In fact," says Newman, "hardly any two persons who took part in the movement, agreed in their view of the limit to which our general principles might legitimately be carried."

Newman tried to picture in his *via media* "a living Church, made of flesh and blood, with voice, complexion, motion and action, and a will of its own." His study of the writings of the early Fathers (always as interpreted by the Caroline divines) seems to have convinced him that any National Church "in possession" within a country, if it taught Catholic doctrines, possessed authoritative jurisdiction in that country. Though certain elements in a National Church were teaching heretical doctrines —even if this was done by its bishops—this did not vitiate the fundamental Catholicity of that Church. The contrary claim of Papal jurisdiction over the whole world was therefore, according to his view, utterly fallacious. The mission of the Tractarians was primarily to eliminate such heretical teachings and thus purify the Church—as it had been the mission of St. Augustine and the other great Catholic teachers of the early centuries.

He seems to have felt when he outlined this *via media* theory that it was impregnable. Not so the bulk of the Anglican world, however—nor the Catholic world. It was greeted with incredulity by the latter but with angry protests by the former. Nor did all the Tractarians accept it wholeheartedly; some of them expressed doubts of its soundness—as did Newman himself a few years later. After he became a Catholic, he reissued his book on the *via media* with annotations which point out the weakness of his former arguments.

During all this time Newman was continuing his studies of the early Church Fathers (a favorite pastime) and was now deep in a study of the Monophysite controversies in the Church of the fifth century. He found that he could not fully harmonize the facts of the Monophysite schism with the principles of the *via media*. He puzzled over the subject for some time and then mentioned his difficulty to Robert Williams, an old friend, still a Protestant. Williams brought his attention to an article on the schism of the Donatists written by Dr. Nicholas Wiseman, which had just appeared in the Catholic *Dublin Review*.

The Monophysites were an heretical sect of the fifth century who taught, among other things, that there is but one nature in Christ, some of them rejecting His human nature while others contended that His one nature was both human and divine. The heresy was condemned at the Council of Chalcedon in A.D. 451. The Donatists (fourth century) taught that the validity of the sacraments depended on the moral character of the minister and that sinners should not be recognized as Christians unless their sins were secret. Splitting into warring groups, they also taught other erroneous doctrines. Their views were condemned by St. Augustine and others and pronounced heretical at Carthage. Both of these sects claimed jurisdiction over the Catholic world; both were declared by the Church to be without jurisdiction.

It was in the spring of 1839 that the difficulty regarding the Monophysites confronted him. Referring to this in his *Apologia*, twenty-five years later, he says: "In the spring of 1839 my position in the Anglican Church was at its height. I had supreme confidence in my controversial status, and I had a great and still growing success in recommending it to others." His powerful plea for the *via media* had just been made public, in which he had said: "It will preserve us from what threatens [the drift to Rome] though it cannot restore the dead. The spirit of Luther is dead, but Hildebrand and Loyola are alive. Is it sensible, sober, judicious, to be so very angry with those writers of the day, who point to the fact that our divines of the seventeenth century have occupied a ground which is the true and intelligible mean between extremes? . . . Is it true moderation, instead of trying to fortify a middle doctrine, to fling stones at those who do? . . . Would you rather have your sons and daughters members of the Church of England or of the Church of Rome?"

Now he had insisted all along, as the basis of his *via media,* that his "stronghold was Antiquity." But his study of the Monophysite controversy was undermining that basis. And when he read the Wiseman article on the Donatist contentions, his faith in his theory was still further shaken. For he found a surprising similarity in the position of the Donatists, when declared in schism, with that of the Anglican Church in relation to Rome.

His view had firmly been that recognition by the rest of the Catholic world was not necessary for membership of the Catholic Church. But now he discovered that the same plea had been made by the Donatists when their own bishops asserted jurisdiction in all parts of the Catholic world. It was precisely the same claim that he had made for the Anglicans.

This claim, however, had been effectively refuted by St. Augustine and the very Fathers on whom Newman had been leaning for the support of his own theory. St. Augustine's position had been that any attempted jurisdiction in defiance of the Holy See was fallacious everywhere—even when a National Church was already established. Any National Church was in schism if it claimed jurisdiction without the consent of the historic Catholic Church. And Newman now discovered, when he studied the Wiseman article, that this was precisely the claim of the Donatists when St. Augustine gave his verdict (which must necessarily apply to the Anglican as well as any other Churches that defied the Holy See): *"Quapropter securus judicat orbis terrarum, bonos non esse qui se dividunt ab orbe terrarum quacumque parte orbis terrarum."* ("The entire world judges with security that they are not good, who separate themselves from the entire world in whatever part of the entire world.")

The *Dublin Review* article had emphasized that answer, saying that "by the Fathers the question was considered one of fact rather than of right; that is to say, the very fact of one particular Church being out of the aggregation of other Churches, constituted these judges over this other, and left no room for questioning the justice of the condemnation."

Newman was indeed startled when he realized that the early Church Fathers, on whose supposed attitude his theory had been erected, had again and again given as the real test of Catholicity, recognition of and communion with the See of Peter as the authoritative possessor of worldwide jurisdiction. St. Augustine gave this as the mark of the true vine on which all local or national Churches must be grafted; St. Ambrose did the same, as did many other Fathers.

And necessarily so. The Anglican "branch theory" was indeed a paper theory, with no tangible evidence to support it. As stated in the *Catholic Encyclopaedia*: "The consequences of the doctrine constitute a manifest proof of its falsity. The unity of the Catholic Church in every part of the world is the sign of the brotherhood which binds together the children of God. More than this, Christ Himself declared that it would be a proof to all men of His divine mission. . . . Contrariwise, this theory, first advanced to justify a state of things having Henry VIII as its author, would make the Christian Church, not a witness to the brotherhood of God's children, but a standing proof that even the Son of God had failed to withstand the spirit of discord amongst men. Were the theory true, so far from the unity of the Church testifying to the Divine mission of Jesus Christ, its severed and broken condition would be a potent argument in the hands of unbelief."

It was the complete undermining, by the decisions of the greatest of the Fathers, of a *via media* such as Newman had been advocating. For the condemnation of St. Augustine applied fully as much to the position of the Monophysites as it did to that of the Donatists; and his study of the former had already unsettled him.

The friend who had called his attention to the Wiseman article had emphasized these words—*"securus judicat orbis terrarum"*—and these words seemed to haunt him from that hour. Long years after he wrote of this incident:

"He [Williams] repeated these words again and again, and when he was gone, they kept ringing in my ears. 'Securus judicat orbis terrarum'; they were words which went beyond the occasion of the Donatists; they applied to that of the Monophysites.

They gave a cogency to the Article which had escaped me at first. They decided ecclesiastical questions on a simpler rule than that of Antiquity; nay, St. Augustine was one of the prime oracles of Antiquity; here then, Antiquity was deciding against itself. What a light was hereby thrown upon every controversy in the Church; not that, for the moment, the multitude may not falter in their judgment; not that, in the Arian hurricane, Sees more than can be numbered did not bend before its fury, and fall off from St. Athanasius; not that the crowd of Oriental bishops did not need to be sustained during the contest by the voice and the eye of St. Leo; but that the deliberate judgment, in which the whole Church at length rests and acquiesces, is an infallible prescription and a final sentence against such portions of it as protest and secede.

"Who can account for the impressions which are made on him? For a mere sentence, the words of St. Augustine, struck me with a power which I never had felt from any words before. To take a familiar instance, they were like the 'Turn again Whittington,' of the chime; or, to take a more serious one, they were like the 'Tolle, lege—tolle, lege,' of the child, which converted St. Augustine himself. 'Securus judicat orbis terrarum.' By these great words of the ancient Father, interpreting and summing up the long and varied course of ecclesiastical history, the theory of the *via media* was absolutely pulverized."

Although he tried to minimize his discovery on reflection, the Wiseman argument continued to trouble him. In September he wrote his friend Frederick Rogers: "I have had the first real hit from Romanism which has happened to me. . . . I must confess it has given me a stomach ache. You see the whole history of the Monophysites has been a sort of alterative. And now comes this dose at the end of it. It does certainly come upon one that we are not at the bottom of things. At this moment we have sprung a leak; and the worst of it is that those sharp fellows, Ward, Stanley & Co., will not let one go to sleep upon it. . . . I seriously think this a most uncomfortable article on every account, though of course it is *ex parte*. I think I shall get Keble to answer it. As for Pusey, I am curious to see how it acts with him. . . .[1] And now, Carissime, goodby. It is no laughing matter. I will not blink the question, so be it; but don't you suppose I am a madcap to take up actions suddenly—only there is an uncomfortable vista which was closed before."

He tried to close his eyes to this "uncomfortable vista." But he was not very successful; it undermined his confidence and weakened his enthusiasm. For he realized that if the position of the Monophysites was disallowed in their time and that of the Donatists in St. Augustine's time, then the present day Anglicans, as well as these others, were not truly Catholic, for to be a part of the Catholic Church, any religious society must bow to the jurisdiction of that Church. And he now realized that his former parallel of the Arian period—on which he had long placed so much weight—did not at all cover the facts of the Anglican position.

It was about this time that he confided to his intimate friend Henry Wilberforce (an active Tractarian) that "in the end he might find it his duty to join the Roman Catholic Church"—a statement which utterly dismayed the latter. But when Wilberforce said he would rather see him die than take such a step, Newman added that if ever the time should come when he was in serious danger, he would ask his friends to pray that, if it was indeed the will of God, he might be taken away before he did it. Deep indeed were still his prejudices against the Catholic Church.

---

[1] In the event, Keble failed to answer it. As for Pusey, he evidently sidestepped it—a habit of Pusey's which grew on him with the years. There was much truth in what Newman said of Pusey years later. People said that Pusey had been much nearer the Catholic Church during the Oxford Movement than later on. In commenting on this Newman remarked: "I pray God that he may one day be nearer to the Catholic Church than he was then; for I believe that, in his reason and judgment, all the time that I knew him, he was never near it at all."

2

After that summer had passed he was calmer, evidently feeling that his emotions had got the better of him. He says, "When I got back to Oxford in October, 1839, I found a general talk on the subject of the article in the *Dublin Review*. If it affected me, it is not wonderful that it affected others also." But he goes on to say that after mature reflection, he "felt no kind of certainty that the argument in it was conclusive. Taking it at the worst, granting that the Anglican Church had not the Note of Catholicity, yet there were many other Notes of the Church. Some belonged to one age or place, some to another. Bellarmine had reckoned Temporal Prosperity among the Notes of the Church; but the Roman Church had not any great popularity, wealth, glory, power, or prospects in the nineteenth century. It was not at all certain as yet, even that we had not the Note of Catholicity; but, if not this, we had others. . . . My first business then, was to examine this question carefully, and see whether a great deal could not be said after all for the Anglican Church, in spite of its acknowledged shortcomings. This I did in an article on the 'Catholicity of the English Church,' which appeared in the *British Critic* of January, 1840. As to my personal distress on the point, I think it had gone by February 21st in that year, for I wrote then to Mr. Bowden . . . thus:—'It made a great impression here, and I say what of course I would only say to such as yourself, it made me for a while very uncomfortable in my own mind. The great speciousness of his argument is one of the things which have made me despond so much, that is, as anticipating its effect upon others.'"

Yet he must have felt that Wiseman's argument was not so "specious," for he continued to worry. But he was still strongly anti-Roman in his general attitude. Perhaps it was partly his desire (though unconsciously) to demonstrate his firm anti-Romanism to himself, as well as to others, that accounts for his rather amusingly antagonistic attitude when, about this time, a Catholic Passionist priest, Father Ignatius Spencer, came to Oxford and wished to meet him.

George Spencer, a son of the second Earl Spencer of Althorp, was born in 1799, was educated at Cambridge, and took Orders in the Anglican Church in 1820. He was a High Churchman long before the Oxford awakening but was strongly attracted to the Catholic Church as a result of spending his holidays abroad. He was also much influenced by another Cambridge student, Ambrose Phillips. The latter was converted to Catholicism very early. Spencer followed him into the Church in 1830. He became a Passionist, taking the name of Ignatius, and was now spiritual director at Oscott, the Catholic College near Birmingham. As a convert from Anglicanism, he was naturally interested in the progress of the Oxford Movement, feeling that it presaged the return of England as a whole to the Catholic Faith. And now he had started in Catholic circles a crusade of prayer for England's conversion. His visit to Oxford was inspired by the hope of inducing the Tractarians to join in this crusade.

In a letter to Rogers, Newman describes his meeting with Father Spencer: "Palmer of Magdalen College asked me to dine with him, Spencer being present. I said I did not like to put myself out of the way—that if Roman Catholics and Anglo-Catholics met together, it should be in sackcloth, rather than at a pleasant party, and so forth. I said I had no right to ask such a thing of Mr. Spencer, that it was pompous of me. But it was arranged, and today he called with Palmer and sat an hour. He is a gentlemanlike, mild, pleasing man, but sadly smooth. I wonder whether it is their habit of internal discipline, the necessity of confession, and so forth, which makes them so?"

Viewing Spencer as an apostate from the Anglican Church, Newman was cold and rude to him. But he later relented and sent him a letter of apology. Yet he could not resist the temptation in this letter to show his animus towards the Catholic Church. He said, "Your acts are contrary to your words. You invite us to a union of hearts, at the same time that you are doing all you can, not to restore, not to reform, not to reunite, but to destroy our Church. . . . I cannot meet familiarly any leading persons of the Roman communion, and least of all when they come to me on a religious errand. You go further than your principles require. You are leagued with our enemies. 'The voice is Jacob's voice, but the hands are the hands of Esau.' " And then he closed with some bitter words about the political alignments of Daniel O'Connell, the Irish Catholic agitator, with the Liberals of the English Parliament.

As far as Newman was concerned, Spencer's mission to Oxford was a failure. Both Newman and Palmer consumed Spencer's limited time by discussing the "branch theory" and subtle theological questions. After returning to Oscott, Spencer wrote to his friend Ambrose Phillips (who had urged the visit to Oxford) : "I was brought during the first days of the fight to the most astonishing point not only of having my battery regularly silenced, but of being in a complete maze in my own mind."

However, Newman and Spencer will in time meet again under very different circumstances.

Despite what Hurrell Froude had long before taught him of the proper attitude of High Anglicans towards the Catholic Church, it is obvious that what Newman later described as his "false conscience" in relation to the Antichrist absurdity—as well as his distorted notions regarding the "Mariolatry" of the Catholic Church—was still potent. Though suffering inwardly from the uncertainties created by his recent discovery that his whole *via media* theory had been "pulverized," his normal attitude was still that of a vigorous champion of the Tractarian, or "Anglo-Catholic" movement.

The article he had written for the *British Critic,* on the

"Catholicity of the English Church," was not any too convincing regarding its Catholicity, but it did seem more successful in its emphasis on the Notes of Life and Sanctity. He now concentrated on this theme, developing his ideas in a number of able discourses. He also attempted to demonstrate the continuity of Life and Sanctity in the Anglican communion by promoting the issuance of a series of lives of English saints—those who worked and wrought for Catholic truth prior to the upheavals of the sixteenth century. To arouse public interest in the English saints of old would, he hoped, help to show that sanctity had been the great antidote to heresy and corruption; and a demonstration of this fact, by bringing to the front the great spiritual figures of the early and medieval English Church, would tend to stimulate zeal for the traditional Catholic characteristics of the Church in England.

It soon became apparent, however, that the lives of English saints who lived before Reformation days awakened no interest among the Anglicans of the nineteenth century. One of the first issued, the life of a famous monk, St. Stephen Harding, was condemned by critics as being "of a character inconsistent with its proceeding from an Anglican publisher." It too strongly reminded the reader of the famous monks of the early ages, whose ascetic lives and alleged miracles appealed not to the Protestant John Bulls of the Anglican Establishment.

It was a wet blanket. If the Church of England, Newman concluded, could not stand the biographies of those who were officially recognized as her own saints—well, what was the use of going on with the series? Further volumes were issued, but he retired from the editorship after two or three of the series had appeared.

Yet he still continued to hope for better things and, despite misgivings, worked hard for the movement. But his mind was never at rest; the "ghost" of uncertainty was ever disturbing him. His feelings were later described in the following passage: "My stronghold was Antiquity; now here, in the middle of the fifth century, I found, as it seemed to me, Christendom of the sixteenth and nineteenth centuries reflected. I saw my face in that mirror, and I was a Monophysite! The Church of the *via media* was in the position of the Oriental communion; Rome was where she now is and the Protestants were the Eutychians. . . . Of all the passages of history, since history has begun, who would have thought of going to the sayings of old Eutyches,[1] that *delirus senex*, as (I think) Petavius calls him, and to the enormities of the unprincipled Dioscorus, in order to be converted to Rome?"

3

After 1839 set in, the trend of the movement—as already indicated—was undergoing a radical change. Among its leaders at least, it had developed into a struggle more to keep its following from flocking to the Catholic Church than to center attention, as during the first years, on the Protestant fallacies within the fold.

As a direct result of this menace to the movement, it seemed extremely important to devise in some way a genuine Catholic interpretation of the official Anglican formularies—the famous Thirty-Nine Articles of Religion, which had been adopted by the Anglican Church at the time of the Tudor Settlement in the sixteenth century. These Articles had been compiled and unanimously endorsed by the extreme Protestant elements at that time as a demonstration of the Church's opposition to Catholicism.

And so it was that, early in 1841, came forth Tract Ninety, written by Newman. It was a remarkable attempt to give these Articles a definite Catholic interpretation. Newman, Pusey and Keble, leaders of the more conservative Tractarians, had begun

---

[1] Eutyches was a heretic of the fifth century; Dioscorus was an anti-pope of the same period.

to realize that if some such attempt as this was not soon made, the more radical men in the movement would soon be flocking to the Catholic Church. The situation was lucidly stated by Newman years later in the *Apologia,* from which the following is quoted.

"It was urged that here was a positive note *against* Anglicanism. Anglicanism [the "Anglo-Catholic" group] claimed to hold, that the Church of England was nothing else than a continuation in this country (as the Church of Rome might be in France or Spain) of that one Church of which in old times Athanasius and Augustine were members. But, if so, the doctrine must be the same; the doctrine of the Old Church must live and speak in Anglican formularies—in the Thirty Nine Articles. Did it? Yes, it did; that is what I maintained; it did in substance, in a true sense. Man had done his worst to disfigure, to mutilate, the old Catholic Truth; but there it was, in spite of them, in the Articles still. It was there—but this must be shown. It was a matter of life or death to us to show it. And I believed that it could be shown; I considered that those grounds of justification, which I gave above—when I was speaking of Tract Ninety—were sufficient for the purpose; and therefore I set about showing it at once. . . . I had in mind to remove all such obstacles as lay in the way of holding the Apostolic and Catholic character of the Anglican teaching; to assert the right of all who chose, to say in the face of day—'Our Church teaches the Primitive Ancient Faith.' I did not conceal this; in Tract Ninety, it is put forward as the first principle of all, 'It is a duty which we owe both to the Catholic Church, and to our own, to take our reformed confessions in the most Catholic sense they will admit; we have no duties towards their framers; . . . that whereas it is usual at this day to make the *particular belief of their writers* their true interpretation, I would make *the belief of the Catholic Church* such. That is, as it is often said that infants are regenerated in Baptism, not on the faith of their parents, but of the Church, so in like manner I would say that the Articles are received, not in the sense of their framers, but (as far as the wording will admit or any ambiguity requires it) in the one Catholic sense."

Newman was passionately in earnest in this attempt to interpret a set of religious formularies, many of which, as the records plainly show, admitted of no such interpretation; in fact some of them admitted of no clear interpretation at all—so obvious was the intent of their framers to throw dust in the eyes of the doubtful while anchoring fundamental Protestantism to the Church. As Richard Holt Hutton, a Protestant admirer of Newman, said in 1890: "It is never a very pleasant office for a man who is himself in passionate earnest, as Newman was, to take refuge behind the ambiguities of a creed artfully devised to suit the views of two distinct parties, whose whole drift was at bottom irreconcilable. I have never quite understood how, with Newman's view of the Church, he was willing to belong to one which had gone so far in the direction of superficially at least disavowing doctrines which he himself was disposed to hold very sacred." [1]

Perhaps the best answer to this query of Hutton's lies partly in Newman's somewhat romantic hope that he could rescue the Church which he loved so well; but the full answer came later on, as a result of further discoveries of the inherent Protestantism of the Anglican Church; and then he left it without further delay.

The Tract was a brave attempt, but the storm it created in Anglican circles was a whirlwind. A few days after its appearance we find Newman writing to his intimate friend Bowles: "Do you know I am getting into a scrape about Tract Ninety? Yes, it must be; I cannot repent it a bit; unless, indeed, it should get Pusey involved in it. . . . People are so angry they will attempt to do anything. I have just heard that the Board of Heads of

---

[1] Richard Holt Hutton, *Cardinal Newman*.

Houses is *most fierce* with the Tract, and Tracts generally, and means to do something."

The Tract amazed all Oxford and alarmed the Church authorities. The Bishop of Oxford, Dr. Bagot, at once called Newman to account; an official censure came from the Heads of Houses like a thunderclap; angry remonstrances arose from all parts of England, every newspaper in the land taking up the cry. What? Tamper with the Thirty-Nine Articles, on which our Protestant structure rests? Away with this Romanizing hypocrite who would undermine our Protestantism in the interest of Popery! This was the all but universal temper; and the more moderate High Churchmen furtively whispered, "Newman has gone too far."

In Oxford, Tait of Balliol (the future Archbishop of Canterbury) openly charged Newman with dishonest quibbling, and this charge was echoed by many of the bishops. At an interview with his own bishop, Newman agreed to discontinue issuing the Tracts but declined to withdraw the opinions expressed in them. But most of the bishops were not content with this promised discontinuance of the Tracts; one after another they issued charges against them, in which they all emphasized the fundamental Protestantism of the Anglican Establishment.

Dean Church, in his history of the *Oxford Movement,* comments on this action of the bishops and University authorities as follows:

"The first bishop to condemn the movement was the bishop of Chester, J. Bird Sumner; in a later charge he came to describe it as the work of Satan; he denounced 'the undermining of our Protestant Church by men who dwell within her walls,' and the bad faith of those 'who sit in the Reformers' seat, and traduce the Reformation.' Unhappily Tract Ninety was met at Oxford, not by argument, but by panic and wrath. . . . Tract Ninety was charged of course with false history and with false reasoning; but the emphatic part of the charge, the short and easy method which dispensed from the necessity of theological examination and argument, was that it was dishonest and immoral."

The antagonism of the bishops is best indicated by quoting the comments of several. One of them quoted from Cranmer's Homily: "Let us diligently search the well of life, and not run after the stinking puddles of tradition devised by man's imagination." Another said: "It is a subject of deep concern that any of our body should prepare men of ardent feelings and warm imaginations for a return to the Roman mass-book." Another bishop wrote: "Already are the foundations of apostasy laid; if we once admit another Gospel, Antichrist is at the door. I am full of fear; everything is at stake; there seems to be something judicial in the rapid spread of these opinions." And still another: "It is impossible not to remark on the subtle wile of the adversary; it has been signally and unexpectedly exemplified in the present day by the revival of errors which might have been supposed buried forever." And finally I quote a loquacious one: "Among many marvels of the present day may be accounted the irreverent and unbecoming language applied to the chief promoters of the Reformation in this land. The quick and extensive propagation of opinions tending to exalt the claims of the Church and of the clergy, can be no proof of their soundness."

It was indeed a tragedy for the Tractarians, and especially for Newman. A letter to his friend J. R. Hope indicates his dismay and confusion. "As for the bishops' charges," he says, "this must be remembered—that they have no authority except in their own dioceses. A bishop's word is to be obeyed, not as to doctrine, but as a part of discipline. Till truth is silenced among us, I do not see that Catholic minds need be in a difficulty. . . . Having said this, I will go on to own that the said charges are a very serious matter; as virtually silencing portions of the truth in particular dioceses, and as showing that it is not impossible that our Church *may* lapse into heresy. I cannot deny that a great and anxious experiment is going on, whether our Church be or not be

Catholic; the issue may not be in our day. But I must be plain in saying that if it does issue in Protestantism, I shall think it my duty, if alive, to leave it."

Perhaps most Catholics reading to this point will wonder how there could have been any doubt about its "issuing in Protestantism"! But some converts of Anglican background will understand!

That the Anglican Church, insofar as its ruling powers were concerned, was roundly Protestant was further demonstrated at this time by the establishment of an Anglican bishopric in Jerusalem, which was to recognize Lutherans, Calvinists and heaven knows what others as communicants on the same basis as confirmed Anglicans. In connection with this venture, Newman wrote to a friend: "Have you heard of this fearful business of the Bishopric of Jerusalem? It seems that we are in the way to fraternize with Protestants of all sorts—Monophysites, half-converted Jews and Druses. If any such event should take place, I shall not be able to keep a single man from Rome. They will all be trooping off sooner or later."

Still another event which a little later indicated that the authorities were bent on crushing the Tractarian movement was that when Dr. Pusey ventured to preach a sermon at Oxford in which he spoke in support of the doctrine of the Real Presence in the Holy Eucharist, he was forthwith suspended for two years from preaching at the University.

It may well be imagined that it was not William George Ward and his school of "advanced" Tractarians who were critical of Tract Ninety. They wildly applauded it; but Ward, with his great dialectical skill, pushed Newman's arguments much further, claiming tolerance for Rome which Newman had in no sense intended. As a result, Ward found himself in a violent controversy with Pusey. He had published a pamphlet making extraordinary claims for the Tract, which Pusey, being far more cautious, at once criticised. Ward was beginning to doubt the validity of Anglican sacraments, and he said that Newman's view was much the same. "I have heard Newman say," he told Pusey, "that it is, to say the least, doubtful whether there can be said to be a valid sacrament unless the priest adds mentally what our Eucharistic service omits. Williams of King's College, Cambridge, mentioned to Newman in my hearing, that the Bishop of Lincoln, in speaking to him at the time of his ordination, laughed at the notion of an Apostolical succession as having passed through 'Pope Joan,' and that Newman said, 'If even the Bishop of Lincoln talks so, what must we say of the remainder of our bishops?'—or words even rather stronger."

Thus was acrimonious discussion about doctrinal matters going on in typical Anglican fashion. Yet how could it be otherwise in a Church made up of contradictory schools of thought? The majority of the bishops of those days (and perhaps a majority of the laity also) were really Arminians, viewing the Articles as harmlessly Lutheran, though the Calvinists had claimed their authorship from the first. As for the Evangelicals, they had difficulty in accepting the doctrine of Baptism as defined in the Articles—not to mention that the doctrine of the Holy Eucharist was too muddled to suit their Protestant minds. But perhaps the most aggressive critics were the divines of Whately's school (the future Broad Churchmen), who were even then undermining the authority of all creeds and articles and proclaiming their dislike of the Athanasian Creed, to which the Prayer Book and the Articles bound them. It was in this sort of *milieu* that the "Anglo-Catholics" were trying to live and move and have their being— as it is even to this day.

Although Ward quarrelled with Pusey and defended Newman at this time, he realized, perhaps sooner than Newman, the weaknesses of Tract Ninety as an effort to prove the Catholicity of the Anglican Church. At any rate they had their differences, and Newman was greatly annoyed at the free way in which Ward quoted him. But Ward went boldly and persistently on with violent discussion, more and more aggressively proclaiming his pro-Catholic leanings. Finally, after two or three years of this, in the summer of 1844 he threw all Oxford into a ferment by the issuance of a polemical book, *Ideal of a Christian Church*, an exhaustive, erudite volume in which he asserted, among many other "heresies," his right to continue as a clergyman in the Anglican Church "while holding the whole cycle of Roman Doctrine." This was too much for the University to stand; it was the straw that broke the camel's back. Ward was dismissed from his Professorship and deprived of his University degrees.

Evidently these actions of the University delighted rather than dismayed him. For he was far advanced on the road to the Catholic Church well before there were any tangible signs that Newman would take the same road. He was received into the Church soon after his book had been put on the University "index"—not, however, until he had done something which amazed, where it did not dismay, his Tractarian friends; he married! He had preached clerical celibacy, but had now concluded that Anglican Orders did not make him a priest. It was his marriage rather than his conversion which inspired Arthur Stanley (a Tractarian who had lapsed) to declare, "It marks the end of the Oxford movement!"

Several of Ward's sympathizers, as well as certain other Tractarians, had preceded him into the Catholic Church during the previous two years. In fact, well before Ward's exit, there had been a growing leakage to Rome—inspired, no doubt, by the wholesale condemnation of Tract Ninety. These events greatly depressed Dr. Pusey; he was quite broken-hearted, not only because of these conversions, but also because of lapses of many of the weaker brethren, who had become timid before the onslaughts of the bishops. It was all but ten years since the optimistic Dr. Pusey had predicted that the entire Anglican Church could be brought around to the views of the Caroline divines—and now his dream had crashed to the ground. Ward, who was blessed with an enormous sense of humor, told with delight how Pusey had said:

"It is all very sad. And all who are leaving us have deteriorated so much—all, that is, with two exceptions. One exception is Newman, whose nature is so beautiful, so perfect, that nothing, not even his going over to Rome, could change him. The other exception is Ward. Ward has got so bad already that with him further deterioration would be impossible!"

If the defection of Ward was expected and caused humorous remarks, rumors which had long been rife regarding Newman were being discounted by a host of people who would not believe that he would ever leave the Anglican Church. But at the time of which we are writing, he did not himself know what his future course would be.

After the condemnation of Tract Ninety and the discontinuance of the Tracts, he continued to preach at St. Mary's; but, as an observer has said, his sermons "assumed an uneasy tone which perplexed his followers." For years he had been trying to lead his people with the confidence that he was strengthening Anglicanism against both Rome and popular Protestantism; but now, he could neither urge his followers to advance closer to Rome nor keep back with convincing arguments those who were going to Rome; and he was also losing the support of many timid and frightened men, who were creeping back under the wings of the bishops. He began to feel that to remain in Oxford with his views so definitely condemned by the authorities was little short of paradoxical; and he was seriously thinking of resigning his station at St. Mary's.

4

In the village of Littlemore, a suburb two or three miles from Oxford, he had been giving catechetical instructions on Sunday evenings for five or six years and in 1836 had established a chapel there as an adjunct to St. Mary's. Later he acquired some cottages and erected extensions, planning a sort of religious center, perhaps a retreat house with an oratory and other appurtenances. Beginning with 1840 he spent more and more time at this Littlemore retreat and provided a curate for St. Mary's. After the condemnation of Tract Ninety, he was seldom to be found at Oxford but kept "open house" at Littlemore, frequently preaching in the small chapel there, where many flocked to hear him. He now did the greater part of his writing at Littlemore, having moved his very extensive library from his rooms at Oriel in Oxford.

The public curiosity which was excited by his removal was later described by him in the *Apologia*. I will let him speak for himself:

"After Tract Ninety," he says, "the Protestant world would not let me alone; they pursued me in the public journals to Littlemore. Reports of all kinds were circulated about me. 'Imprimis, why did I go up to Littlemore at all? For no good purpose, certainly; I dared not tell why.' Why, to be sure, it was hard that I should be obliged to say to the editors of newspapers that I went up there to say my prayers; it was hard to tell the world in confidence, that I had a certain doubt about the Anglican system, and could not at that moment resolve it, or say what would come of it; it was hard to have to confess that I had thought of giving up my Living a year or two before, and that this was a first step to it. It was hard to have to plead that, for what I knew, my doubts would vanish, if the newspapers would be so good as to give me time and let me alone. Who would ever dream of making the world his confidant? Yet I was considered insidious, sly, dishonest, if I would not open my heart to the tender mercies of the world. . . . 'What was I doing at Littlemore?' . . . Am I . . . not to have the privilege to go where I will? Am I alone to be followed about by jealous prying eyes? . . . I cannot walk into or out of my house, but curious eyes are upon me. Why will you not let me die in peace? Wounded brutes creep into some hole to die in, and no one grudges it them. Let me alone, I shall not trouble you long. . . . This was the keen feeling which pierced me, and, I think, these are the very words in which I expressed it to myself. I asked, in the words of a great motto, 'Ubi lapsus? Quid feci?' . . . I had thought that an Englishman's house was his castle, but the newspapers thought otherwise. . . ."

Long before he had given up his living at St. Mary's the gossips were busy, and even his own bishop felt constrained to ask him how much truth there was in a newspaper story that "a so-called Anglo-Catholic monastery is in process of erection at Littlemore, and the cells of dormitories, the chapel, the refectory, the cloisters may be seen advancing to perfection, under the eye of a parish priest of the diocese of Oxford." The bishop said that while he never placed credence in mere gossip, yet he wished to inquire if there was any basis for this statement. It gave Newman an opportunity to write the bishop a long explanatory letter, in which, among other things, he said:

"As to my intentions, I purpose to live there myself a good deal, as I have a resident curate at Oxford. In doing this, I believe I am consulting the good of my parish, as my population at Littlemore is at least equal to that of St. Mary's in Oxford. . . . At the same time it has appeared to me that a partial or temporary retirement from St. Mary's Church might be expedient under prevailing excitement. . . . Your Lordship will perceive from what I have said that no 'monastery is in process of erection'; there is no 'chapel,' no 'refectory,' hardly a dining-room or parlor. The 'cloisters' are my shed connecting the cottages. I do not understand what 'cells of dormitories' means. . . . I am attempting nothing ecclesiastical, but something personal and private, and which can only be made public, not private, by newspapers and letter writers, in which sense the most sacred and conscientious resolves and acts may certainly be made the objects of an unmannerly and unfeeling curiosity."

The bishop was surely mollified by this letter, for from that time on their relations were friendly and sympathetic. In fact, although the Bishop of Oxford was certainly not sympathetic towards Tractarianism, he always held Newman in high regard. Long after, Newman was to write of him: "My duty to him was my point of honor; his disapprobation was the one thing I could not bear. I believe it to have been a generous and honest feeling; and in consequence I was rewarded by having all my time for ecclesiastical superior a man, whom had I had a choice, I should have preferred, out and out, to any other Bishop on the Bench, and for whose memory I have a special affection; Dr. Bagot—a man of noble mind, and as kind hearted and as considerate as he was noble. He ever sympathized with me in my trials which followed. . . . May his name be ever blessed."

By 1842 certain of his old associates seem to have lost faith in him (at least they were puzzled and mystified), while those of strong Catholicizing tendencies were disappointed in his failing to assume a more friendly attitude towards Rome. But the truth was that his own mind was far from clarified, and he could not take a definite stand until he had solved the problems which were troubling him. His more worthwhile friends, Keble and Pusey particularly, clearly understood his attitude. As he later said, "I had to make up my mind for myself, and others could not help me. I determined to be guided, not by my imagination, but by my reason." And this is said over and over again in the years that followed, both in conversation and private letters. "Had it not been for this severe resolve, I should have been a Catholic sooner than I was."

He was still Vicar of St. Mary's, but a letter to Keble written somewhat earlier contains passages which indicate how troubled he was in regard to this situation.

"For a year past a feeling has been growing on me that I ought to give up St. Mary's, but I am no fit judge in the matter. I cannot ascertain accurately my own impressions and convictions, which are the basis of the difficulty, and though you cannot of course do this for me, yet you may help me generally, and perhaps supersede the necessity of my going by them at all. . . . [The] authorities of the University, the appointed guardians of those who form great part of the attendants on my sermons, have shown a dislike of my preaching. It seems then, on the whole, that I am using St. Mary's to the neglect of its direct duties for objects not belonging to it. . . . One dissuades men from coming; the late Vice-Chancellor threatens to take his own children away from the church; and the present [Vice Chancellor], having an opportunity last spring of preaching in my parish pulpit, gets up and preaches against doctrines with which I am in good measure identified. No plainer proof can be given of the feeling in these quarters, than the absurd myth, now for a second time put forward, that Vice-Chancellors cannot be got to take office on account of 'Puseyism.' . . . But this is not all. I fear I must allow that, whether I will or no, I am disposing them [his hearers] towards Rome. First, because Rome is the only representative of the Primitive Church besides ourselves; in proportion then as they are loosened from one, they will go to the other. Next, because many doctrines which I have held have far greater, or their only scope, in the Roman system. . . . People tell me that I am . . . exerting at St. Mary's a beneficial influence on our prospective clergy; but what if I take to myself the credit of seeing further than they, and of having in the course of the last year discovered that what they approve so much is very likely to end in Romanism? . . . Nor can I counteract the danger by preaching or writing against Rome. I seem to myself almost to have shot my last arrow in the article on English Catholicity. It must be added, that the very circumstance that I have committed

myself against Rome has the effect of setting to sleep people suspicious about me, which is very painful now that I begin to have
suspicions about myself!"

Keble, of course, poured oil on the troubled waters, urging
him to stay at St. Mary's, with the hope, no doubt, that his difficulties would pass in time. Actually, Newman delayed in leaving
until 1843.

One story circulated by the gossips particularly infuriated
him: "It was that I was actually in the service of the enemy. I
had forsooth been already received into the Catholic Church,
and was rearing at Littlemore a nest of Papists, who, like me,
were to take Anglican Orders in which they disbelieved, by virtue
of a dispensation from Rome, and thus in due course to bring
over to that unprincipled Church great numbers of the Anglican
clergy and laity! . . ."

In this connection he says: "The case was simply this: as I
made Littlemore a place of retirement for myself, so did I offer it
to others. There were young men in Oxford, whose testimonials
for Orders had been refused by their colleges; there were young
clergymen, who had found themselves unable from conscience to
go on with their duties, and had thrown up their parochial
engagements. Such men were already going straight to Rome,
and I interposed. . . . Their friends besought me to quiet them,
if I could. Some of them came to live with me at Littlemore.
They were laymen, or in the place of laymen. I kept some of
them back for several years from being received into the Catholic
Church. Even when I had given up my living, I was still bound
by my duty to their parents or friends, and I did not forget still
to do what I could for them. The immediate occasion of my
resigning St. Mary's, was the unexpected conversion of one of
them. After that, I felt it was impossible to keep my post there,
for I had been unable to keep my word with my Bishop."

5

It would serve little purpose to detail here all the annoying incidents that confronted Newman during these troubled years. He was continuously being charged with duplicity and cowardice, whereas in truth he was simply trying to resolve his doubts regarding the Catholicity of the Anglican Church. But as for his conniving to lead people to Rome, this, in view of his inborn and deep-seated prejudices against the Catholic Church, was grotesquely absurd.

His mind was still "stained" by his notion, imbibed in his youth, that the Pope was Antichrist, and also by his ignorant prejudices regarding the "Mariolatry" which he believed was taught by the Catholic Church. Thus he says in his *Apologia*:

"I could not go to Rome while I thought what I did of the devotions she sanctioned to the Blessed Virgin and the Saints. . . . But it was made a subject of reproach to me at the time, and is at this day, that I did not leave the Anglican Church sooner. To me this seems a wonderful charge; why, even had I been quite sure that Rome was the true Church, the Anglican bishops would have had no just subject of complaint against me, provided I took no Anglican oath, no clerical duty, no ecclesiastical administration. [After his last sermon, "The Parting of Friends," which he delivered in 1843, he had retired to lay communion.] However, I was to have other measure dealt to me; great authorities ruled it so; and a great controversialist thought it a shame that I did not leave the Church of England as much as ten years sooner than I did."

In response to the charge that he was a "concealed Romanist" for ten years prior to his actual conversion, he was explicitly to state: "For the first four years [1835 to 1839] I honestly wished to benefit the Church of England at the expense of the Church of Rome; for the second four years I wished to benefit the Church of England without prejudice to the Church of Rome; at the beginning of the ninth year I began to despair of the Church of England and gave up all clerical duty; and then, what I wrote and did was influenced by a mere wish not to injure it, and not by the wish to benefit it. At the beginning of the tenth year I distinctly contemplated leaving it, but I also distinctly told my friends that it was in my contemplation. Lastly, during the last half of that tenth year, I was engaged in writing a book [*Essay on Development*] in favor of the Roman Church, and indirectly against the English; but even then, till it was finished, I had not absolutely intended to publish it, wishing to reserve to myself the chance of changing my mind when the argumentative views which were actuating me, had been distinctly brought out before me in writing."

Although with the completing of his *Essay on Development* in the autumn of 1845 Newman was brought to his final decision, other influences had also been working on his mind. As early as the summer of 1841 he had become acquainted with Dr. Charles William Russell, later the President of Maynooth. A warm friendship gradually developed, and in the course of time Newman raised with him the question of "Mariolatry" in the Catholic Church. Russell gave him some books on the subject, including a volume of sermons of St. Alfonso Liguori. As a result, for the first time the true attitude of the Catholic Church regarding the Blessed Virgin became clear to him. Thus he says, "Dr. Russell, perhaps, had more to do with my conversion than anyone else."

A somewhat lengthy comment concerning his enlightenment on this subject is found in the *Apologia,* from which these brief excerpts are quoted:

"This I know full well now, and did not know then, that the Catholic Church allows no image of any sort, material or immaterial, no dogmatic symbol, no rite, no sacrament, no saint, not even the Blessed Virgin herself, to come between the soul and

its Creator. It is face to face, 'solus cum solo,' in all matters between man and his God. He alone creates; He alone has re-
deemed; before His awful eyes we go in death; in the vision of
Him is our eternal beatitude. . . .

"The devotion then to Angels and Saints as little interfere
with the incommunicable glory of the Eternal, as the love which
we bear our friends and relations, our tender human sympathies,
are inconsistent with that supreme homage of the heart to the
Unseen, which really does but sanctify and exalt, not jealously
destroy, what is of earth. At a later date Dr. Russell sent me a
large bundle of penny or half-penny books of devotion, of all
sorts, as they are found in the booksellers' shops at Rome; and,
on looking them over, I was quite astonished to find how different they were from what I had fancied, how little there was in
them to which I could really object. . . . Dr. Russell sent me
St. Alfonso's book at the end of 1842. It was still a long time
before I got over my difficulty, on the score of the devotions paid
to the saints; perhaps . . . it was some way into 1844, before I
could be said fully to have got over it."

Quite typical is this of converts who, in utter ignorance of the
truth, have carried false notions for years. From boyhood Newman had carried the notion (imbibed in his Protestant upbringing), which seems to have waxed stronger during his early Anglican years, that the Catholic Church teaches worship of the
Mother of God, not as a creature, but as an equal to God—a
"goddess," no less!—and worship of all other saints in a similar
category.

As for his lifelong conviction that the Pope was Antichrist, this
notion had now faded from his mind; probably it had been fad-
ing since the days of Hurrell Froude—though he insists that it
lingered long as a sort of "false conscience."

His studies during this last year in the Anglican communion,
which were now leading him to reach his final goal by way of his
great *Essay on Development,* undoubtedly did much at this time

to help him to a proper perspective in the matter of the Blessed Virgin and the saints. Apropos of this he says: "The idea of the Blessed Virgin was, as it were, *magnified* in the Church of Rome as time went on—but so were all the Christian ideas; as that of the Blessed Eucharist. The whole scene of pale, faint, distant Apostolic Christianity is seen in Rome, as through a telescope or magnifier. The harmony of the whole, however, is of course what it was. It is unfair, then, to take one Roman idea, that of the Blessed Virgin, out of what may be called its context."

Then he adds by way of explanation: "Thus I am brought to the principle of Development of Doctrine in the Christian Church, to which I gave my mind at the end of 1842 . . . even at an earlier date I had introduced it into my *History of the Arians* . . . nor had I ever lost sight of it in my speculations. And it is certainly recognized in the *Treatise of Vincent of Lerins,* which has so often been taken as the basis of Anglicanism."

In this connection might be added this further quotation from his *Apologia*: "So, at the end of 1844, I came to the resolution of writing an Essay on Doctrinal Development; and then, if at the end of it, my convictions in favor of the Roman Church were not weaker, of taking the necessary steps for admission into her fold." [1]

---

[1] To avoid interruption of the personal narrative, an explanation of this notable work, *Development of Christian Doctrine,* is deferred until Chapter Six. The actual conversion of Newman and his reception into the Catholic Church should first be described.

CHAPTER FIVE

"THE BLESSED VISION OF PEACE"

1

"FROM THE END OF 1841, I was on my deathbed, as regards my membership with the Anglican Church—though at that time I became aware of it only by degrees." With these words Newman begins the chapter in his *Apologia* covering the years 1841 to 1845. Then he goes on to say:

"A deathbed has scarcely a history; it is a tedious decline, with seasons of rallying and seasons of falling back; and since the end is foreseen, or what is called a matter of time, it has little interest for the reader, especially if he has a kind heart. Moreover, it is a season when doors are closed and curtains drawn, and when the sick man neither cares nor is able to record the stages of his malady. I was in these circumstances, except so far as I was not allowed to die in peace—except so far as friends, who had still a full right to come in upon me, and the public world, which had not, have given a sort of history to those four last years."

It was at Littlemore that he was on his Anglican "deathbed" during these years. At first he had stayed there only for short periods and still was frequently seen at Oxford. But as time went on, more days were spent at Littlemore, and only occasionally was he to be found in Oxford. But perhaps it was not until after he resigned his living of St. Mary's in the year 1843 that he was permanently lodged at Littlemore. Here he lived with a group of his closest friends and sympathizers, Ambrose St. John, J. D. Dalgairns, E. S. Bowles and Richard Stanton (Albany Christie and John Walker were frequent visitors). This group, with the gradual augmentation of younger men who were still students, made up the little community, which led a life of the utmost simplicity and self-denial. The Divine Office was said daily, and certain simple rules of living prevailed. As they were still Anglicans, they made use of the Littlemore chapel, where W. J. Copeland, Newman's curate, remained after Newman's retirement to lay communion.

Prayers, reading and writing filled the mornings of the group in residence. In the afternoon they usually took long strolls, when Newman led the conversation on topics of interest—a lifelong habit of his acquired in college days. His talks on these strolls were always of a general or secular nature—politics, literature, current events were ordinarily the subjects under discussion. Only to Ambrose St. John did he in these days open his heart on the all-important topic of Anglicanism versus Catholicism. The others had to guess his thoughts.

Often he was a guest of William George Ward, who now had a cottage nearby. Other friends, like Oakeley, who came over from Rose Hill, and Mark Pattison, R. W. Church and W. J. Copeland, were frequent visitors. But most of his own free hours were spent at work in his library alone, where he was struggling to untangle the threads of the great problem which was still troubling him.

Nearly all the friends who lived with or visited him from time to time were struggling with the same problem; but, like Newman, they all hesitated to break the links with the past. For these men all loved the Church which they had been trying so hard to serve. Though they had met with rebuffs from bishops and others, yet to them the Anglican body was a beautiful and venerable institution. In a passage written long afterward, Newman answered the question whether, had the ruling powers of the Establishment been more sympathetic or tolerant towards their work, they would have remained within the fold. "Many a man," he said, "might have held an abstract theory about the Catholic Church to which it was difficult to adjust the Anglican, might have admitted a suspicion or even a painful doubt about the latter, yet never have been impelled onwards, had our rulers preserved the quiescence of former years; but it is the corroboration of a great living and energetic heterodoxy that realizes and makes such doubts practical. It has been the recent speeches and acts of authorities who had so long been tolerant of Protestant error, which has given to inquiry and to theory its force and edge."

Newman's studies of fundamentals forced him to abandon the Church of his youth and the scenes and people he had loved for many years. We need not wonder that he looked back wistfully to the past. He knew that he was a stumbling block to all who were opposed to him and his views. With his delicate, sensitive nature, he must have suffered intensely. It was hard to turn his back on so much beauty and affection, to cut himself off from the inspiring Oxford life where, with the little group of like-minded companions—like Pusey and Keble and Copeland and Henry Wilberforce—he had been doing yeoman service for the cause which was so close to all their hearts. There had been the keen joy with which he had written the Tracts, the ardor with which he had worked on those wonderful sermons delivered at St. Mary's, the crusader-like spirit that had animated them all in their struggle to bring to the mind of their Church, the Apostolic and spiritual truths which had been so largely lost.

Years later, after he had entered the Catholic Church, in one of the lectures of the series called "Difficulties of Anglicans," delivered in London before Anglican audiences, he spoke of those Oxford days of his youth as follows:

"Can I forget—I never can forget—the days when, in my youth, I found myself bound to the ministry of God in that old church of St. Frideswide, the patroness of Oxford. Nor how I wept most abundant and most sweet tears when I thought of what I had become; though I looked on ordination as no sacramental rite, nor even to baptism ascribed any supernatural virtue. Can I wipe out from my memory, or wish to wipe out, those happy Sunday mornings, light or dark, year after year, when I celebrated your communion-rite, in my own church of St. Mary's; and in the pleasantness and joy of it heard nothing of the strife of tongues which surrounded its walls? When, too, shall I not feel the soothing recollection of those dear years which I spent in retirement, in preparation for my deliverance from Egypt, asking for light and by degrees gaining it, with less of temptation in my heart, and sin on my conscience, than ever before? O my dear brethren, my Anglican friends, I easily give you credit for what I have experienced myself. . . ."

In the autumn of 1843 he resigned his living of St. Mary's and at the same time preached, in the Littlemore church, his famous sermon on "The Parting of Friends." The church that day was overflowing with flowers; it was the seventh anniversary of its consecration. In this little church was the tomb of his own mother; when she died in 1836 she had been living not far from the village of Littlemore. The church was crowded that day, not only with local parishioners, but with many from Oxford, many of Newman's old Tractarian friends, including Dr. Pusey, Copeland, Wilberforce, Williams and others. Although he had said nothing to indicate it, this was to be the last sermon he was ever to preach as an Anglican. Perhaps this was instinctively felt by his great audience, even before he announced it. For by this time it seemed obvious to most of them that his severance from Anglicanism would not be long delayed.

This sermon was one of the most touching discourses of his

entire career. One would wish to quote it in full, but space limits me to two brief excerpts.

"O my mother," he exclaimed in the anguish of farewell to this Church of his youth; "whence is this unto thee that thou hast good things poured out upon thee and canst not keep them, and bearest children, yet darest not own them? Why hast thou not the skill to use their services, nor the heart to rejoice in their love? How is it that whatever is generous in purpose, and tender or deep in devotion, thy flower and thy promise, falls from thy bosom and finds no home within thine arms?"

The closing passage, addressed particularly to old and affectionate friends, not only brought tears to his own eyes and caused his voice to falter, but his audience could scarcely restrain their own tears as they listened to this touching farewell:

"O my brethren," he said in a gentle voice, as he leaned over the pulpit, "O kind and affectionate hearts, O loving friends, should you know any one whose lot it has been, by writing or by word of mouth, in some degree to help you thus to act; if he has ever told you what you knew about yourselves, or what you did not know; has read to you your wants or feelings, and comforted you by the very reading; has made you feel that there is a higher life than this daily one, and a brighter world than that you see; or encouraged you, or sobered you, or opened a way to the inquiring, or soothed the perplexed; if what he has said or done has ever made you take an interest in him, and feel well inclined towards him;—remember such a one in time to come, though you hear him not, and pray for him, that in all things he may know God's will, and at all times be ready to fulfill it."

That moving appeal to his friends that they try to understand him touched many hearts. But the attitude of many other of his former friends was one of disappointment rather than sympathy. His long silence, which was to follow the delivery of this last address, tended to chill the hearts of many who, Sunday after

Sunday at Littlemore as well as at St. Mary's, Oxford, had hung upon his words. Many whom he had greatly loved stood off and merely looked at him with sorrowing eyes. "How vividly," says one observer, "comes back the remembrance of the aching blank, the awful pause, which fell on Oxford when that voice had ceased, and we knew that we should hear it no more. It was as when, to one kneeling by night, in the silence of some vast cathedral, the great bell tolling solemnly overhead has suddenly gone still. To many, no doubt, the pause was not of long continuance. Soon they began to look this way and that for new teachers, and to rush vehemently to opposite extremes of thought. But there were those who could not so lightly forget. . . . On Sunday forenoons and evenings, in the retirement of their rooms, the printed words of those marvellous sermons would thrill them till they wept 'abundant and most sweet tears'! Since then many voices of powerful teachers they may have heard, but none that ever penetrated the soul like his."

It was not alone that doubting or critical attitudes of former friends distressed him during these last days; his own sisters, as usual, were viewing his course in a critical and unsympathetic mood. In a touching letter to his sister Jemima, who had written at length expressing her distress at his (to her) disastrous course, he writes at the end of August, 1843:

"My dear Jemima:—I am sorry to put you to such pain. Your letter and ——'s to you [which she had enclosed] would have brought me to many tears unless I had so hard a heart. You must take what I do in faith, at least; if not, I fear I cannot find a better way of consoling you. . . . My dearest Jemima, my circumstances are not of my making. One's duty is to act under circumstances. Is it a light thing to give up Littlemore? Am I not providing dreariness for myself? If others, whom I am pierced to think about, because I cannot help them, suffer, shall not I suffer in my own way? Everything that one does honestly, sincerely, with prayer, with advice, must turn to good. In what am I not likely to be as good a judge as another? In the consequences? True, but is not this what I have been ever protesting against?—the going by expedience, not by principle? My sweetest Jemima, of whom I am quite unworthy, rather pray that I may be directed aright, rather pray that something may occur to hinder me if I am wrong, than take the matter into your own hands."

Distressful as his situation was, with his sisters worrying him, his brothers abusing him, gossips spreading all sorts of absurd stories about him, and many of his friends seeming to lose faith in him, yet until his mind was fully clarified he felt he could make no positive move. The coldness and disapproval, or indifference, of many who had formerly seen eye to eye with him, added greatly to his perplexity—for his nature was one which always needed friends. True, he still had many who sympathized, but aside from Ambrose St. John, he did not feel able to open his heart fully to them; a certain reticence held him back. Actually, he felt he must make his journey through the shadows alone. "How dreadful it is," he wrote Henry Wilberforce in the spring of 1845, *apropos* of his old friend Blanco White, who, after drifting from Christianity to agnosticism, had just passed away; "how dreadful it is to have to act on great matters so much in the dark—yet I, who have preached so much on the duty of following in the night whenever God may call, am the last person who have a right to complain."

We may glimpse his mental state at this time from an introspective passage in his journal. It vividly reflects his distress in this hour of tribulation:

"What hope have I but in Him? To whom should I go? Who can do me any good? Who can speak a word of comfort but He? Who is there but looks on me with sorrowful face? But He can lift up the light of His countenance upon me. . . . All is against me—may He not add Himself as an adversary. May He tell me, may I listen to Him, if His will be other than I think it be!"

2

But the end of his long vigil was now not far away. By the late summer of 1845 he was near the end of his "death struggle." He had busied himself throughout the winter and spring with the writing of his essay on the Development of Doctrine. He became so absorbed in this work that he scarcely noticed what was going on around him. There had been many more conversions of Tractarians, but he had all but ignored them.

There was now a period of suspense among his Tractarian friends. "There was a pause," says Dean Church, "but it was no secret what was coming; it was not until the summer that the first drops of the storm began to fall. Then, through the autumn and next year, friends whose names and forms were familiar in Oxford, one by one disappeared and were lost to it. Fellowships, livings, curacies, intended careers were given up. We sat glumly at our breakfasts every morning, and then someone came in with the news of something disagreeable—someone gone, someone sure to go." [1]

Newman was deeply touched by the receipt of a long, affectionate letter from John Keble, which came to him just as he was about to cross the Rubicon. Among many kindly lines in it may be quoted the following. They display the true Christian humility so characteristic of Keble, as well as his affection for Newman:

"Besides the deep grief of losing you for a guide and helper, and scarcely knowing which way to look, you may guess what uncomfortable feelings haunt me, as if I, more than anyone else, was answerable for whatever of distress or scandal may occur. I keep on thinking, 'If I had been different, perhaps Newman would have been guided to see things differently, and we might have been spared so many broken hearts and bewildered spirits.'

[1] Church, *The Oxford Movement.*

. . . And now I wish you to help me. That way of help, at any rate, is not forbidden you in respect of any of us.

"My dearest Newman, you have been a kind and helpful friend to me in a way in which scarce anyone else could have been, and you are so mixed up in my mind with old and dear and sacred thoughts, that I cannot well bear to part with you, most unworthy as I know myself to be. And yet I cannot go along with you. I must cling to the belief that we are not really parted; you have taught me so, and I scarce think you can unteach me.

"And having relieved my mind with this little word, I will only say, God bless you and reward you a thousand fold for all your help in every way to me unworthy, and to many others. May you have peace where you are gone, and help us in some way to get peace; but somehow I scarce think it will be in the way of controversy. And so, with somewhat of a feeling as if the spring had been taken out of the year, I am, as always, your affectionate and grateful,—J. Keble."

Newman must have shed abundant tears over this letter. He kept it until after Keble's death, finally depositing it in the archives of Keble College, Oxford, where it still may be seen. Indeed, his love for John Keble continued through all the years to come. A letter from Rome to his sister in January 1847 contains a passage which indicates his continuing affection for his old friend of Tractarian days. Speaking of St. Philip Neri he says:

"This great saint reminds me in so many ways of Keble, that I fancy what Keble would have been if God's will had been that he should have been born in another place and age; he [St. Philip] was formed on the same type of extreme hatred of humbug, playfulness, nay, oddity, tender love for others, and severity, which are lineaments of Keble."

After the parting of their ways, Newman and Keble—as well as Pusey—saw little of one another for many years, although there was a reunion in 1865. But as late as 1877, long after Keble's death, we find Newman writing affectionately of him, mentioning "the sweet gravity with which he spoke," and that he had lost none of his love and admiration for him. He also spoke affectionately of Dr. Pusey, as "so full of the love of God," when the latter passed away. He never had, however, the *personal* affection for Pusey that he had for Keble.

3

During the last months of intense labor, working on his development essay often as much as fourteen hours a day and far into the night, Newman seldom left the neighborhood of Littlemore, except to take brief afternoon walks for exercise and perhaps go in to Oxford occasionally to see Dr. Pusey. Old friends, R. W. Church, Mark Pattison and Isaac Williams, or perhaps Henry Wilberforce, called and dined with him now and then; and his sister Jemima came to spend a few weeks in the village to be near by. Most of these visits were, in a way, regarded by the guests as leave-takings; they all seemed to feel, though Newman had yet said nothing, that their paths were soon to divide. Yet Dr. Pusey, with his perennial optimism, continued to express the belief that "we shall not lose him."

Then came the first of October, and with it the completion of the *Essay on Development*—that is to say, completion to the point where he deemed it unnecessary to go on. He never completed it beyond the point where he found himself fully convinced of the truth and his last doubts and difficulties set at rest. Even so, this long "essay" of over four hundred pages is "all but" complete!

His final decision had now been reached. It was ten o'clock at night when he laid down his pen. Then he mailed a letter resigning his Oriel Fellowship. Four days later he told Ambrose St. John of his decision. The latter had been away on a holiday, and while gone (unknown to Newman until his return), had been re-

ceived into the Catholic Church. Dalgairns also, who had long
been at the point of making the break, had just been received at
Aston by Father Dominic Barberi, an Italian Passionist priest.

John Dalgairns, before he joined the Littlemore community
and while still a student at Oxford, had started a correspondence
with Father Dominic, and an intimate friendship had since grown
up between them. First stationed in Belgium, Father Dominic had
later founded a monastic center at Aston and, partly owing to
help from Ambrose Philips, Father Ignatius Spencer and others,
was carrying this work on with remarkable success. He had long
been watching the Oxford Movement, and his contacts with
young Dalgairns had kept his interest at white heat. A year
before this time, Dalgairns had induced Father Dominic to visit
Littlemore; Newman had then met him and liked him.

And now, going off on a short holiday without telling Newman
of his purpose, Dalgairns had gone straight to Aston, and there
Father Dominic received him into the Church. Evidently Dalgairns had but slight misgivings as to how the Littlemore community would view his precipitate act: they were all getting ready
to do the same thing!

And now occurred an incident which Newman viewed as
Providential. Dalgairns, just returned, announced that Father
Dominic would stop at Littlemore on a journey he was about
to make to Belgium and would arrive on the evening of October
8. Nothing had been said to the Father about receiving Newman
into the Church, for he had said nothing to Dalgairns. But on
the evening before the priest's arrival, he wrote his friend Henry
Wilberforce (and also several others):

"Father Dominic the Passionist is passing this way, on his way
from Aston in Staffordshire to Belgium, where a Chapter of his
Order is to be held at this time. He is to come to Littlemore for
the night as a guest of one of us whom he has admitted at Aston.
He does not know of my intention, but I shall ask of him admission into the One true Fold of the Redeemer. . . . Father

Dominic has had his thoughts turned to England from a youth, in a distinct and remarkable way. For thirty years he had expected to be sent to England, and, about three years since, was sent, without any act of his own, by his Superior. . . . On Thursday or Friday, if it be God's will, I shall be received."

Early in the evening of October 8, Dalgairns went over to Oxford to meet Father Dominic, who was to arrive by the coach. There was a great downpour of rain, and when they got to Littlemore shortly before midnight, their clothes were sodden, and they tried to dry themselves before a blazing fire. In a letter to his Superior in Rome, Father Dominic describes the event in detail. I quote the following passage:

"We reached Littlemore about an hour before midnight, and I took up my position before the fire to dry myself. The door opened—and what a spectacle it was for me to see at my feet John Henry Newman, begging me to hear his confession and admit him into the bosom of the Catholic Church! And there by the fire he began his general confession with extraordinary humility and devotion. In the morning I betook myself to Oxford to say Mass in a Catholic Church there, and returned to Littlemore once more in the pouring rain. There I terminated Mr. Newman's confession, and heard the confessions of two other gentlemen who were there, namely, Stanton and Bowles, both of them, like Newman, ministers of the Church of England. That same evening at about six o'clock I received the profession of faith of all three, and gave them conditional baptism. On the following morning, the Feast of St. Francis Borgia, I said Holy Mass for the first time in their private Oratory. . . . At the Mass I gave Holy Communion to Mr. Newman and four other companions of his, formerly Protestants, and now most fervent Catholics." [1]

Thus simply and quietly, without pomp of circumstance or any

---

[1] Urban Young, ed., *Dominic Barberi in England.*

unnecessary formalities, Newman crossed the frontier to the Catholic Church of the Ages, passing peacefully from the old life to the new. He had at last reached the end of the long dark road, so strewn with doubts and difficulties, and now emerged into the light of certitude and peace.

The manuscript of his *Essay on Development* lay on his desk the morning after he had received his First Communion in the Catholic Church. Entering the room, he hurriedly took up his pen and wrote the following lines as an epilogue to the essay:

"Such were the thoughts concerning the 'Blessed Vision of Peace,' of one whose long continued petition had been that the Most Merciful would not despise the work of His own hands, nor leave him to himself; while yet his eyes were dim, and his breast laden, and he could but employ Reason in the things of Faith.

"And now, dear Reader, time is short, eternity is long. Put not from you what you have here found; regard it not as a mere matter of present controversy; set not out resolved to refute it, and looking about for the best way of doing so; seduce not yourself with the imagination that it comes of disappointment, or disgust, or restlessness, or wounded feeling, or undue sensibility, or other weakness. Wrap not yourself round in the associations of years past, nor determine that to be truth which you wish to be so, nor make an idol of cherished anticipations. Time is short, eternity is long.

> *Nunc dimittis servum tuum, Domine,*
> *Secundum verbum tuum in pace:*
> *Quia viderunt oculi mei salutare tuum."*

CHAPTER SIX

THE CATHOLIC CHURCH OF THE AGES

1

THE TURNING POINT in Newman's religious life was marked as we have seen by the practical completion of his *Essay on Development of Christian Doctrine*. It was not until he had laid down his pen on the night of October 1, 1845, that he took measures for seeking admission into the Catholic Church.

It is a truism that there are many "gates" through which converts pass to the Catholic Church. Some of these gates are seldom used, though always open: the average pilgrim enters by one of the well traveled routes. But Newman's approach was unique; he entered the Church quite the way he might have done had he lived in the fourth century instead of the nineteenth.

If one glances back over his religious evolution in earlier years, from his Calvinistic Protestantism to a gradual realization of Catholic truth, one notes that his starting point was in his study of early Church history, more particularly the period prior to and during the spread of Arianism in the fourth and fifth centuries. Basically, it was really St. Athanasius and the Alexandrian Fathers who made him a Catholic. One may say, therefore, that Newman's "gate" to the Church was the "fourth century gate." Moreover, his journey to that gate was over a road not well-worn, but almost untrodden until he had himself traversed it. Then others, in increasing numbers, followed the same route. They are doing so still.

Long before he wrote the *Development,* he had caught many glimpses of this road to Rome. But he found himself living in the nineteenth and not the fourth century; and to him the Catholic Church of the nineteenth century had looked not at all like the "Church of Antiquity" which had long fascinated him and to which he had devoted years of study. Modern Catholicism seemed to be marked by accretions and corruptions in doctrine quite foreign to the Church's original state. Consequently, instead of being led directly to the Catholic Church when his Protestantism fell away, he embarked on the *via media* between Catholicism and Protestantism, as championed by the Oxford Movement, thus placing his reliance, not directly on the testimony of the early Church Fathers, but on the interpretations of those Fathers by the Anglican divines—who taught that the Catholic Church, from the fifth century on, had been "corrupting" the pure faith of the primitive Church.

But as we have seen, his confidence in the *via media* theory, first developed by the Caroline divines, began to be shaken in 1839 by the words of St. Augustine; and subsequent discoveries and events shook it still more. He was later to describe this collapse of confidence in the Anglican divines in a vivid passage in his *Apologia*:

"I will freely confess . . . that I was angry with the Anglican divines. I thought they had taken me in; I had read the Fathers with their eyes; I had sometimes trusted their quotations or their reasonings; and from reliance on them, I had used words or made statements which by right I ought rigidly to have examined myself. . . . As a matter of feeling and duty, I threw myself into the system I found myself in; I saw that the English Church had a theological idea or theory as such, and I took it up. I read Laud on Tradition and thought it very . . . masterly. The Anglican theory was very distinctive. . . . It did not (I think) occur to me to doubt it; I saw that it was able, and supported by learning, and I felt it a duty to maintain it. Further, on looking into Antiquity and reading the Fathers, I saw such portions of it as I examined, fully confirmed. There was only one question about which I had a doubt, viz., whether it would work, for it has never been more than a paper system."

This had been his mood when, after 1841, his doubts had grown portentous, and he had finally decided to go over the heads of the Anglican divines and study the whole problem at first-hand. This led him, of course, to try to account for the apparent changes in Christian doctrine so noticeable in the Catholic Church, as compared with the simplicity of doctrine he had found in the Church of Antiquity. Thus was he led to the study of the *development* of Christian doctrine. As early as 1842, in one of his last sermons as an Anglican, he set forth the idea of development in considerable detail. The subject began to fascinate him, for it seemed to explain many things as true about Catholic teachings, which he and all his Tractarian companions had sweepingly condemned as "Roman corruptions, accretions and decays."

Such was the theme which he determined to carry to its ultimate conclusion when, in 1844, he set to work on his essay. It was a novel method for demonstrating the truth of the Catholic claims; and even when he began he was not sure that he would convince himself, let alone others, of its soundness. He was seeking an answer which would give him the certitude he longed for, and not mere unsupported probabilities. Still, as he has said in a notable passage, "accumulated probabilities do aid in arriving at certitude."

As he has stated: "God cooperates with us in our acting and thereby enables us to do that which He wills us to do, if our will but cooperate with Him, to a certitude which rises higher than the logical force of our conclusions. And thus I came to see clearly, and to have a satisfaction in seeing, that in being led into the Church of Rome, I was not proceeding on any secondary or isolated grounds of reason, or by controversial points in detail, but was protected and justified, even in the use of those secondary and particular arguments, by a great and broad principle. But, let it be observed that I am stating a fact. not defending it; and if any Catholic says in consequence, that I have been converted in a wrong way, I cannot help that now."

In the event, some Catholics did say that he had been converted in a wrong way, and for years certain of them found fault with his reasoning, as well as with his novel point of view. Even in Rome his book was criticized. But, as he was to say thirty years later: "So orthodox has it [the theory of development of dogma] been found in principle," that at the Vatican Council of 1870, when the Infallibility of the Pope in *ex cathedra* pronouncements was formally defined, it was charged that Newman's theory of doctrinal development was responsible for the definition!

2

For a clear conception of his thesis in the *Development of Christian Doctrine,* one should read the entire book. It is not difficult and abounds in passages of great beauty and power. It is a liberal education in Christian history, embracing, as it does, a panorama extending across the centuries. Here only a brief outline, with a few passages, is possible.[1]

He begins with a definition of "development." As the full-grown tree bears no resemblance to the acorn from which it springs, it seems amazing that the giant tree is a development of that which lived in the seed of its origin. So with Christian doctrine. But the real problem is how to distinguish true develop-

---

[1] In these quotations I have followed the edition of 1878.

ments from corruptions and decays. It is this problem that he sets out to solve.

Revelation is the "seed" of Christianity. From this basic fact he goes on to distinguish true developments from changes and growths, which might justly be called accretions and corruptions, or outright decays, if any, in the doctrines and dogmas held by the Catholic Church.

"To find what corruption or perversion of the truth is," he says, "let us enquire what the word means when used literally of material substances. Now, it is plain, first of all, that corruption is a word attached to organized matter only; a stone may be crushed to powder, but it cannot be corrupted. Corruption, on the contrary, is the breaking up of life preparatory to its dissolution. The resolution of the body into its component parts is the stage before its dissolution; it begins when life has reached its perfection, and it is the sequel, or rather the continuation, of that process towards perfection, being at the same time the reversal and undoing of what went before. . . . Taking this analogy as a whole, I venture to set down seven Notes of varying cogency, independence and applicability, to discriminate healthy developments of an idea from its state of corruption and decay,—as follows:

"There is no corruption if it retains one and the same type, the same principle, the same organization; if its beginnings anticipate its subsequent phases, and its later phenomena protect and subserve its earlier; if it has a power of assimilation and revival and a vigorous action first and last."

From that starting point, the essay becomes a sweeping review of the growth and development of doctrine and dogma in the Catholic Church, from the days of the Apostles down through the centuries, with the aim of demonstrating that a "law of development" has been in operation during her entire life, protecting the Faith once delivered to the saints from real corruption and corrosion. And necessarily so. For, as he says, "Whereas Revelation is a Heavenly gift, He who gave it virtually has not given it, unless He has also secured it from perversion or corruption, in all such developments as may come upon it by the necessity of its nature. That intellectual action through successive generations, which is the organ of development, must be in its determinations infallible. . . ."

He then shows, by presenting vivid examples, how far non-Catholics have wandered from recognition of this principle, and the dire results which have followed. Thus Luther tossed away or distorted the interpretations of the Church Fathers and proclaimed the principle of private judgment in interpreting the Scriptures. Calvin, Zwingli and other reformers did the same, some carrying the principle to grotesque extremes. As for the Anglican view of Archbishop Laud, commonly called the *Via Media*, or the middle way between Catholicism and Protestantism, it at least had the virtue of teaching that the Scriptures should be interpreted by Tradition, particularly emphasizing the importance of the "rule" of St. Vincent of Lerins, which was, "That is the Christian faith which has been taught always, everywhere and by all."

Newman emphasizes, however, the fact that as a defender of the Catholic principle of Tradition, St. Vincent is not altogether a safe guide; as a matter of fact, he was a semi-Pelagian. As an Anglican who followed Laud, Newman had accepted this vague "rule" of St. Vincent; but he had found that "Antiquity" did not present itself at all as St. Vincent implied; even Vincent himself had wandered into heresy. At that time, there were Councils against Councils and Fathers against Fathers. The Caroline divines of the seventeenth century had really not answered the question—what was the basic "rule" on which Christianity proceeded? They had merely followed St. Vincent.

The true answer, Newman insists, is found in the principle of development. What are often condemned as Roman corruptions of the primitive Creed, are really logical developments of the original Deposit of Faith. He points out that the Anglicans had accepted many developments; the councils of Ephesus and Chalcedon in the fifth century had developed definitions as well as the Council of Trent in the sixteenth century. But while the Caroline divines arbitrarily rejected this rule of normal growth or development after the first few centuries, the Catholic Church has always allowed true development to proceed.

3

Newman emphasizes, with wonderful lucidity, the great principle of life, and consequently growth, as the true test of Catholic truth. He points out that in all *living* systems there are bound to be the changes which are natural to a living social body. As circumstances change with men, "old principles reappear under new forms. It changes with them in order to remain the same. In a higher world it is otherwise, but here below to live is to change, and to be perfect is to have changed often." This, he explains, in no way vitiates the claim of the Catholic Church to be divine. In spite of changes in form and polity as, for example, fuller definitions of dogma (indeed, because of such changes), the Faith is kept alive and uncorrupted.

He insists that the Scriptures were really written on the principle of development, a fact which non-Catholics (particularly the sixteenth century reformers) utterly ignored. "Can any history," he asks, "wear a more human appearance than that of the rise and growth of the chosen people?" And as with the Old, so with the New Testament, with the Creed and with the Church. "No one doctrine," he says, "can be named, which starts complete at first, and gains nothing afterwards from the investigations of faith and attacks of heresy." . . . And then he insists that "there can be no combination of truth without an organ of truth." Otherwise confusion is worse confounded. "What power," he asks, "will suffice to meet and do justice to these conflicting conditions, but a supreme authority ruling and reconciling individual judgments by a Divine right?" That authority is lodged, of course, only in the See of Peter in Rome.

He devotes many pages to show the identity of the Church which is in communion with Rome with the Church of the earlier ages. He does this by presenting historical parallels between the Catholic Church of the nineteenth century and the Church as it was viewed by the outside world in other periods of her history— the Church of the Apostolic period, of the Nicene period, and of the fifth and sixth centuries. In each of these parallels he writes as an historian with masses of facts at his fingers'-end, which he presents with all the power of lucidity for which he was famous. These several parallels are too long to quote; but I give space to one—that of the worldly view of the Church in the Nicene period as compared with the nineteenth century view.

"There is a religious communion, claiming a divine commission, and holding all other religious bodies around it heretical or infidel; it is a well organized, well disciplined body; it is a sort of secret society, binding together its members by influences and by engagements which it is difficult for strangers to ascertain. It is spread over the known world; it may be weak or insignificant locally, but it is strong on the whole from its continuity; it may be smaller than all other religious bodies added together, but it is larger than each separately. It is a natural enemy to governments external to itself; it is intolerant and engrossing, and tends to a new modelling of society; it breaks laws, it divides families. . . . It is a gross superstition; it is charged with the foulest crimes; it is despised by the intellect of the day; it is frightful to the imagination of many. And there is but one communion such. . . . Place this description before Pliny or Julian; place it before Frederick Second or Guizot. 'Apparent dirae facies.' Each knows at once, without asking a question, who is meant by it. One object, and one only, absorbs the delineation."

4

The last chapter of the book is on "Chronic Vigour" and is, in the opinion of many, the most brilliant of all. I will quote a passage bearing on alleged corruptions in the Church versus true developments.

"When we consider the succession of ages during which the Catholic system has endured, the severity of the trials it has undergone, the sudden and wonderful changes without and within which have befallen it, the incessant mental activity and the intellectual gifts of its maintainers, the enthusiasm which it has kindled, the fury of the controversies which have been carried on among its professors, the impetuosity of the assaults made upon it, the ever increasing responsibilities to which it has been committed by the continuous development of its dogmas, it is quite inconceivable that it should not have been broken up and lost, were it a corruption of Christianity. Yet it is still living, if there be a living religion or philosophy in the world; vigorous, energetic, persuasive, progressive; *vires acquirit eundo;* it grows and is not overgrown; it spreads out yet is not enfeebled; it is ever germinating, yet ever consistent with itself. Corruptions indeed are to be found which sleep and are suspended; and these, as I have said, are usually called 'decays.' Such is not the case with Catholicity; it does not sleep, it is not stationary even now; and that its long series of developments should be corruptions would be an instance of sustained error, so novel, so unaccountable, so preternatural, as to be little short of a miracle, and to rival those manifestations of Divine Power which constitute the evidence of Christianity. We sometimes view with surprise and awe the degree of pain which the human frame can undergo without succumbing; yet at length there comes an end. Fevers have their crisis, fatal or favorable; but this 'corruption' of a thousand years, if corruption it be, has ever been growing nearer death, yet never reaches it, and has been strengthened, not debilitated, by its excesses."

Without doubt one of the most convincing things in the *Essay on Development of Christian Doctrine* is the powerful way in which it demonstrates the truth that nowhere can the Church founded by Christ be found except under the jurisdiction of the Holy See. It demonstrates that rejection of the Papal jurisdiction has been the basic flaw which has vitiated all independent ventures in Christianity—even those which adhere to much Catholic doctrine. The author says, "If Christianity is both social and dogmatic, and intended for all ages, it must, humanly speaking, have an infallible expounder. Else you will secure unity of form at the loss of unity of doctrine, or unity of doctrine at the loss of unity of form; you will have to choose between a comprehension of opinions and a resolution into parties, between latitudinarian and sectarian error." No truer words were ever uttered by Newman than these: "You must accept the whole or reject the whole; attenuation does but enfeeble and amputation mutilate; it is trifling to receive all but something which is as integral as any other portion." Thus it is trifling to accept everything Catholic except the Head of the Body of Christ upon earth. As well may we expect the human frame to retain life and function without its head.

The closing passage of the book (never quite finished, though nearly so) must end my quotations:

"It is true there have been seasons when, from the operation of external or internal causes, the Church has been thrown into what was almost a state of *deliquium*; but her wonderful revivals, while the world was triumphing over her, is a further evidence of the absence of corruptions in a system of doctrine and worship into which she has developed. If corruption be an incipient disorganization, surely an abrupt and absolute recurrence to the former state of vigor, after an interval, is even less conceivable than a corruption that is permanent. Now this is the case with the revivals I speak of. After violent exertion men are exhausted and fall asleep; they awake the same as before, refreshed by the temporary cessation of their activity; and such has been the slumber and such the restoration of the Church. She pauses in her course, and almost suspends her functions; she rises again, and she is herself once more; all things are in their place and ready for action. Doctrine is where it was, and usage, and precedence; and principle and policy; there may be changes, but they are consolidations or adaptations; all is unequivocal and determinate, with an identity which there is no disputing. Indeed, it is one of the most popular charges against the Catholic Church at this very time, that she is 'incorrigible';—change she cannot, if we listen to St. Athanasius and St. Leo; change she never will, if we believe the controversialist or alarmist of the present day."

One can picture the effect on Newman's mind, as he unrolled his panorama of the Catholic Church's history from the days of the Apostles down to the reigning pontiff of his time. All the past comes alive under his pen, wrinkles of history are smoothed out, and the difficulties which he had carried in his mind for so long are one by one clarified. He had said, in his Epilogue, that he could only employ reason in the things of Faith, while yet his eyes were dim and his heart laden. Employ reason he did, and the result was the *Development of Christian Doctrine*.

To the casual outside observer, the complicated history of the Catholic Church, with its array of doctrinal teaching, is often puzzling; but this great essay, whether or not one accepts as a whole this theory of development, throws a vivid light on the Living Church in all her phases for every person who would sincerely wish to understand the what, why, and wherefore of this great organism of two thousand years. It is not surprising that this exhaustive study brought Newman to his great decision.

CHAPTER SEVEN

THE EXODUS TO ROME

1

FOR A COMPLETE VIEW of the circumstances under which the Oxford Movement struggled for place and power, and then collapsed in 1845, it is necessary to make some reference to the position of the English Catholics at that time. We also need to know how it came about that the English Catholics were emancipated from the age-long repressive laws at the precise time when scepticism and general indifference to orthodox Christianity were creating havoc in the Anglican communion itself.

The persecution of Catholics from the days of Henry VIII, with its growing intensity during the reign of Queen Elizabeth, and its continuance even into the eighteenth century, makes a long and tragic story. It would require hundreds of pages to tell it in full. It is not my intention to elaborate on it here, but at least something must be said regarding the English Catholic revival of the nineteenth century.

It was not until 1778 that a Special Relief Act repealed the laws for the persecution of "Catholic bishops, priests and Jesuits," which had been enacted in the time of William III near the end of the seventeenth century. This Relief Act of 1778 permitted Catholics to open and operate schools and to acquire and hold real property. A second act in 1791 gave them some further liberties. A potent reason for these relaxations was, of course, that after the repression of the Catholic Church for nearly two and a half centuries, the Catholic body had so dwindled that Protestants had come to view it as no longer a serious menace, even though fear of "papalism" was still strong.

Near the end of the century, during the French Revolution, the government committed itself to befriend French refugees, and many priests and religious were permitted to enter England without protest. Fleeing from a terror which was viewed by the British as worse than Catholicism, they gained much sympathy. At this time the teachers and students of the English College at Douay, founded by Cardinal Allen in 1579 to train priests for the English mission, were allowed to transfer their work to English soil; and in 1792 the Jesuits at St. Omer were permitted to do the same. The Jesuits settled at Stonyhurst, where Thomas Weld, a wealthy Catholic layman, gave them his fine Tudor home. Other colleges, St. Edmunds at Ware, and Ushaw in county Durham, were opened for students in 1795.

With the opening of the nineteenth century, sentiment was increasing in favor of granting further relief to the Catholics, but this was definitely opposed by King George III and later by George IV and his Prime Minister, Lord Liverpool. But what seem irrelevant incidents sometimes have unexpected consequences. In the year 1815, what was called the Veto Controversy arose in Parliament. This had relation to the appointment of Catholic bishops and other Church dignitaries in Ireland. The British Parliament demanded the right to veto, if it saw fit, such appointments as might from time to time be made by the Pope for the Irish Catholic Church.

In those days the Irish were in a weak state, having been crushed in attempted insurrections a few years before, and it was assumed by the British Parliament that their spirit had been broken. It was thought that they might be induced to look with favor on the proposal, especially because of the fact that it carried an endowment to the Irish Catholic Church to be supplied from government funds—giving them the same sort of support of a financial nature as Protestants received. Would not the hard-pressed Irish Catholic hierarchy welcome this olive branch? Certain members of the suffering remnant of English Catholics appeared to view the idea sympathetically.

But the Irish clergy and people indignantly rejected the proposal; their Catholic liberty meant more to them than any benefits to be derived from a plan which would tie down their Church to the British Parliament. It was now that the great Catholic agitator Daniel O'Connell appeared on the scene to defend the independence of the Irish Church. He brought the Catholic question before both English and Irish as a major issue. Without detailing here the violent controversies which followed, it is important to emphasize the fact that from this time on the fighting spirit of Daniel O'Connell kept the entire question of Catholic Emancipation to the fore.

Ultimately the English and Irish Catholics got together on the matter; and when, in 1827, Lord Liverpool relinquished power and was succeeded by George Canning as Prime Minister, the question came up in a new form. Canning favored Catholic relief and found much support, but he was bitterly opposed by the Duke of Wellington and Sir Robert Peel. With such opposition it was not believed that anything important could be accomplished; and had it not been for the aggressive agitation of O'Connell, perhaps Canning would soon have abandoned the attempt.

An event shortly followed, however, which changed the outlook. In 1827 the Duke of York died, so that the heir to the throne was now the Duke of Clarence, William IV, who had already announced that he was in favor of relief for the Catholics. But before anything could be accomplished, Canning also died, and the Duke of Wellington became the Prime Minister. Wellington had always strongly opposed any Catholic relief, and O'Connell viewed his appointment as a declaration of war against the Irish Catholics. He led a political uprising in Ireland which soon had great repercussions in the English Parliament. Least of all, at that particular time, did the British government wish to be confronted with war in Ireland. After much agitation among both Whigs and Tories (which need not be detailed here), Sir Robert Peel, the most forceful man in Wellington's Cabinet, persuaded the Duke that if peace in Ireland was to be preserved, some form of Catholic relief should not be long delayed.

And so it was that, to the horror of the English Protestants, there was submitted to King George IV on January 29, 1829, a memorandum drawn up by Peel, urging that the question of granting Catholics greater freedom be favorably considered. The King was strongly opposed, but under pressure he yielded with bad grace. At the opening of Parliament the speech from the throne recommended that the laws which imposed disabilities on His Majesty's Catholic subjects be considered in connection with the question "whether the removal of these disabilities can be effected consistently and with the full and permanent security of our establishments of Church and State."

This astounding change of front caused a furious public outburst against the ministry, and particularly against Sir Robert Peel, who was then a candidate for re-election to Parliament for the constituency of Oxford. He was defeated by a heavy vote. Yet this did not deter him. Shortly thereafter he gave notice of his intention to bring the Catholic question before the House of Commons. The King made a final attempt to oppose this, but the ministry offered its resignation as a protest, and the King— who dreaded a Whig ministry—felt obliged to yield.

The bill passed the House by a large majority, and in April it passed the House of Lords. It became law on April 15, 1829.

The aftermath was anything but a happy one for the Tory ministry. The Anglican bishops had long been demanding that the government repel "the lawless demands of the Papists." And now the Archbishop of Canterbury, with the entire bench of bishops in the House of Lords, worked hard for the overthrow of Wellington and Peel. As it was, the Wellington government staggered in its efforts to keep from falling; but it had a prop in the King, who, though bitterly resentful of the adoption of the Catholic relief bill, preferred the existing ministry to one composed of the Whig opposition. But on June 26, 1830, King George IV died, and William IV, who was sympathetic to Catholic emancipation, succeeded to the throne. From that time the reform was secure.

The Catholic Emancipation Bill had not, of course, granted full justice to the Catholics. It relieved them from penalties, financial and other, for being Catholics, gave them the right to sit in Parliament, and opened to them (with some exceptions) the great offices of State. But it left Catholic marriages still illegal, and Catholic soldiers and sailors were still required to attend Protestant Church services.

Nevertheless the English Catholics were indeed grateful. For the first time since the 1560's they now enjoyed freedom to practice their religion openly. As they wisely refrained from displaying any great exultation, the Protestant population, after the first shock, seems to have accepted the new situation with more or less tolerance and good will. No doubt this was based partly on the widespread belief that there was little likelihood of any important growth in the small Catholic population.[1]

2

It was indeed a surprise to all Protestants, and a shock to many Anglicans, when there was an evident stirring of life among the old English Catholic group after the Emancipation Bill had been

---

[1] A valuable study (to which I am indebted) of the events which led to Catholic Emancipation is contained in *The Catholic Question*, by Philip Hughes.

passed. Even the Liberals (those of no particular religious affiliations, who had, for the most part, favored Catholic relief as simple justice to a small group of law-abiding citizens) hardly anticipated that this new freedom would be followed by great expansion in their numbers and activities.

It was not immediately so followed, but within one short decade the expansion had begun to be quite perceptible. And this startled the Tractarians. Not that they had any fear at first that there would be any leakage from their own ranks into the English Catholic Church, for they considered themselves more truly "Catholic" than the Church of Rome. But in their eyes, this Catholic Church was a disturber of both religious and political peace in England. To them, the agitation led by Daniel O'Connell was a monstrous thing; for O'Connell had allied himself politically with non-Catholics and even with Liberals. Oxford was intensely Tory and had expressed its attitude in no uncertain way through the crushing defeat of Sir Robert Peel. At that time Newman had written to his mother: "We have gathered a glorious victory; it is the first public event I have been concerned in, and I thank God from my heart both for my cause and for its success. We have proved the independence of the Church and of Oxford."

The Tractarians had no real fear during the early years that a Catholic revival would interfere with their movement; it was some years later that Newman said, "The problem of the Romanists has overtaken us like a summer cloud." Even though, long before Emancipation, the Catholics had shown some sign of life with the return from Douay of the English college and the others settled at Ushaw and Stonyhurst (and at Oscott), they viewed these incidents as of little significance.

As for the attitude toward the Tractarians of the old English Catholics themselves, they looked with suspicion on the Oxford Movement. They thought it was quite insincere and would soon peter out. This feeling was doubtless partly due to the fact that the anti-Catholic attitude early displayed by the Oxford reformers was no different from that which had always characterized the Protestants. These Catholics saw that the Tractarians were appealing primarily to the Anglican divines of the seventeenth century; and these divines had favored the crushing out of the Catholic Church in England, just as had the Puritans of those days. That alone was enough to arouse their antagonism and distrust.

But this negative attitude of the English Catholics towards the stirrings at Oxford ultimately underwent considerable change. This was due largely to the activities of one man—Dr. Nicholas Wiseman, the young monsignor whom Newman and the Froudes had met in Rome in 1833 and with whom they had then discussed the status of their own and the Catholic Church in England. It is important to say a few words regarding him at this point.

Nicholas Wiseman, born in Seville, Spain, in 1802, was of Irish parentage. His grandfather, a native of Waterford, Ireland, had emigrated to Seville in the mid-eighteenth century to enter into business there. His son, who succeeded him in his business in Seville, first married a Spanish woman; but she soon died. Then he married a Miss Strange of county Kilkenny, Ireland, and from this union Nicholas was born. A few years, and his father died; the mother brought the child home to Waterford, and when he was eight years old she sent Nicholas to school at Ushaw, England. Here he remained until his sixteenth year, then deciding that he had a vocation for the priesthood. With several other youths, shortly after this he journeyed to Rome and became a student in the English College for seminarians (which was now reopened after having been closed during the Napoleonic wars). After finishing his studies, he was ordained to the priesthood in 1825, being at the time but twenty-three years old. A brilliant scholar, he promptly attained a doctorate of divinity. He had specialized in oriental history and languages and proved so proficient that he was made a tutor at the college. Within a year he had become its vice-rector; by 1828 he had advanced to the rectorship.

With an exclusively scholastic career ahead of him, young Wiseman did not expect to return to England, where he knew little of Catholic conditions. The agitation over Catholic Emancipation had awakened some interest; but since he had seen it only from afar, it had made no lasting impression. Not until 1830 did he evince any particular interest in the possibilities of an English Catholic revival. But in that year George Spencer, the Cambridge convert who had been an Anglican clergyman, now about thirty years old, arrived at the English College to study for the Catholic priesthood. As he was thought to be too old to be placed with the junior students, Wiseman supervised his instruction privately. They quickly became great friends, and Wiseman was soon impressed with Spencer's enthusiasm regarding the hope of a great Catholic revival in England; and his own interest awakened.

Some time after ordination, Spencer joined the Passionists, becoming Father Ignatius Spencer, and even thus early he met Father Dominic Barberi, who, fifteen years later, was to receive Newman into the Catholic Church. But even before his ordination, Spencer had convinced Dr. Wiseman that he should be employing his great talents in assisting in the conversion of England rather than as a mere professor in a Roman college. As an outcome of Spencer's persuasion, Dr. Wiseman now began to preach sermons to English audiences in Roman churches, and he also began to contribute articles to a Catholic magazine in London. His interest in the English situation increased, and by 1833, when Newman and the Froudes visited Rome, it had taken the uppermost place in his thoughts.

In 1835 Wiseman visited England. He was practically a stranger to English Catholics, for it had been seventeen years since he had stood on English soil. He was welcomed with but little enthusiasm by these old Catholics, who viewed him with noticeable indifference when he expressed particular interest in the Anglican revival at Oxford. They all told him it was visionary to expect converts from that quarter.

But he was not discouraged. After a brief tour of Catholic institutions throughout the Provinces, he returned to London and was invited to deliver a series of Advent lectures in the Sardinian chapel at Lincoln's Inn Fields. They were well advertised and attracted many Protestants, and he made a great impression. Remaining in London until the spring of 1836, he was induced by Bishop Bramston to repeat these lectures during Lent at St. Mary's, Moorfield, and was equally successful. His audiences included many non-Catholics, and several conversions followed. This startled the Tractarians. But Newman expressed the view that while "Romanism may spread among Dissenters and irregulars," he had no fears for the right-minded among the Tractarians.

In 1837 Wiseman again visited England and made an equally good impression. The old Catholics still were sceptical; but as more progress in stirring up outside interest in the Church became evident, many of them admitted that his efforts were not proving entirely futile. Conversions were now occurring in increasing numbers. And no doubt the so-called Cambridge converts, Ignatius Spencer and Ambrose Phillips—and the notably boisterous convert architect, Augustus Welby Pugin—added much to keep alive Wiseman's enthusiasm.

Dr. Wiseman made a third visit in 1839, and in 1840 he was consecrated a bishop and sent permanently to England as coadjutor of the aging Bishop Walsh, Vicar Apostolic of the Central District. At the same time he was made President of Oscott College, located near Birmingham, not far from Oxford. It was now not long before his influence spread widely. As we have seen, in 1839 he wrote, for the *Dublin Review*, his article on the Donatist controversy, which had so greatly stirred the Tractarians and profoundly shaken Newman's belief in his *via media*.

Conversions from the Anglican Church became more frequent; within the next two years the trend increased and began to awaken wide interest among the old-line English Catholics. Wiseman became possessed of the dream that Oscott might become the Catholic center to which would be drawn, in the years to come, a vast movement from the Tractarian groups. Within a year thereafter Newman's famous Tract Ninety appeared; the reaction to it in the Anglican Church was very significant to him. He watched Newman's attitude with deep interest and now felt certain—long before anything of the sort transpired—that Newman was definitely on the road to the Church. A memorandum written by Wiseman at Oscott shows his deep conviction that a great movement from Anglicanism to Catholicism was pending. I quote excerpts from this.

"There was one thought that cheered and supported me . . . from the first dawn of hope which visited me in Italy, from the day of Newman's and Froude's visit there. Never, never for an instant did I waver in my full conviction that a new era had commenced in England. . . . To the promotion of this grand object of England's hopes I had devoted myself. Puny and worthless as might be my efforts, they had been offered to this one end. Among the providential agencies that had seemed justly timed and even necessary for it, appeared to me the erection of this noble College in the very heart of England. . . . Often in my darkest days and hours, feeling as if alone in my hopes, have I walked in front of it, casting my eyes towards it and repeatedly exclaiming to myself, 'No, it was not to educate a few boys that this College was erected, but to be the rallying point of the yet silent but vast movement towards the Catholic Church which has commenced and must prosper.' I felt as assured of this as if the word of prophecy had spoken it."

3

After 1843 and throughout 1844 and 1845, it seemed to Wiseman that his dream was coming true. One after another, converts from the Tractarians had been received. William George Ward was followed by J. M. Capes, a scholarly layman; Frederick Oakeley resigned Margaret chapel and came in; also about this time came Frederick William Faber, Robert Coffin, Ambrose St. John, J. D. Dalgairns, Albany Christie, George Ryder, James Spencer Northcote, J. B. Morris, Richard Simpson of Oriel, followed by dozens of others, both clerical and lay. The flow, first a mere trickle, had now become a full stream, and by the time of Newman's conversion, it had become a torrent.

Newman having remained silent during this entire period, Wiseman was in no position to read his mind. But months before his reception actually took place, Newman had written the following letter to a friend, which indicates the imminence of his change.

"As far as I know myself," he said, "my one great distress is the perplexity, unsettlement, alarm, which I am causing to so many, known or unknown, who have wished well of me. . . . My one paramount reason for contemplating a change is my deep, unvarying conviction that our Church is in schism, and that my salvation depends on my joining the Church of Rome. I have no visions whatever of hope, no schemes of action in any other sphere more suited to me. I have no existing sympathies with Roman Catholics; I hardly ever, even when abroad, was at one of their services. And then, how much I am giving up in so many ways . . . sacrifices innumerable, not only from my age, when people hate changing, but from my especial love of old associations and the pleasures of memory. Nor am I conscious of any feeling, enthusiastic or heroic, of pleasure in the sacrifice; I have nothing to support me here."

Most of the Tractarians who had been flocking in during this period of Newman's hesitancy later became prominent in Catholic Church activities. Frederick Oakeley became Canon of Westminster; Robert Coffin became the Superior of the Redemptorists and later Bishop of Southwark; Spencer Northcote became President of Oscott; J. D. Dalgairns became famous as a great preacher at the Brompton Oratory; Thomas Meyrick became a distinguished Jesuit; and George Dudley Ryder was father of Ignatius Ryder, who many years later succeeded Newman at the Birmingham Oratory as its Superior. Ambrose St. John worked with Newman all his days.

The exodus of Anglicans to Rome went far beyond what most of the old generation of Catholics had believed possible. But it by no means reached the volume dreamed of by Dr. Wiseman. He had envisioned the entire body of Tractarians coming over within a few years. But while this conversion movement did continue indefinitely, a large number of the Tractarians remained behind. Only one of the three great leaders—Newman—made his exodus; the other two—Pusey and Keble—did not stir, but during the remainder of their lives they kept up the struggle (which is still being carried on) to promote within the Anglican Church a *via media* between Protestantism and Catholicism— with varying success but with much opposition.

The great increase in the number of Catholics in England which occurred in these years was only indirectly and partially due to the influx of many Anglicans. It was primarily a result of the immigration of Catholics from other countries—particularly from Ireland. The arrival of Catholic refugees in great numbers from France and other Continental countries during and after the long Napoleonic regime, of course, was important; but the startling growth in Catholic population during the late 1830's and the 1840's was largely due to the expansion of the factory system and the growth of great industrial centers, Liverpool, Manchester and so on. Immigrants from Ireland in great numbers were attracted by the possibilities of employment in these industrial centers. Moreover, immigration of Irish Catholics vastly increased during the years of the Irish potato famine, which extended from 1844 to 1847.

Around the end of the eighteenth century, the English Catholics had so shrivelled in numbers, after two and a half centuries of the penal laws, that they may not have numbered over sixty thousand souls in all England. But by 1850 this total had been increased perhaps tenfold, or more. There was a heavy Catholic population in the London district as well as in all the industrial towns, and the growth was continuous thereafter. In our time it is estimated that in England, Scotland and Wales there are more than three million practicing Catholics. The convert movement which started in the 1840's is still going on.

4

Before leaving Newman's Anglican years, it may be well briefly to picture his position in the midst of this exodus to Rome.

In July, 1845, Bernard Smith, a militant convert, tried to stir Newman up. A former curate of St. Mary's, Smith felt confident that he would be welcomed at Littlemore, for he had long known well all the inmates. But Newman had been most indignant with him when he had become a Catholic. And now, while the others were very cordial, Newman was frigid, and soon left the room. But that evening he rejoined them at dinner. Smith noted that he appeared in gray trousers; a fact which he construed as a hint from Newman that he no longer considered himself an Anglican priest. Despite his frigidity, Newman was giving him a sign. He hastened to report the incident to Bishop Wiseman, exultantly exclaiming, "I know the man, and I know what it means; he will come, and soon." (He did not know that Newman had been wearing gray trousers ever since he had ceased all clerical duty. Perhaps Wiseman knew it; for he was not impressed.)

After his reception by Father Dominic, Newman had remained at Littlemore until the end of October. It was then arranged that he go to Oscott to receive Confirmation at the hands of Bishop Wiseman. He arrived with Ambrose St. John and John Walker, who also were to be confirmed. But what was his surprise when he found that Father Ignatius Spencer and Father Bernard Smith were to be "masters of ceremony" at his own Confirmation! The last time he had seen Spencer was when he had frozen him out at Oxford, years before; and frigidity had prevailed at his last meeting with Smith. But now the ice simply had to melt.

Newman and Wiseman scarcely knew each other. It was more than twelve years since that meeting in Rome. Though they had exchanged a few letters, there had always been, till now, the traditional wall between them. And even now, although cordial messages had come from the Bishop, to which Newman had sent equally cordial replies, this meeting was to be embarrassing to them both. Years later, Bernard Smith described their meeting to Wilfrid Ward:

"The meeting between the two men was characteristic. The great Oxford leader, who had at last owned that Rome had conquered, had come, as it were, to surrender his sword to the man who had so strenuously urged surrender as his only course. Orders disowned, preferments resigned, he came in poverty and simplicity to ask for Confirmation at the hands of the bishop. His faith and conviction brought him to Oscott, but they could not untie his tongue or rid him of the embarrassment which belonged to the situation. In company with John Walker and Ambrose St. John, he was ushered into the Oscott guest-room, and in a few minutes Bishop Wiseman, with Bernard Smith and Father Ignatius Spencer, entered the room. The embarrassment was mutual, and Wiseman could scarcely find words for more than formal inquiries about the journey. Any touch of exultation, or any expression of commonplace and conventional congratulation, would, as all felt instinctively, outrage a situation in which the leading mind was so highly wrought, that silence seemed the only possible course. The two principal figures sat almost silent, while their companions talked more readily to each other. A message which announced that a boy was waiting to go to Confession to the bishop, gave Wiseman an excuse for retiring, which he accepted with significant alacrity."

The Confirmation took place on the Feast of All Saints, November 1, three others, Oakeley, St. John and Walker, being confirmed at the same time. After that, the ice was broken, and both Newman and Wiseman were thoroughly at ease with each other. The latter now wrote an account of the occasion to Dr. Russell of Maynooth, who had long known Newman and had been an important instrument in his conversion in clearing his mind on the subject of the Blessed Virgin.

"Newman," he wrote, "came on the Eve of All Saints with St. John and Walker, and was followed by Mr. Oakeley. Those from Littlemore had been confirmed here the Sunday before. On All Saints, Newman, Oakeley, and the other two were confirmed, and we had *ten* quondam Anglican clergymen in the chapel. Has this ever happened before, since the Reformation? Newman took the name of Mary; Oakeley, Bernard and Mary. Newman stayed with us Sunday and half of Monday, and he and all his party then expressed themselves, and have done so since, as highly gratified by all they saw and felt. Oakeley stays with us altogether. Newman's plans are not finally determined, nor will they be till his book is published. But he opened his mind completely to me; and I assure you the Church has not received, at any time, a convert who has joined her in more docility and simplicity of faith than Newman."

Newman now began in earnest his life as a Catholic. No plans for the future were as yet matured, and he did not leave Littlemore for good until the following February, though in the meanwhile he traveled about, visiting the leading Catholic colleges and centers, and meeting the various bishops and other important Churchmen. While he was still uncertain of his future activities, at least it can be said that his second spring had begun.

CARDINAL NEWMAN

From a painting by W. W. Ouless, R. A., at the Oratory,
Birmingham.

PART TWO

THE CATHOLIC YEARS

CHAPTER EIGHT

SECOND SPRING

1

Many people consider the little story *Loss and Gain,* which Newman wrote shortly after he had entered the Catholic Church, as not only essentially his own story, but a more readable revelation of his struggles to overcome prejudices and grasp truth than is to be found in his famous *Apologia,* written many years later. It has indeed a greater appeal for the multitude who find it difficult to understand Anglican disputations and quarrels—unless they themselves happen to have an Anglican background. A similar difficulty confronts many regarding his *Development of Christian Doctrine.* Both of these books are best understood by those whose interest in religious doctrine, as doctrine, is paramount. But the simpler story *Loss and Gain* is marked with human interest of an everyday kind, and as a reflection of John Henry Newman's own life, brings his struggles vividly before the everyday reader of the type of Tom, Dick and Harry and, perhaps of you and me!

In this book, which is the story of a young Oxford student who is studying for the Anglican ministry, he makes his hero say to a Catholic friend, as he is at the point of leaving the Anglican Church and entering the Catholic communion:

"Yes, I give up home; I give up all who have ever known me, loved me, wished me well; I know I am making myself a by-word and an outcast." Later, when he breaks the news to his mother, she reproaches him bitterly, as do his sisters also. A tragic scene follows. There was of course nothing that he prized like his home and the love and sympathy of his mother and sisters. But now he was to be shut out from that forever.

It reflected Newman's own situation exactly. He had no hope that any of his family would follow him; but they displayed no sympathy whatever nor even tolerant interest. Henceforth he was to be all but a stranger to them. We find his sister Jemima writing him in a reproachful strain: "When you spoke in the name of *our* Church your exhortations were all powerful, your voice seemed the voice of an angel, you touched a chord in all our hearts—you seemed to know our very hearts. Since your new views have gained the ascendancy, how great the change! Your talents, experience, and depth of mind may make your words powerful, but you will not influence the same class of minds that you have in the past!"

His sister Harriet was equally unsympathetic. As for his two brothers-in-law, the Mozleys, both clergymen in the Anglican Church, who were supposed to be good "Anglo-Catholics" and had cooperated with him in promoting the Tractarian movement, they now turned their backs on the High Church philosophy to a large extent, taking advantage of this occasion to become a species of Broad Churchmen—perhaps relieved at the opportunity.

Of course both his brothers scoffed, Francis accusing him of having been "a secret Romanist" for many years. And so far as the general public was concerned—the cultured groups, the Lords and Ladies, the bishops and University heads, the elite of the town and country parishes—they, with a few exceptions, washed their hands of him. Only among the rank and file, the common people, did he find much sympathy.

Despite the widespread rumors of his impending change, which had been in circulation more or less for three or four years, the effect on the English public of his actual conversion had been startling. Said Mark Pattison, one of the ablest of the Tractarians, who later lapsed and became a sceptic: "It is impossible to describe the enormous effect, I may say throughout all England, of one man's changing his religion." Gladstone was in such dismay that he wrote to his friend Archdeacon Manning: "I stagger to and fro like a drunken man, and am at my wits' end." Arthur Stanley (the future Dean of Westminster) averred that Newman's exodus, with the death at this time of Dr. Arnold, "could not but look ominous, like the rattle of the departing chariots that was heard on the eve of the downfall of the Temple of Jerusalem." Of course, the secular press pounced on Newman, calling him a knave, a secret Jesuit, and a coward who had surrendered to the Pope because he lacked courage to think for himself—and so on and so on.

This fury of abuse, and the general public disdain, hurt him deeply; but his sensitive soul had already suffered profoundly, and his new happiness in his "blessed vision of peace" cast into shadow the abuse. Criticism and castigation were to be expected, and he strove to live above them. But to leave his beloved Littlemore was indeed a trial. He had returned home after his Confirmation in November; but now, the day before his forty-fifth birthday, February 21, 1846, he was leaving for good—going to "Old Oscott". His feelings at this time are reflected in the following excerpts from letters to friends and from items in his journal:

"I have had a very trying time, parting from the people. I came into this bower by myself; I quit it by myself. Very happy times have I had here (though in such doubt) and I am loath to leave it. Shall I ever see Littlemore again? I went off at eight-thirty with Bowles, for Maryvale via Leamington. I quite tore myself away and could not help kissing my bed and mantelpiece, and other parts of the house. I have been most happy there, though in a state of suspense. . . ."

To Copeland, his former curate, he wrote: "Without having

any plan or shadow of view on the subject, I cannot help thinking that I shall one day see Littlemore again, and see its dear
inhabitants, including yourself, once again one with me in the
bosom of the true Church of Christ. . . ."

Shortly after reaching Oscott, where he was to remain until
his future course was decided upon, he wrote to his dear friend
Henry Wilberforce (still an Anglican clergyman) thus affectionately:

"Carissime,—I write my first letter from my new home to
you. Pusey is my oldest friend since dear Bowden was taken away
—you come next. I am going to write to him, and had got out my
paper, but somehow my fingers have slipped away from my purpose, and I write to you, who have ever been so faithful to me.
No one can be truer or more faithful to me than Pusey himself—
but Aristotle says something about our hearts going out more with
those younger than ourselves than with others; and of those who
in any sense have been providentially placed under me, you alone
have been affectionate to me. And that is the reason, perhaps, why
I love Ambrose St. John so much, because he comes from you and
your teaching. O that he might be a pledge to me that you are
yourself to repair that breach which you sorrow over, by doing
what he has done—but I say the above whatever you resolve
upon, Carissime, great indeed, as must be my distress, as well as
yours, while we are divided. . . . I have brought here your little
reading desk, which was Wood's. I had not the heart to leave it
behind. It formed part of the altar on which Father Dominic offered Mass, and from which I received my First Communion,
October 10th. Please come and fetch it. I cannot help saying
so. . . ."

In the event, Henry Wilberforce *did* repair the breach which
he sorrowed over. About four years later he and his wife were
received into the Catholic Church.

2

Why did Newman go to Oscott? The critics-at-any-price still say he went there "under orders" from Bishop Wiseman, who did not quite trust these Oxford converts and wished to keep his eye on them and choose their careers for them; especially, was it said, he wished to keep his eye on Newman through fear that he might lapse! But as a matter of fact, Wiseman was at his wits' end to know what to do with the flood which was then rolling in on him. Old Oscott seemed to be a good temporary headquarters for at least a limited number.

Old Oscott was a pleasant little spot, nestling in the wooded slopes of Warwickshire; and it had an interesting history. Here, back in the seventeenth century, the priest Andrew Bromwich had had a little secret mission, and during the notorious Titus Oates scare, he had nearly lost his head. On the site of this little mission a house was built in the middle of the eighteenth century as a residence for the vicars apostolic; the famous Bishop Challoner, and later, Bishop John Milner, resided here. At the time of the French Revolution, when the English seminary in Douay, France, was closed, the building at Oscott was taken over for educational purposes. Extensions were then made; but by 1820 it was too small to accommodate all the pupils, and a new college building was erected about two miles away, leaving this building standing as "Old Oscott."

It was an ideal place for the new converts to be temporarily housed. They gave it the name of Maryvale. At first there were but eight occupants, who refurbished the rooms, with Newman filling the place with books—for he had brought his entire library from Littlemore. Here they "organized" their activities, with a religious schedule, beginning with Mass every morning at seven and crowding the days with study and meditation—and, of course, planning for the longer future.

Newman was not at all certain as yet that he would seek Holy Orders. Physically he was much run down; he needed a long rest after his trying time at Littlemore, with his feverish work on his *Development,* which sometimes ran through an entire night.

But as is the fate of every convert who has a writing bent, he had scarcely got settled at Maryvale when he was being urged to write the story of his conversion. Dr. Wiseman, with Father Spencer and others, eager to make the most of the convert trend at that particular time, begged him to write something, to strike while the iron was hot. But he was cold to their appeals, insisting that his *Development* (just then appearing in print) answered all questions about his conversion. To Spencer Northcote, who was especially insistent that he write something, he wrote the following letter, which I quote in part.

"Catholicism is a deep matter, you cannot take it up in a tea-cup. Any dogmatic or sententious proposition would too surely be misunderstood. If I said, for instance, 'I have become a Catholic, because I must be either a Catholic or an infidel,' men would cry out, 'So he has flung himself into the Catholic Church to escape infidelity'; whereas I should only mean that Catholicism and Christianity had in my mind become identical, so that to give up the one was to give up the other. I do not know how to do justice to my reasons for becoming a Catholic in ever so many words—but if I attempted to do so in few, and that in print, I should wantonly expose myself and my cause to the hasty and prejudiced criticisms of opponents. This I will not do. People shall not say, 'We have now got his reasons, and know their worth.' No, you have not got them. You cannot get them except at the cost of some portion of the trouble I have been at myself. . . . You must consent to *think*—and you must exercise such resignation to the Divine Hand which leads you, as to follow it any whither. I am not assuming that my reasons are sufficient or unanswerable, when I say this—but describing the way in which alone our intellect can be successfully exercised on the great subject in question, if the intellect is to be the instrument of conversion. Moral proofs are grown into, not learnt by heart."

His scruples, however, about taking Orders for the priesthood did not last very long, and within a few months his mind had been made up. After this was rumored about, his brother Francis threatened to journey to Maryvale, evidently to protest. Newman writes St. John from London: "My brother is coming to see me at Maryvale. . . . Why should he come? I think he has some obscure idea about thumbscrews."

During his first months at Maryvale he avoided all controversial writing; but his interests there did not prevent him from keeping up correspondence with old friends like Keble and Pusey; and when at this time Pusey fell seriously ill, he hastened to his bedside. But now their paths had divided, and after Pusey's recovery they were not to meet again for many years. This was true regarding John Keble also.

In early June of 1846 the reigning Pope, Gregory XVI, died, and a new Pope ascended the throne—the courageous, long-lived Pius IX. Early in July he sent Newman his special blessing. The latter had now matured his plans, and on September 7, 1846, with Ambrose St. John and Richard Stanton, he started on his journey to Rome, crossing to Dieppe and going on to Paris. There they were met by Robert Coffin, all four visiting the Archbishop and other dignitaries. A few days later they pushed on to Milan by way of the Simplon, which they reached on September 20 in time for Sunday Mass at the Duomo. They reached Rome October 26, went immediately to St. Peter's and found the Pope offering Mass at the tomb of the Apostles. After this they met Cardinal Fransoni and Cardinal Brunelli, the latter being Secretary of the College of Propaganda, where they would now spend more than a year. They were soon presented to the Holy Father, who welcomed them with great cordiality.

At the College of Propaganda, they immediately became students to prepare for their ordination to the priesthood; middle-aged men among a multitude of young seminarians, some of them mere boys. Ambrose St. John writes home: "Newman does edify them [the teachers] in the true sense of the word, by turning schoolboy at his age."

They tried to balance this schoolboy role by seeing Rome thoroughly and making friends among the ecclesiastics. Oddly enough, Newman met in Rome at this time two men, one a convert and one a convert-to-be, who would give him more trouble in future years than any other individuals in the Church. One was Father George Talbot, a former Anglican, who would presently become a monsignor. He was already close to Pius IX and would soon be a power at the Vatican. Newman had met him for a few moments at Oscott in February, but only now did he really get to know him. The other was Henry Edward Manning, still an Anglican archdeacon. He was hovering over the Roman scene, greatly edified by all he saw and charmed with Pope Pius IX—whose ear he would get many times in future years.

After not very long, Newman and his companions were ordained. For months they had been receptive to the idea of joining a preaching or teaching Order, the Dominicans or the Jesuits. But now Newman, who had long been an admirer of that charming sixteenth century saint Philip Romolo Neri, the famous Apostle of Rome and founder of the Oratorians, fell in love with the idea of following in his footsteps by becoming an Oratorian himself. As early as January 1847, we find him writing to Dalgairns: "How would it suit us to be Oratorians? First, we must give up our Dominican notion of teachers of divinity in schools of classics or philosophy. The Oratorian rule does not admit of it. . . . Secondly, we must be located in a town. These are two conditions which seem to me unavoidable, if we are to be Oratorians at all. And now to see how we can adjust ourselves to them. . . ."

Newman's interest in St. Philip Neri seems to have settled the matter. This we may well understand if we take a glance at that most attractive saint.

St. Philip Neri lived in that tempestuous period when the Lutheran revolt had at last awakened the Church authorities to the urgent need of cleaning house and repairing the damage done to the Church and her discipline during the days of the worldly and careless Renaissance Pontiffs, many of whom had been more interested in temporalities than in the spiritual life. Born in Florence in 1515, he grew up amid the memories of Savonarola, and much of his boyhood was spent among the Dominican friars of San Marco, thus giving him early a strong religious bent. He was well educated as he matured, but he seems to have had no thought of becoming a priest. When he was sixteen he was sent by his father to devote himself to business in Cassino, in southern Italy. There he acquired the habit of going often to the great Benedictine monastery of Monte Cassino for prayer; and here in time his true vocation in life seems to have come clear to him.

In 1533 Philip left Cassino, going to Rome, where he lived for the following eighteen years as a layman, devoting his time to study, to the greater sanctification of his own soul, and to missionary work among the poor and sick. He induced others to follow a similar apostolate until, after some years, he had formed a nucleus of what became the Brotherhood of the Little Oratory. His following steadily increased, and in 1548 he founded the Confraternity of the Most Holy Trinity, for taking care of pilgrims and convalescents, its members specializing in devotion to the Blessed Sacrament. Of a cheerful nature and sociable disposition, he became famous for the conversion of worldly people, and especially dissolute youth. Finally, in 1551, at the urging of his confessor, he entered the priesthood. For the remainder of his life he carried on a mighty apostolate in Rome, bringing back to the Faith thousands of souls. Always kind and gentle, his golden rule with sinners was—"First let a little love find entrance into their hearts, and the rest will follow."

Out of the work of this holy man grew the famous Oratorian Foundation, approved by the Pope after St. Philip's death. It was a form of "congregation" rather than an Order in the strict sense of the word; a community of priests living under obedience but taking no vows. St. Philip had insisted that in forming an Oratory, each house should be independent. "Let each house live by its own vitality, or perish by its own decrepitude." A wise principle, for it excluded the danger of a strong house being dragged down by the weakness or decay of another.

That Newman fell in love with St. Philip is indicated by his description of him years later in one of his Dublin lectures:

"He suited himself to noble and ignoble, young and old, subjects and prelates, learned and ignorant, and received those who were strangers to him with singular benignity, and embraced them with as much love and charity as if he had been a long time expecting them. When he was called upon to be merry, he was so; if there was a demand upon his sympathy, he was equally ready. He gave the same welcome to all, caressing the poor equally with the rich and wearying himself to assist all to the utmost of his power. In consequence of his being so accessible and willing to receive all comers, many went to him every day, and some continued for the space of thirty, nay, forty years, to visit him very often both morning and evening, so that his rooms went by the agreeable nickname of the home of Christian mirth."

Newman later described St. Philip in verse:

This is the saint of gentleness and kindness,
Cheerful in penance and in precept winning,
Patiently healing of their pride and blindness,
*   Souls that are sinning.*

This is the saint who, when the world allures us,
Cries her false wares and opens her magic coffers,
Points to a better city, and secures us
*   With richer offers.*

He was inspired to try to follow in the footsteps of this unique saint and perpetuate his name and fame in England. He was not slow in preparing his plans. The Pope was favorable to Newman's idea of founding an Oratory in England and when, shortly after the ordination of himself and his companions, they left for home (early in 1848) he brought with him a Brief from the Pope authorizing him to establish the English Community of the Oratory of St. Philip Neri.

Immediately after their arrival home, there gathered with Newman at Old Oscott, Ambrose St. John, J. D. Dalgairns, Robert Coffin, Richard Stanton and W. G. Penny—now all priests—with their first novice, Father Francis Knox, and three lay brothers, to organize and set in motion their new Oratory. The formal inauguration took place on the Feast of the Purification, February 2, "under the protection of Our Lady and St. Philip." Before that month was over, the new community was fully functioning, and in March, Newman was able to write: "We are very busy, as you may think; I as Superior, as Novice Master, as Lecturer in Theology—besides chance matters and going to Birmingham. We have, I believe, eighteen priests in fact, or *potentialiter*."

3

How sensitive and diffident Newman was, wishing to avoid anything which might make him appear peculiar or unconventional or be the subject of curious comment, must surely be clear to the reader. An amusing side-light on his modesty and embarrassment is seen in his reluctance to appear in public when he first adopted the clerical garb of the Catholic priesthood in place of the old-fashioned ministerial dress then worn by Anglican clergy. When, after his return from Rome, he was obliged to exhibit himself on the London streets in his new attire, it induced him to make this comment to a friend:

"My dislike of marching up the London streets is considerable; not indeed that I have any reluctance in wearing a clerical dress, for I need not unless I wished it, but I am so awkward and gawky that I feel ashamed of myself. The only make-up is that the poor Catholics recognize it and touch their hats to me; but imagine *me*, who have never been in costume, wearing a straight cut collar to my coat, and having a long skirt to it. I know I look like a fool, from my own intrinsic absurdity."

The march of time surely does bring surprising changes in customs—and costumes! If, in those days, Protestants ridiculed or frowned upon the dress worn by Catholic priests, how different it is today. Even fifty years ago it was safe to assume that any man with a Roman collar was a Catholic priest—or at least a High Anglican. But nowadays he may turn out to be, not even an Episcopalian, but a Methodist, Presbyterian, Baptist, Congregationalist, or indeed some unlabeled lay preacher. No "Anglo-Catholic" would now say, as Newman did, that a Catholic clerical garb makes him "look like a fool." He is sure it makes him look like a priest—and feel like a priest. How it makes the out-and-out Protestant feel is more of a mystery.

During his sojourn in Rome, despite his keen interest and his absorbing experiences, Newman often found himself homesick. His knowledge of the Italian language was limited, and while he made many new friends, his thoughts often centered on the English environment which was his home. As he wrote from Rome to Henry Wilberforce:

"New friends cannot love one, if they would; they know nothing of one: but to one who has known another twenty years, his face and his name are a history; a long series of associations is bound up with every word or deed which comes from him. . . . And then I feel that no one here can sympathize with me duly— for even those who think highly of me have the vaguest, most shadowy and fantastic notions attached to their idea of me, and feel a respect, not for me, but for some imagination of their own which bears my name." Then he adds, quite characteristically— "But what people here can do for me and what they cannot, carries off my mind to Him Who 'has fed me all my life until this day,' Whom I find protecting me most wonderfully under such new circumstances, just as He ever has before, and Who can give me that sympathy which men cannot give."

But even in Rome, busy as he was with matters connected with his preparation for the priesthood, planning his Oratory and making contacts with many people, he was filling his leisure moments with his pen. This was never idle; that "passion for scribbling" which he says possessed him in his boyhood days was as potent as ever. And although before he left for Rome he had declined to write anything bearing on his conversion, he was inspired, while viewing the Roman scene (yet longing for home and the still-loved Oxford), to turn his thoughts to the writing of a book. The result was *Loss and Gain,* which, if not completed in Rome, must have been planned and outlined there. It appeared shortly after his return home and achieved a wide circulation. It was immediately accepted as Newman's own story, or at least as basically autobiographical, which indeed it was. Bishop Wiseman, whom Newman had repulsed at Oscott for urging him to write his conversion story, must now have indulged in a quiet chuckle.

In this little book the hero, Charles Reding, is studying for the Anglican ministry at Oxford. But in his researches in Christian history he soon becomes entangled in the same difficulties that had troubled Newman himself. He has doubts about the Thirty-Nine Articles and these doubts lead to others. The Tractarian controversy is under way, and the air is charged with incessant discussion. He has many talks with other young men, some still students like himself, some already ordained. Among his friends is one Willis, who finally succumbs to Rome; but nearly all his friends are anti-Catholic. In the event, the arguments of these Protestant friends prove fruitless, for after two years of struggle, during which he studies the Caroline divines to bolster his declining Anglican beliefs, he finds himself at the door of the Catholic Church.

There is little action in the story aside from Reding's struggles; but the tale is beautifully told. Again and again we see Newman's own struggles vividly pictured. Indeed, Charles Reding is his *alter ego*; like Newman himself he is deeply introspective, ever concerned with his consciousness of the Divine Presence "which was the pillar of the cloud before him and guiding him." In all essentials we have a picture of the storm and stress period of Oxford and Littlemore. How exactly he limns the emotions which were his own on leaving Littlemore: "He crossed the meadow, and walked steadily down to the junction of the Cherwell and the Isis. Then he turned back. What thoughts came upon him—for the last time? There was no one to see him; he threw his arms around the willows so dear to him and kissed them; he tore off some of their black leaves and put them in his bosom."

Aside from this intensely human story, there are other virtues not to be overlooked. The book is studded with some of the most brilliant passages that Newman ever wrote. There is, for example, a remarkable passage on the Mass. Reding, before his conversion, is seeing the Mass only as a Roman superstition, as do others present; but the Catholic convert, Willis, comes to its defence:

"I declare to you," he says, "to me nothing is so consoling, so piercing, so thrilling, so overcoming, as the Mass, said as it is among us. I could attend Masses forever and not be tired. It is not a mere form of words—it is a great Action, the greatest action that there can be on earth. It is not the invocation merely, but, if I dare use the word, the evocation of the Eternal. He becomes present on the altar in flesh and blood, before whom angels bow and devils tremble. This is that awful event which is the end, and is the interpretation, of every part of the solemnity.

Words are necessary, but as means, not as ends; they are not mere addresses to the throne of Grace, they are the instruments of what is far higher, of consecration, of sacrifice. They hurry on as if impatient to fulfill their mission. Quickly they go; the whole is quick; for they are all parts of one integral action. Quickly they go; for they are awful words of sacrifice, they are a work too great to delay upon; as when it was said in the beginning, 'What thou doest, do quickly.' Quickly they pass; for the Lord Jesus goes with them, as He passed along the lake in the days of His flesh, quickly calling first one and then another. Quickly they pass, because as the lightning which shineth from one part of the heaven to another, so is the coming of the Son of Man. Quickly they pass, for they are as the words of Moses, when the Lord came down in the cloud, calling on the Name of the Lord as He passed by, 'The Lord, the Lord God, merciful and gracious, long suffering, and abundant in goodness and truth.' And as Moses on the mountain, so we too 'make haste and bow our heads and adore.' So we, all around, each in his place, look out for the great Advent, 'waiting for the moving of the water.' Each in his place, with his own heart, with his own wants, with his own thoughts, with his own intention, with his own prayers, separate but concordant, watching what is going on, watching its progress, uniting in its consummation;—not painfully and hopelessly following a hard form of prayer from beginning to end, but like a concert of musical instruments, each different, but concurring in a sweet harmony, we take our part with God's priest, supporting him, yet guided by him. There are little children there, and old men, and simple laborers, and students in seminaries, priests preparing for Mass, priests making their thanksgiving; there are innocent maidens, and there are penitents; but out of these many minds rises one eucharistic hymn, and the great Action is the measure and the scope of it. . . ."

That vivid description of the Mass and its significance was surely conceived by Newman while in Rome, where, for the first time, in his rounds of the great Roman churches, he absorbed atmosphere and scenes which he never could have absorbed at home.

There is another (briefer) passage I must quote. Reding and Willis are traveling homeward, and as they part, Willis says to Reding in subdued tones: "Oh, that you were one of us! You have it in you. I have thought of you at Mass many times. Our priest has said Mass for you. Oh, my dear friend, quench not God's grace; listen to His call; you have had what others have not. What you want is faith. I suspect you have quite proof enough; enough to be converted on. But faith is a gift; pray for that great gift, without which you cannot come to the Church; without which you cannot walk aright when you are in the Church. And now farewell; alas, our path divides; all is easy to him that believeth. May God give you that gift of faith, as He has given me! Farewell again; who knows when I may see you again, and where? May it be in the courts of the true Jerusalem, the Queen of Saints, the Holy Roman Church, the Mother of us all!" Then Willis left him without another word.

This was the turning point for Charles Reding. He hurried along in the twilight at a brisk pace, enthusiastic in his consciousness that now faith was within his grasp. "He felt himself possessed, he knew not how, by a high superhuman power, which seemed able to push through mountains, and walk the sea. 'O mighty Mother,' burst from his lips; he quickened his pace almost to a trot, scaling the steep ascents and diving into the hollows which lay between him and Boughton. 'O mighty Mother,' he still said half-unconsciously; 'O mighty Mother, I come; but I am far from home. Spare me a little; I come with what speed I may, but I am slow of feet, and not as others, O mighty Mother!' "

It was still to be some time before Charles Reding entered the Church. Like Newman, his reason—not merely his heart but his head—must guide his will.

4

And now, back from Rome as a Catholic priest, we do not find
Newman leading a great crusade, as in the early days of the Oxford Movement, but, as had been the case at Littlemore, living
apart from the noise and tumult of the world. This he would continue to do for nearly all the years of his Catholic life. For he was
by nature a solitary, dreading turmoil and the annoyances of the
battling life.

But this does not mean that he idled away his time. His pen
was as busy as ever. Indeed, when we glance over the writings of
his Catholic days, with his immense correspondence, we can only
marvel at his industry; and especially so during the early years of
his Catholic life, when his Oratory was under development, ultimately settling permanently at Edgbaston, a suburb of Birmingham. There was also, at first, the London Oratory. This, however, was developed independently of the Birmingham House,
with Father Frederick Faber at its head, assisted by Dalgairns and
one or two others from the Birmingham House. First in temporary quarters in King William Street, Strand, the London Oratory
later removed to Brompton Road, where the present Brompton
Oratory now stands. This London House specialized in charitable
activities in the London slums and became famous for this type
of work. Nor were such activities neglected by the Birmingham
House. When cholera broke out at Bilston near Birmingham,
Newman and St. John were seen visiting the sick and dying in
the most dangerous districts, daily spending long hours in these
works of mercy.

But what Newman longed for in these first years was quietude
and harmony, after his long tempestuous period in the Anglican
communion. Not that he wished to avoid toil, but, as he said to
Father St. John: "How much happier for me to have no liabilities
(so to speak) but to be a single unfettered convert." His health

was very poor at this time and he easily succumbed to weariness; the vigor of his earlier years seemed to be passing; old age, he felt, was crowding on. It was always "crowding on" for this gentle soul, even in this comparatively youthful period of his long life. "At times," he says, "the weight of responsibility and desolateness has come upon me so strongly that I could fancy it might be equal to any pain; and I thought what the Pope must suffer." [1]

This wished-for season of rest and relaxation, however, seems not to have been realized to any marked extent. For besides the necessary and constantly increased demands on his time in connection with the Oratory, he was writing and delivering sermons and lectures. In 1849 he preached in Birmingham a series of great sermons which resulted in many conversions, among both the poor and well-to-do; at that time Lady Arundel, the future Duchess of Norfolk, entered the Church. These sermons, published later as *Discourses to Mixed Congregations,* are in some ways superior to his great Oxford University sermons; they possess that quality of verve so characteristic of the new convert, who feels a sense of freedom and certitude regarding the Faith which he had never known before. As a competent Protestant observer has said: "These sermons have a definite tone and genius of their own. They represent more adequately Dr. Newman as he was when he first felt himself 'unmuzzled,' than any of his other writings; and though they have not to me quite the delicate charm or the reserve, and I might almost say the shy passion, of his Oxford sermons, they represent the full-blown blossoming of his genius, while the former show it only in bud." [2] Dr. Jowett, that very conspicuous member of the Broad Church Anglican school, said of them: "I think that Romanism was never so glorified before."

---

[1] Pope Pius IX at this time was struggling with the Italian political turmoils. He had been banished from Rome and was carrying on for the time being at Gaeta, in southern Italy.
[2] Hutton, *Cardinal Newman.*

As a result of these discourses, several prominent Puseyites were converted, including T. W. Allies, Sir George Bowyer, William Monsell and H. F. Bellasis. This was the time when Henry Wilberforce and his wife were received. A little later, Robert Wilberforce and Henry Edward Manning were to follow—though the latter had his particular reasons (which will be detailed later) for his conversion.[1]

Newman was now well started in the work which he was well fitted for—preaching and lecturing. In the spring of 1850 he was induced to deliver at the temporary Oratory Church in King William Street, Strand, a series of lectures which he felt diffident about undertaking. It consisted of twelve lectures primarily addressed to Anglicans and designed to clarify the minds of those Tractarians who had not come into the Catholic Church but who were supposed to be hanging on the brink. Bishop Wiseman was sure there were many such; Newman himself was not so sure—he knew them! At the time, he remarked to Father Faber: "I am writing them intellectually against the grain more than I recollect ever doing anything." He wanted to avoid controversy with the Tractarians.

In these lectures, which were of high literary quality and resulted in several important conversions, he displayed his talent for piercing irony, humor, and ability for stating unpleasant truths with sweet and gentle discrimination. But even though this undertaking warmed the heart of Bishop Wiseman, Newman did not like the job. Never again was he drawn into this type of controversy with Anglicans—unless we might so designate his last, friendly controversy with Dr. Pusey, many years later.

Far more congenial to him were his series on "The Present Position of Catholics in England," delivered at the Corn Exchange in Birmingham in June of 1851. While they did not get

---

[1] T. W. Allies, like Manning, was greatly influenced by the "Gorham judgment" in the Anglican Church. Later he became eminent as a writer.

the newspaper publicity accorded his "Difficulties of Anglicans," delivered in London the year before, they did much to discredit the arguments of the fanatical and ignorant against the Catholic Church. The following brief passage, in which he undertakes to contrast the ideals of the Church with those of the world, is typical of the series.

"The Church aims not at making a show," he says, "but doing a work. She regards this world, and all that is in it, as a mere shadow, as dust, compared with the value of one human soul. She holds that, unless she can, in her own way, do good to souls, it is no use her doing anything; she holds that it were better for the sun and moon to drop from heaven, for the earth to fail, and for all the many millions who are upon it to die of starvation in the extremest agony as far as temporal affliction goes, than that one soul, I will not say, should be lost, but should commit one single venial sin, should tell one wilful untruth, though it harmed no one, or steal one poor farthing without excuse. She considers the action of the world and the action of the soul simply incommensurable, viewed in their respective spheres; she would rather save the soul of one single bandit of Calabria, or whining beggar of Palermo, than draw a hundred lines of railroad through the length of Italy, or carry on a sanitary reform in fullest details in every city of Sicily, except so far as these great natural works tended to some spiritual good beyond them."

That was tough meat indeed for the typical English John Bull, so prone to confuse Christian standards and ideals with his current conceptions of material progress as the test for righteous Christian life.

One of Newman's lectures in this series got him into serious trouble—the so-called Achilli affair. But I must defer explanation of that until the next chapter. I first proceed to an event of far greater significance: the restoration of the Catholic hierarchy in England in 1850 and the appointment of Bishop Wiseman as Cardinal Archbishop of Westminster—the first English cardinal archbishop since the days of Cardinal Pole, before the accession of Queen Elizabeth in the sixteenth century. Though the Catholic Church had survived in England during the long period of the persecution, her traditional form of government had been eliminated. In its restoration, hangs a story well worth the telling.

5

The increase in the Catholic population in England had been so marked after 1840 that it was thought necessary to take steps to expand the system of Church government. Since 1688 the Church in England had been under the supervision of four vicars apostolic.[1] The number of vicars apostolic was now increased to eight. Dr. Wiseman had succeeded Bishop Walsh as Vicar Apostolic of the London district on the latter's death. But by 1848, this district, with its vast and increasing Catholic population, had become very difficult to manage.

With his usual energy, Wiseman had done much to promote the erection of new churches. One of the most important of the new edifices was St. George's, Southwark, which was opened with a great ceremony in July, 1848. The fact that this church was erected on a site which had been the center of the famous Lord George Gordon anti-Catholic riots of 1780 caused wide comment. The *Illustrated London News* (featuring a Catholic function for the first time) printed a series of pictures of this great event, in which fourteen Catholic bishops and two hundred and forty priests took part. "Strange indeed," commented this journal, "are the mutations of localities in this vast metropolis, and not the least of them is that the focus of the famous 'No popery'

[1] Vicars apostolic are appointed by the Holy See to govern churches in districts or countries where no regular hierarchy exists—as was the case in England during the long period of persecution of the Church.

riots of 1780 should within a lifetime become the site of a Roman Catholic Church—the largest erected in England since the Reformation."

Agitation in favor of restoring the hierarchy had arisen several years before, but action had been delayed, due perhaps to the unsettled conditions in Italy, with the Italian wars beginning and the Pope in exile. A definite move, however, was made when the Pope returned to Rome in 1850 and proclaimed a Jubilee year. In September of that year, it was announced in Rome (where Dr. Wiseman was at the time) that Bishop Nicholas Wiseman was to become Cardinal Archbishop of Westminster.

The British public received this news calmly and with considerable interest, evidently viewing it as a compliment that Rome should confer this honor on an illustrious Englishman. But Wiseman's tone of exultation in a pastoral letter to his flock, "from out the Flaminian Gate of Rome," with the Pope's Brief authorizing the re-establishment of the hierarchy, resulted in an amazing revulsion of feeling. In his pastoral letter, Wiseman had announced: "His Holiness was pleased to appoint us, though most unworthy, to the Archiepiscopal See of Westminster . . . giving us at the same time the administration of the Episcopal See of Southwark. So that at present . . . we govern, and shall continue to govern, the counties of Middlesex, Hertford and Essex, as Ordinary thereof, and those of Surrey, Kent, Sussex, Berkshire and Hampshire, with the islands annexed, as Administrator with Ordinary jurisdiction."

He went on to say: "The great work, then, is complete; what you have long desired and prayed for is granted. Your beloved country has received a place among the fair Churches which, normally constituted, form the splendid aggregate of the Catholic Communion; Catholic England has been restored to its orbit in the ecclesiastical firmament, from which its light had long vanished, and begins now anew its course of regularly adjusted action round the center of unity, the source of jurisdiction, of light and vigor. . . ."

It is perhaps not surprising that this exultant announcement should have been misinterpreted by Protestant England. In any event, the *Times* saw fit to misinterpret it in an inflammatory editorial, and this awoke the Anglican bishops. The Bishop of Durham at once sent an angry protest to the Prime Minister, Lord John Russell, asserting that this "Papal aggression" was an outrageous and unlawful intrusion on the preserves of the Anglican Church. Both the bishop's letter and the Prime Minister's reply to it were immediately published. Lord John Russell's reply was in the best style of the old anti-papal bigotry.

"My dear Lord,—I agree with you in considering the late aggression of the Pope upon our Protestantism as 'insolent and insidious,' and therefore I feel as indignant as you can do upon the subject. . . . There is an assumption of power in all the documents which have come from Rome—a pretension to supremacy over the realm of England, and a claim to sole and undivided sway, which is inconsistent with the Queen's supremacy, with the rights of our bishops and clergy, and with the spiritual independence of the nation, as asserted even in Roman Catholic times. . . . The liberty of Protestantism has been too long enjoyed in England to allow any successful attempt to impose a foreign yoke upon our minds and consciences. No foreign prince or potentate will be permitted to fasten his fetters upon a nation which has so long and so nobly vindicated its right to freedom of opinion, civil, political and religious."

But in his panic, the worthy Prime Minister mixed his metaphors, firing an even heavier volley at the innocent Puseyites, who really had no more use for the Papacy than had the Bishop of Durham. He lashed out at them in the following words:

"There is a danger, however, which alarms me much more than any aggression of a foreign sovereign. Clergymen of our own

Church, who have subscribed the Thirty-Nine Articles, and acknowledged in explicit terms the Queen's supremacy, have been the most forward in leading their flocks, step by step, to the brink of the precipice. The honor paid to saints, the superstitious use of the sign of the Cross, the mutterings of the Liturgy, so as to disguise the language in which it is written, the recommendation of auricular confession—all these things are pointed out by clergymen of the Church of England as worthy of adoption, and are now openly reprehended by the Bishop of London in his charge to the clergy of his diocese. What then, is the danger to be apprehended from a foreign prince of no great power, compared to the danger within the gates from the unworthy sons of the Church of England herself? I have little hope that the founders and framers of these innovations will desist from their insidious course. But I rely with confidence on the people of England, and I will not bate a jot of heart or hope so long as the glorious principles and the immortal martyrs of the Reformation shall be held in reverence by the great mass of a nation which looks with contempt on the mummeries of superstition, and with scorn at the laborious endeavors which are now making to confine the intellect and enslave the soul."

Obviously the Prime Minister was not a Puseyite. Nor was the queen. Nor were the bishops, who, with but two exceptions, signed a joint letter to the queen which ran in this wise:

"We consider it our duty to record our united protest against this attempt to subject our people to a spiritual tyranny from which they were freed at the Reformation, and we make our humble petition to your Majesty to discountenance by all constitutional means the claims and usurpations of the Church of Rome, by which religious divisions are fostered and the labors of our clergy impeded in their endeavors to diffuse the light of true religion."

With characteristic solemnity, Queen Victoria endorsed this manifesto. Quite naturally the newspapers followed with a great hue and cry, and taking their cue from Lord John Russell, did not fail to vilify the Puseyites. Indignation meetings were held in London and other cities, the Pope was burned in effigy, and priests and their congregations hooted. Cardinal Wiseman was insulted on the streets; and Newman, in Birmingham, had a bag of flour dumped on his head from an upper window. Nor did the Puseyites escape. Mobs stormed St. Alban's Church, Margaret Street, London, making it impossible to conduct services, and its rector, who was under the jurisdiction of the Anglican Bishop of London (bitterly anti-Catholic), was forced to resign his living.

This so-called "Papal aggression" was nothing more than the establishment in England of a Catholic hierarchy similar to that which already existed in several of the British colonies, including Australia and Canada. But the public, aroused by the *Times* attack and Lord John Russell's letter, half expected that Cardinal Wiseman intended to evict the Dean and Canons of Westminster Abbey and celebrate his triumph by holding a Pontifical Mass there. Perhaps they thought the Pope was about to land at Dover!

The Cardinal's pastoral was, of course, addressed not to the British public or to the government, but simply to his own Catholic flock, and was not designed for general publication. But being read in the churches, its contents became public, and as the Cardinal had not yet returned from Rome, he was not at the moment in a position to explain to the general public the meaning of the pastoral letter. When he did reach London a week or two later, it required his best literary talent to convince the English public in an open letter that no "aggression" was planned. He also wrote a brilliant explanation to the *Times*, which published it in full and then formally recalled its own absurd earlier charges and criticisms and unwarranted assertions.

The panic now gradually subsided. The Cardinal's explanation embraced a notable passage which must have been quite illumi-

nating to the frightened Protestant population. This passage I
quote.

"The diocese (of Westminster) consists of two very different
parts," he said. "One comprises the stately Abbey, with its adja-
cent palaces and its royal parks. To this portion the duties and
occupation of the Dean and Chapter are mainly confined, and
they shall range there undisturbed. To the venerable old Church
I may repair, as I have been wont to do. I may visit the old Abbey,
and say my prayers by the shrine of good St. Edward; and medi-
tate on the olden times, when the church filled without a coro-
nation, and multitudes hourly worshipped without a service. Yet
this splendid monument, its treasures of art, and its fitting endow-
ments, form the part of Westminster which will not concern me.
For there is another part which stands in frightful contrast,
though in immediate contact with this magnificence. Close under
the Abbey of Westminster there lie concealed labyrinths of lanes
and courts, and alleys and slums, nests of ignorance, vice, depravity, and crime, as well as of squalor, wretchedness and
disease; whose atmosphere is typhus, whose ventilation is cholera;
in which swarms a huge and almost countless population, nomi-
nally, at least, Catholic: haunts of filth which no Sewage Com-
mittee can reach, dark corners which no Lighting Board can
brighten. *This* is the part of Westminster which alone I covet, and
which I shall be glad to claim and visit as a blessed pasture in
which sheep of Holy Church are to be tended, in which a bishop's
godly work has to be done."

That vivid picture of a London slum area was surely an indict-
ment of the so-called "march of progress"—less than twenty
years after the passage of the first Reform Bill, of which Lord
John Russell had been one of the outstanding advocates.

A strong reaction set in after the excitement of the "Papal
Aggression" flare had died down; and there followed a new influx
of distinguished converts to the Catholic Church. These included
a number of Puseyites. Lord John Russell's tirade against them

inspired more than one conversion to the more secure and serene atmosphere of the Catholic Church, where they would not be charged with "leading their flocks to the brink of the precipice" by prime ministers or bishops.

The "Papal Aggression" panic gave Newman an opportunity, when later delivering his lectures on "The Present Position of Catholics in England," to put forth an exquisitely humorous description of the way the incident had been greeted by the traditional Protestant majority:

"Heresy and schism, and infidelity, and fanaticism may challenge [the Establishment] in vain; but fling upon the gale the faintest whisper of Catholicism, and it recognizes by instinct its connatural foe. Forthwith, as during the last year, the atmosphere is tremulous with agitation, and discharges its vibrations far and wide. . . . Spontaneously the bells of the steeples begin to sound. Not by an act of volition, but by a sort of mechanical impulse, bishop and dean, archbishop and canon, rector and curate, one after another, each on his high tower, off they set, swinging and booming, tolling and chiming, with nervous intenseness and thickening emotion, and deafening volume, the old dingdong which has scared town and country this weary time; tolling and chiming away, jingling and clamoring, and ringing the changes on their half dozen poor notes, all about the 'Papal aggression,' 'insolent and insidious,' 'insolent and atrocious,' 'foul and offensive,' 'pestilent and horrid,' 'subtle and unholy,' 'audacious and revolting,' 'contemptible and shameless,' 'malignant,' 'frightful,' 'mad,' 'meretricious'—bobs (I think the ringers call them), bobs and bobs royal, and triple bob-majors and grandsires,—to the extent of their compass, and the full ring of their metal, in honour of Queen Bess, and to the confusion of the Pope and the Princes of the Church."

As already indicated, one of Newman's purposes in the series of lectures on "The Present Position of Catholics in England," was to bring to light the primary cause of the colossal prejudice against the Catholic Church in England—ignorance of her teachings and of her standards. He had begun by announcing, "I am going to enquire why it is that in this intelligent nation and in the nineteenth century, we Catholics are despised and hated by our own countrymen. Why they are prompt to believe any story, however extravagant, that is told to our disadvantage; as if, beyond a doubt, we were everyone of us, either brutishly deluded or preternaturally hypocritical, and they themselves, on the contrary, were in comparison of us, absolute specimens of sagacity, wisdom, uprightness, manly virtues and enlightened Christianity. I am not enquiring why they are not Catholics themselves, but why they are so angry with those who are."

Some of these lectures, replete with humor, good-natured satire and amusing illustrations of anti-Catholic prejudice based on pure ignorance, had a telling effect. Perhaps for the first time in that generation many a critic of the Church was made uncomfortable at this exposure of his own ignorance.

6

Soon after the establishment of the new hierarchy, an event of great importance took place. This was the First Provincial Synod of Westminster, held at Oscott in July 1852, at which assembled all the English Catholic bishops, with their new Cardinal Archbishop, and a vast gathering of priests and other dignitaries of the Church, including nearly all the Oxford converts who had become priests. On this occasion, Newman delivered his famous address, "Second Spring," one of the greatest orations of his career. It was no less memorable than that earlier masterpiece "The Parting of Friends," preached at Littlemore nearly ten years before. But then he had lamented over a loss; now he was to exult over a triumph, proclaiming, in lyrical note, the resurrection to life of that which had seemed well nigh unto death.

This English Catholic body, now free to express its will openly, though still filled with bitter memories of the age-long persecution of the Church, opened its proceedings by carrying out the full ancient ceremonial as used before the days of suppression in the sixteenth century. The Mass of the Holy Spirit was celebrated with full music and liturgy. Newman's address made an extraordinary impression. As Bishop Ullathorne later said: "The sentiments of that moment will never be forgotten; for deep and soul stirring as they were, they found their expression in Dr. Newman's exquisite discourse. . . . During its delivery, Cardinal Wiseman, in the Presidential chair, wept tears of consolation. The bishops and clergy were nearly all in tears. And when the preacher came out from the Synod, they crowded upon him, giving full flow to the ardent outpourings of their gratitude. . . ."

The Second Spring address was not only a triumph of religious oratory, but it was a high example of beautiful English prose and filled with the brilliant symbolism of which Newman was so great a master. It was applauded not merely at the Synod, or among Catholics, but all over England. Even the anti-Catholic unbeliever Lord Macaulay said that he had learned it by heart; and George Eliot, another famous sceptic, said she could not read it without tears.

To realize its full beauty as a superb example of Newman's genius as a writer and speaker, one must read it all. He began with a description, in an unforgettable passage, of the world of nature:

"We have familiar experience of the order, the constancy, the perpetual renovation of the material world which surrounds us. Frail and transitory as is every part of it, restless and migratory as are its elements, never ceasing as are its changes, still it abides. It is bound together by a law of permanence, it is set up in unity; and, though it is ever dying, it is ever coming to life again. Dissolution does but give birth to fresh modes of organization, and one death is the parent of a thousand lives. Each hour, as it comes, is but a testimony, how fleeting, yet how secure, how certain, is the great whole. It is like an image on the waters, which is ever the same, though the waters ever flow. Change upon change— yet one change cries out to another, like the alternate Seraphim, in praise and glory of their Maker. The sun sinks to rise again; the day is swallowed up in the gloom of night, to be born out of it, as fresh as if it had never been quenched. Spring passes into summer, and through summer and autumn into winter, only the more surely, by its own ultimate return, to triumph over that grave, towards which it resolutely hastened from its first hour. We mourn over the blossoms of May, because they are to wither; but we know, withal, that May is one day to have its revenge upon November, by the revolution of that solemn circle which never stops—which teaches us in our height of hope, ever to be sober, and in our depth of desolation, never to despair."

And now he proceeds to contrast this with the state of the natural Man, as placed by his Creator in the midst of this material world which surrounds him.

"And forcibly as this [the process of nature] comes home to every one of us, not less forcible is the contrast which exists between this material world, so vigorous, so reproductive, amid all its changes, and the moral world, so feeble, so downward, so resourceless, amid all its aspirations. That which ought to come to naught, endures; that which promises a future, disappoints and is no more. The same sun shines in heaven from first to last, and the blue firmament, the everlasting mountains, reflect his rays; but where is there upon earth the champion, the hero, the lawgiver, the body politic, the sovereign race, which was great three hundred years ago, and is great now? . . . Man rises to fall; he tends to dissolution from the moment he begins to be; he lives on, indeed, in his children; he lives on in his name; he lives not on in his own person. . . . He was young, he is old, he

is never young again. This is the lament over him, poured forth
in verse and in prose, by Christians and by heathen. The greatest work of God's hands under the sun, he, in all the manifestations of his complex being, is born only to die. . . ."

This vivid description of the natural man and his mutability
is leading up, of course, to the main theme of the address—the
restoration of the Catholic hierarchy in England after the lapse
of nearly three centuries. While man and his human devices
grow old and pass away, the Church ever renews her life after
being to all appearances dead, and passes through her winter to
her spring. He describes the status of the English Catholic Church
as it was when men of his own generation were born—an eloquent passage too long to insert here. After picturing her seemingly hopeless prospects as they were at the end of the eighteenth
century, he continues:

"But what is it, my Fathers, my Brothers, what is it that has
happened in England just at this time? Something strange is
passing over this land, by the very surprise, by the very commotion, which it excites. . . . We should judge rightly in our
curiosity about a phenomenon like this; it must be a portentous
event, and it is. It is an innovation, a miracle, I may say, in the
course of human events. The physical world revolves year by year,
and begins again; but the political order of things does not renew
itself, does not return; it continues; but it proceeds, there is no
retrogression. . . . The past is out of date; the past is dead. As
well may the dead live to us, as well may the dead profit us, as
the past return. *This,* then, is the cause of this national transport,
this national cry, which encompasses us. The past *has* returned;
the dead lives. Thrones are overturned, and are never restored;
States live and die, and then are matter only of history. Babylon
was great, and Tyre and Egypt, and Ninive; and shall never be
great again. The English [Catholic] Church was, and the English
[Catholic] Church was not, and the English [Catholic] Church is

once again. This is the portent, worthy of a cry. It is the coming in
of a SECOND SPRING; it is a restoration in the moral world, such
as that which yearly takes place in the physical. . . ."

And now he presents a sweeping picture of the Catholic Church
of the last three centuries, pointing out her handicaps and sufferings in passages of great power. Finally, in bringing his discourse to its close, he abandons the exultant note and is careful
to emphasize, in glancing to the future, the dangers of over-
optimism. He warns his hearers that no period of unmixed serenity for the Church is to be expected, and therefore not boastful-
ness, but thankfulness tempered by faith and hope, must be the
attitude of all English Catholics in that hour.

"Yes, my Fathers and Brothers," he continues, "and if it be
God's blessed will, not Saints alone, not Doctors only, not preachers only, shall be ours—but Martyrs, too, shall reconsecrate the
soil to God. . . . Something, for what we know, remains to be
undergone, to complete the necessary sacrifice. May God forbid
it, for this poor Nation's sake! But still, could we be surprised,
my Fathers and my Brothers, if the winter even now should not
yet be quite over? Have we any right to take it strange, if, in this
English land, the springtime of the Church should turn out to
be an English spring, an uncertain, anxious time of hope and fear,
of joy and suffering,—of bright promise and budding hopes, yet
withal, of keen blasts, and cold showers, and sudden storms?

"One thing alone I know,—that according to our need, so will
be our strength. One thing I am sure of, that the more the enemy
rages against us, so much the more will the Saints in Heaven
plead for us; the more fearful are our trials from the world, the
more present to us will be our Mother Mary, and our good
patrons, and Angel Guardians; the more malicious are the
devices of men against us, the louder the cry of supplication will
ascend from the bosom of the whole Church to God for us. We
shall not be left orphans; we shall have within us the strength

of the Paraclete, promised to the Church and to every member
of it. . . . By the intercession of the Saints on high, by the pen-
ances and good works and the prayers of the people of God on
earth, you would be forcibly borne up as upon the waves of the
mighty deep, and carried on out of yourselves by the fulness of
grace, whether nature wished it or no. I do not mean violently,
or with unseemly struggle, but calmly, gracefully, sweetly, joy-
ously, you would mount up and ride forth to battle, as on the
rush of Angels' wings, as your fathers did before you, and gained
the prize. You, who day by day, offer up the Immaculate Lamb
of God, you who hold in your hands the Incarnate Word under
the visible tokens which He has ordained, you who again and
again drain the chalice of the Great Victim; who is to make you
fear? what is to startle you? what to seduce you? who is to stop
you, whether you are to suffer or to do, whether to lay the foundations of the Church in tears, or to put the crown upon the work
in jubilation? . . ."

This great sermon has been called a prose poem; it is indeed
that, but also much more. It is full of the personality of Newman
himself—saturated with the spiritual vision so characteristic of
him, as well as the realism which was also characteristic. His
descriptive powers are here seen at their best.

He was overwhelmed by the enthusiastic response to this address. All crowded round him to offer their congratulations; reso-
lutions of commendation and gratitude to this great convert were
drawn up and voted unanimously.

An interesting incident of the occasion was that Henry Edward
Manning, who had but recently become a Catholic, stepped to
the front to take possession of the hero of the hour and lead him
to quieter surroundings—an act which was not only characteristic of the future Cardinal of Westminster but which some people
have found it hard to tie into a graceful knot, in view of the
future relations of these men.

7

If this period of revival of the Catholic Church in England is appropriately called her second spring, it can be said with equal truth that this first half-dozen years of Newman's Catholic life was *his* second spring—replete as they were with all the freshness and beauty of a new life budding forth and developing in the bright sunshine of religious certitude and spiritual peace.

These first years had been marked by glowing successes in all his activities: in the congenial work of developing his Oratory, in his achievements in writing and preaching—not to mention the host of new friends of like views with his own, who had now gathered round him. The loss of old friends and loved ones had of course been a trial; and the estrangement from his sisters and brothers must always have been a heavy cross to bear; but the new life of mental and spiritual peace went far to compensate for these losses. Years later, in referring to this time and the years that followed, he wrote: "I have been in perfect peace and contentment; I have never had one doubt. It was like coming into port after a rough sea; and my happiness on that score remains to this day without interruption."

The reader must already have noticed the sharp contrast between his old life and the new. Still, as every convert to the Faith soon finds, the blessed unity of belief within the Catholic Church does not imply unity or uniformity of things on the natural or mundane plane. Individual Catholics, like the rest of humanity, are as diverse in their personal characteristics and temperaments as frail humanity necessarily must be. The notion that individual Catholics are "all alike" is an absurdity. Some Catholics are saints; but there are plenty of sinners. They *should* all be saints; they should all love their neighbor. But many fall short of this counsel of perfection. That is one reason why the Church has confessional boxes!

Newman knew all this, if some of his critics did not. And troubles for him, so happy in the "blessed vision of peace," were soon to begin. In fact, one trouble (the Achilli affair, to be touched on presently) had already begun. The note of caution which he had so strongly emphasized in his "Second Spring" address was equally applicable to his own second spring. This, too, was to prove an English spring, "with keen blasts, and cold showers, and sudden storms."

KEEN BLASTS AND COLD SHOWERS

1

THAT NEWMAN, a man so sensitive, was to meet with keen blasts and cold showers in his newly found Catholic life really should not surprise us. Much of his trouble and distress in the years to come can be traced to the subjective side of his temperament, which often overbalanced his undeniably objective characteristics. Sensitive as a woman, he was prone to exaggerate injuries, whereas a more consistently objective personality—like Cardinal Manning, for instance—would ride over such things as mere incidents in the day's work. Where Newman would be driven in upon himself, Manning would storm. In this is the explanation of many things in the lives of both these men.

There was one fact connected with Newman's frustrations, however, which is frequently overlooked. Most of those who crossed him, and were loudest in criticisms of him, were not life-long Catholics but converts like himself—men who had come into the Church for the most part from the Anglican Establishment, though there were one or two exceptions. Henry Edward Manning, William George Ward, Frederick Faber, George Talbot, John More Capes and Richard Simpson (all trouble-makers for Newman) were ex-Anglicans. Orestes Brownson, however, as bitter a critic of Newman as any, was not an ex-Anglican; he was "ex" everything else!

If Newman was from time to time criticised or frustrated by some hereditary Catholics, it was frequently the result of meddling on the part of converts. One of these converts—William George Ward—who said he wanted a new Papal encyclical to read every morning at breakfast—was of that class of converts who strive to be more Catholic than the Pope. Newman was not one of these. Though so often misunderstood, his principle, which he never abandoned by jot or tittle, was to be *as* Catholic as the the Pope. And before he died, every candid critic (even Ward himself) realized that he had never departed from that principle in any essential particular.

Is there any rational explanation for this tendency of militant converts from Anglicanism to be critical of other converts who have come into the Church from the same background? Perhaps there is. In their former environment, if they took their beliefs at all seriously, the habit of disputation was never at a loss for exercise. If High Church, they were critical of the Lows; if Low Church, they were critical of the Highs; if their bishop was a straddler, he was ever catching it from both sides. And quite naturally, when these militant Anglicans get into the Catholic Church, they carry over this habit of disputation into their new environment. Of course, most of them get over it after they become seasoned Catholics. But a few never get over it; it is in the blood. Lifelong Catholics may smile at this explanation; but, being an ex-Anglican myself, I speak from the book!

To return to the narrative. For Newman there was now to be a multitude of troubles. The distressing Achilli affair; his troubled experience with the new Dublin University; the outcome of the proposal to the Pope that he be made a bishop; the failure of his plan for a new English translation of the Scriptures; the blocking of his plans for establishing an Oratory at Oxford; the undermining at Rome of his reputation for orthodoxy: these were the vicissitudes which made him suffer most. There were also many minor annoyances, as he found himself being tossed hither and thither by the attitudes and scheming of certain militant converts who, for the most part, were by no means his equals intellectually and often twisted his words and actions to a false meaning—not vindictively, but often ignorantly.

It is time to describe some of the keen blasts and cold showers of this period—as well as the brighter spots which intervened. I will first touch on the distressing Achilli affair.

2

The fifth lecture in the series "The Present Position of Catholics in England" included a passage inspired by Cardinal Wiseman. In the *Dublin Review* the Cardinal had exposed the immoralities of an excommunicated priest who called himself Dr. Achilli and was making his living by delivering a series of anti-Catholic lectures under Protestant auspices in London. The Cardinal had in his possession complete proofs of his charges against Achilli. He suggested that Newman expose Achilli in his lecture course, where the facts about him would get wider publicity among Protestants than in the relatively unknown *Dublin Review*.

On principle Newman always avoided attacking individuals, but with Achilli's attacks on the Catholic Church getting so much publicity, the Cardinal insisted that his depravity should be disclosed to his English audience. Therefore Newman inserted in his fifth lecture the following devastating passage:

"Ah! Dr. Achilli: I might have spoken of him last week, had time admitted of it. The Protestant world flocks to hear him, because he has something to tell of the Catholic Church. He has something to tell, it is true; he *has* a scandal to reveal, he *has* an argument to exhibit. It is a simple one, and a powerful one, as far as it goes—and it is *one*. That one argument is himself; it is his presence which is the triumph of Protestants; it is the sight of him which is a Catholic's confusion. It is indeed our great confusion, that our Holy Mother could have had a priest like him." [Here he pictures Achilli himself speaking] . . . " 'You do not see such a sight every day. Can a Church live over the imputation of such a production as I am? I have been a Catholic and an infidel; I have been a Roman priest and a hypocrite; I have been a profligate under a cowl. I am that Father Achilli, who, as early as 1826, was deprived of my faculty to lecture, for an offence which my superiors did their best to conceal; and who, in 1827, had already earned the reputation of a scandalous friar. I am that Achilli, who in the diocese of Viterbo in February, 1831, robbed of her honor a young woman of eighteen; who in September, 1833, was found guilty of a second such crime, in the case of a person of twenty-eight; and who perpetrated a third in July, 1834, in the case of another aged twenty-four. I am he, who afterwards was found guilty of sins, similar or worse, in other towns of the neighborhood. I am that son of St. Dominic who is known to have repeated the offence at Capua, in 1834 and 1835; and at Naples again, in 1840, in the case of a child of fifteen. I am he who chose the sacristy of the Church for one of these crimes, and Good Friday for another. Look on me, ye mothers of England, a confessor against Popery, for ye "ne'er may look upon my like again." I am that veritable priest, who, after all this, began to speak against, not only the Catholic faith, but the moral law, and perverted others by my teaching. I am the Cavaliere Achilli, who then went to Corfu, made the wife of a tailor faithless to her husband, and lived publicly and travelled about with the wife of a chorus singer. I am that Professor in the Protestant College at Malta, who with two others was dismissed from my post for offences which the authorities cannot get themselves to describe. And now attend to me, such as I am, and you shall see what you shall see about the barbarity and profligacy of the Inquisitors of Rome.' "

Achilli and his Protestant backers had ignored the article in the *Dublin Review*, but now that Newman in his lecture had given the facts wide publicity, they thought it necessary to do something. Achilli was induced to bring an action for criminal libel against Newman. It was necessary, of course, for Newman to produce his evidence in support of his charges. And here is where Cardinal Wiseman failed him. He had in his possession the documentary proofs which, at least so Newman believed, would have caused the court to dismiss the charge of criminal libel at the preliminary hearing. But though he scoured his house from cellar to roof he was unable to find them in time. Newman was committed for trial.

In the months between this preliminary hearing and the trial itself, friends of Newman went to Italy to gather evidence, which involved persuading a great many of the women wronged by Achilli to come to London and give evidence. In the event, the evidence was extremely well presented. Not only the Italian women but London servant girls gave evidence of Achilli's immorality. But the jury refused to believe them, and Newman was found guilty. An attempt was made to secure a new trial, but it failed, and Newman came up for sentence. He might well have been sentenced to a term of imprisonment, and was prepared for the possibility. But in the event he was fined only £100, though he also found himself forced to pay all the heavy costs of the trial, amounting to about $60,000.

But if the Cardinal had failed him, a host of friends had not; they assumed the obligation, raising a sum more than adequate to cover all costs, legal and personal.

Judge and jury had shown quite outrageous prejudice. The London *Times* severely criticised this utterly unfair verdict in the following words: "We consider that a great blow has been given the administration of justice in this country, and the Roman Catholics will henceforth have only too good reason for asserting that there is no justice for them in cases tending to arouse Protestant feeling of judges and juries." All reasonable public opinion endorsed this view. Achilli was utterly discredited; his audiences quickly faded away and he disappeared from the public view, never to be heard of in England again.

Cardinal Wiseman, greatly distressed by his own negligence— his records were always disorderly—did his best to make amends; it was partly due to his efforts that the funds for paying the expenses of the trial were promptly raised. Then followed a flood of friendly letters to Newman from many quarters. One letter was from Archbishop Kenrick of Baltimore, which Newman received with special gratitude, for this archbishop had been critical of his *Essay on Development* a few years before. His acknowledgment of Kenrick's letter is worthy of space:

"I think I recollect the saying of a heathen sage, to the effect that the most perfect polity was that in which an injury done to the humblest citizen, was felt as a blow to the whole community; but how much nobler a conception I see fulfilled today when an individual, whose claim on Catholics is not that of a citizen, but of a stranger who has but come (as it were) to their hearth, and embraced their altars, and appealed to their hospitality, is raised by the hand and lifted out of his distress, as if he had been all his life long of the number of the *cives sanctorum domestici Dei.* . . . It is not I who am the real object of the bounty of Catholics; nor is gratitude, such as mine, its true reward. Let me venture to say it: they have been serving Him who accepts as done to Himself mercies bestowed upon even the weakest of His disciples; and they have been securing a recompense from the just Judge who never suffers Himself to be outdone in the interchange of offices of love."

Thus ended the first "keen blast," which had caused much suffering to this innocent priest who had simply conformed to the wishes of his archbishop. Now that it was all over, his peace of mind returned—only to be soon disturbed by a series of cold showers.

Incidentally, one belligerent American convert, who already had been a sore trial to Newman, was Dr. Orestes Brownson. The latter crossed his path very early. When the *Essay on Development of Christian Doctrine* found its way to America in 1847, certain Boston Unitarians, after a shallow examination of the book, asserted that Newman had proved that the Catholic doctrine of the Holy Trinity was merely a "corruption" of the third century—whereas he had clearly shown that it was a true development of the original Deposit of Faith. Brownson, who had formerly been a Unitarian himself and had become a Catholic only one year before Newman, seems to have decided, without much investigation, that the Unitarians had tripped Newman up. He forthwith notified certain American bishops that Newman was teaching heresy, and attacked him in *Brownson's Quarterly Review*. The bishops took Brownson at his word, and the statement was at once delated to Rome.

Fortunately, Newman was in Rome at the time and was able to clarify the matter. Nevertheless, it was many years before certain Roman theologians ceased suspecting Newman's orthodoxy, so effective had been the meddling of Orestes Brownson.

Orestes Brownson was a remarkable character and possessed great intellectual qualities. But he never warmed to the Oxford converts; Anglicanism was a closed world to him. He was of the traditional New England puritanical type. A self-educated man, he had begun life as a journeyman lay preacher. In the course of years he tried out various forms of Protestantism, running all the way from Presbyterianism through Universalism to Unitarianism, interspersing his course with socialism and other 'isms, religious and political. When finally, in middle life, he arrived at Catholicism, it was his last resting place; but he had reached it by his own novel route. He never lost his habit of proclaiming his own home-grown opinions on all subjects, human and divine. He was brilliant, but this was offset by his colossal self-confidence. Like many another militant convert, he loved disputation. He attacked

the Irish when most American Catholics were Irish; he quarrelled with his bishop in Boston, and when he moved to New
York, he quarrelled with Archbishop Hughes. A journalist of
amazing writing capacity, he thundered his anathemas at both
Catholics and Protestants. Militant converts everywhere should
take off their hats to him!

Yet with all his belligerency he never departed one jot from
the Catholic faith after his conversion. His sincerity cannot be
doubted; but he lived not in peace but in war. That Newman
did not understand him any more than he understood Newman
is indicated by the fact that the latter invited him (despite his
attack on the *Development*) to accept a professorship in the new
Dublin University! He continued to find fault with Newman all
through the years to come, although he did concede in 1864 that
he had judged Newman unfairly in 1847!

3

Ireland is proverbially a wet country, but Newman found too
many cold showers there to induce him to stay very long. He
really never wished to go there; he wanted to stay at home and
build up his Oratory and Oratory School; but he was drawn into
a venture which he thought he was called by Providence to
undertake—only to find, after much heart-burning, that this was
not the case at all, but that he had allowed himself to be led into
a mare's nest.

The occasion was this. Two new secular institutions, the
Queen's Colleges, which had been founded in Galway and Cork
in 1846 by Sir Robert Peel, then Prime Minister, to promote
mixed education among Irish Protestants and Catholics, were not
at all satisfactory to the Irish bishops. They feared the bad effects
on Catholic youth of secular institutions which neglected the

teaching of religion. They witnessed what was now happening at Oxford and Cambridge. A profound change had taken place in Oxford since Newman's time. It was commonly said of Oxford that as soon as Newman's star had set, that of John Stuart Mill arose; theology and religion went out and science and free thought came in. It was not many years after Newman's departure that the bars were let down, and the student body was no longer restricted to those who pledged loyalty to the Established Church by signing the Thirty-Nine Articles of Religion. The change in atmosphere was becoming all too evident. Religion was going by the board, and freethinkers were being turned out in increasing numbers at both the old English universities, noticeably so at Oxford—less than twenty years after the start of the Tractarian movement.

It is therefore not surprising that the Queen's Colleges were banned by the Irish bishops. Yet a university for Catholic youth was a crying need in Ireland. And a strong supporter for the establishment of such a university was Dr. Cullen, Archbishop of Armagh, who would shortly be transferred to Dublin and then be made a cardinal.

Dr. Cullen was persuaded that Father Newman should be invited to head the proposed university as its rector. Newman's name stood high in Catholic circles as an outstanding scholar, and with him at its head the new university would get off to a brilliant start.

So it was that in July 1851, Dr. Cullen came to England and made a visit at the Birmingham Oratory. To Newman he then extended his invitation. After some hesitancy, Newman agreed to accept. He also promised to deliver, in Dublin, a series of lectures outlining his own ideas of what a Catholic university should be. And when he learned that the plan for the new undertaking had the full approval of Pope Pius and would be strongly supported at Rome, he became enthusiastic. He decided that it

might perhaps be made the intellectual center for the Catholics
of the entire kingdom.

In May 1852 he visited Dublin and there delivered five lectures
on the proper scope of a university. These lectures made a marked
impression. They were delivered before a scholarly assemblage,
including nearly all the Irish bishops as well as many of the educated Irish laity. Favorable judgment was unanimous and Newman was overjoyed. We find him writing to Dr. Manning: "I
have prospered here in my lectures beyond my most sanguine
anticipations, or rather, beyond my most anxious efforts and
pains; for I have had anxiety and work beyond belief in writing
them,—expectations none. At least my good Lord has never left
me, nor failed me in my whole life, nor has He now. So my
imagination was free from hope or fear about the event. But my
mind has been on my work; no one can tell how it has worn me
down but myself."

In these lectures his ideas are brilliantly stated, and they
seemed to be accepted in high spirit. But almost at once trouble
began. Newman was the supreme scholar, the intellectual genius;
but he was never outstanding as an administrator, and nothing
of a politician. In planning his faculty, he made his first
blunder. He proposed that Cardinal Wiseman be made Chancel-
lor of the university, a proposal immediately frowned upon by
the Irish bishops, who saw no reason why Wiseman in London
(who was not particularly identified with Ireland, even though
he was Irish himself) should be put at the head of a university
in Dublin. He invited Dr. Manning to become Vice-Rector, but
Manning had shown no interest in Ireland; he declined, having
bigger fish to fry. Newman then invited a group of other converts
to join the faculty, William George Ward, Henry Wilberforce,
Dr. Northcote—and Orestes Brownson! But loading the university with English-convert instructors, and the American wild man,
did not appeal to the Irish bishops. Fortunately for Newman's

peace of mind, these men all declined. Dr. Cullen liked New-man's Irish appointments just as little—they were Young Ireland-ers and the Irish Archbishop wanted the new university kept clear of every taint of Fenianism. In the event Newman was relieved of the job of choosing a faculty; and Dr. Patrick Leahy (later Archbishop of Cashel), a stranger to him, was made Vice-Rector, without the Rector's being consulted on the appointment.

Newman soon found that although he was to be the Rector, he was to have little voice in management and less in questions of policy. One difficulty followed another. Dr. Cullen, who had so urgently persuaded him to undertake the task, soon mystified him by his negligence. Newman could not get any answers to urgent letters written to the Archbishop. It had not as yet dawned on him that Dr. Cullen might be developing doubts of his fitness for the position after all.

Archbishop Cullen had recently gone to Rome and there dis-cussed the situation with the authorities, one of these being Mon-signor George Talbot, who, it will be recalled, was also a convert from Anglicanism (he had entered the Catholic Church as re-cently as 1847). The younger son of Lord Talbot of Malahide, he had important connections and advanced rapidly. Remaining in Rome after his ordination, he had become a papal chamberlain, and his position in Vatican circles soon became outstanding. As an adviser to the Pope on English affairs, his influence was not to be minimized. But his judgment of others seems not always to have been of the best. And he seems to have been a receptive listener to gossip. Being an ex-Anglican, he was naturally suspi-cious of converts! Certainly it seems likely that Talbot's doubts about Newman may have had something to do with Dr. Cullen's change of heart.

When the University project was first broached, Cardinal Wiseman had suggested to the Holy Father that Newman be made a bishop, as this would put him on a par with the Irish bishops who were to be trustees. The Holy Father readily assented, and then Wiseman at once wrote Newman: "Ever since the Achilli trial I have felt that a mark of honor and favor, and an expression of sympathy from the Church was requisite, and this seemed to me the proper mode of bestowing it. I have only one thing to add—that I request the consolation and honor of conferring on you the proposed dignity, when the proper time shall come."

But the "proper time" never came. News was circulated in England that the appointment was imminent; congratulations poured in to Newman; friends sent him costly presents in anticipation of the great event. Then, at the last moment, the Pope was induced to change his mind. How much Dr. Cullen had to do with this is not in the record; but Monsignor Talbot may have had something to do with it.

A "cold shower" indeed for Newman. It was not the loss of the bishopric that upset him; it was the embarrassing situation in which he was placed, after the entire English Catholic body had extended its congratulations and the public press had joined in the chorus of approval. As a matter of fact, Newman had no ambition to become a bishop; he had only welcomed the proposal because of his position as Rector of the university. He was profoundly conscious of his lack of administrative ability. In his crusade in the Oxford days, his leadership was never of the managerial sort, but exclusively intellectual. "Out of my own head," he had said, "I started the Tracts"; and it was certainly from out of his own head that his great sermons, which gave the movement its life, had come. And out of his own head had come Tract Ninety!

When his appointment failed to materialize, it was suggested that he be made Bishop of the See of Liverpool, which was at the moment vacant. His reaction to that suggestion was expressed in the following way: "I feel most deeply and habitually that the office of Bishop is not suited to me. Some things one is fit for, other things one is not fit for. To say I am not a thorough theologian, and that I know nothing of Canon Law, is obvious; I do not urge what is plain to everyone. But more than this, I have not the talent, the resource, the spirit, the power of ruling necessary for the high office of a Bishop. This is neither humility nor modesty, but plain commonsense. My mode of influence is in quite another line. And I am sure I should get so oppressed with a sense of my responsibilities and shortcomings that I should have my spirit broken. Every instrument is fitted for its own work;— a spade, a trowel, a sword, a razor, each has its own use. I trust it will not please them at Rome to throw me away when they might turn me to account."

It would serve no purpose to detail in these pages the long delays, confusion and setbacks which led Newman, after a few years, to resign the Rectorship of the Dublin venture. Suffice it to say that during his sojourn there the university was started and expanded in a limited way, and some of his ideas were partially carried out. But it proved a hopeless task at that time to build a student body adequate for its larger success. One monument to Newman's work in Dublin survives. The handsome church on St. Stephen's Green, built as the university chapel, was partly paid for by him from the surplus left over of the large sums subscribed for meeting the expenses of the Achilli trial, which had been contributed by Catholics the world over in 1852.

In 1858 Newman returned from Dublin to his Oratory at Birmingham, sick at heart over the failure of his "Irish Campaign," as he called it. It seemed to him he had been a wretched failure. Administratively, perhaps, he had been partly that, but in another sense he had registered a marked success. It was during these difficult years that his famous lectures on university training, later published under the title *Idea of A University*, were delivered, with many other related discourses of high quality. Nearly a century has gone by since these lectures were first published, but they are still read and studied, not only in scholastic circles but by a far wider audience. Really to know the scholarly Newman, one can do no better than study his *Idea of A University*. It is as timely today as it was in the mid-nineteenth century.

4

Back to his Oratory and at peace once more, Newman turned his attention to a subject which had for years been on his mind—the problem of Faith and Reason. He had tried to develop this theme years before in some of his University sermons, but he now planned to write a book on the subject. No sooner, however, had he got well started on this congenial task, than an invitation came from Cardinal Wiseman to undertake a new English translation of the Old and New Testaments.

Needless to say, this superb master of English prose was the ideal scholar for such an important undertaking. He was thrilled at the prospect; he laid aside his projected work on Faith and Reason and instantly accepted, writing to the Cardinal, "A greater honor, I feel, could not possibly have been done me than that which your Eminence has conferred in selecting me for preparing an annotated version of the Bible."

He threw himself into this task with great energy, gathering at once a group of competent assistants. Then he wrote an exhaustive introduction to be prefixed to the new translation, a masterly essay designed primarily to counteract the effects on the public of the rapidly increasing agnostic propaganda, which, with the rising German modernistic interpretations of the Bible, was creating much havoc among traditional Christian believers. In the meantime he set his group of specialists to work and spent considerable money.

Everything was moving serenely and steady progress was being made. Then, out of a clear sky, the Cardinal forwarded him a letter from a group of American bishops, deprecating the proposed translation on the ground that a similar work was being carried on by Archbishop Kenrick of Baltimore and would soon be completed and published. Cardinal Wiseman did not think it wise to ignore the objections of the American bishops; he thought it best for Newman to drop the whole matter.

Newman was broken-hearted. An undertaking for which he was peculiarly fitted had to be abandoned. It was indeed a pity; not only because the American version, on which Kenrick was said to be far advanced, never saw the light of day (it was only the old Douay version, after all), but because a new English edition of the Bible edited by Newman would have been of priceless value to the English-reading world.

This was one of the most tragic disappointments of his entire life. He never quite got over it. Twenty years later, when he was invited to join with a group who planned a similar task, he abruptly declined. He anticipated that it would have the same outcome as his own attempt—and it did.

After this fiasco, he turned back to his Oratory work, where he was now organizing his school for boys at Edgbaston on an enlarged and permanent basis—only to be promptly confronted by another cold shower. John More Capes, a lay convert who had entered the Church with the original Oxford groups, had in 1848 started a Catholic magazine called the *Rambler*. For some years it had struggled for existence, but Newman had recently encouraged Capes in his effort to establish a high-class literary journal for the Catholic laity and finally contributed some articles. Then, on Capes' urging, he acted as editor of the magazine for a short time. He was succeeded very soon by Richard Simpson, also a convert.

But Capes was a militant convert with a strong bent for criticising his co-religionists, not excepting priests, bishops, and finally the Holy See itself. This sort of thing got him into trouble with the authorities, and, like Orestes Brownson, he "talked back."

But he had not the staying power of Brownson. In 1858 he resigned the editorship of the *Rambler*. (Later he lapsed back to Protestantism, though he returned to the Church and died a Catholic.) He was succeeded by Richard Simpson, a more brilliant man and not less harassing to authority. Within a year Simpson too resigned, as the only means of saving the paper from episcopal condemnation.

Newman, though he deplored the spirit in which much of the *Rambler* was written, still felt that there was a place for such a periodical. Upon the resignation of Simpson, Newman himself most reluctantly became editor, but brought out only two numbers, because Bishop Ullathorne approached him after the first and suggested that he give it up—on the general ground that the Catholic laity was not yet ready for that kind of discussion of religious questions. But in the last number he edited, that of July 1859, he wrote an article "On Consulting the Faithful in Matters of Doctrine." It was delated to Rome, and though Rome took no action, it was reported that the Pope was pained. Here was a situation for Monsignor Talbot to handle. In his gossipy way he insinuated that Newman was responsible for all the faults of the *Rambler*—and then, it was said, added fuel to the flame by repeating a false rumor that Newman had subscribed to a fund being raised in England in support of Garibaldi, who was at that time carrying on war against the Papacy!

Without his at first realizing it, Newman was losing his high status among the Roman ecclesiastics. The fact that Newman had become intimate with Sir John Acton (later Lord Acton), a brilliant young Catholic layman who also had his Roman troubles, and with Dr. Döllinger of Munich, later a critic of many things in Rome, surely did not help the situation. But his intimacy with these men, both of whom wrote for the *Rambler*, was based, not upon any sympathy with their alleged heterodox views, but rather upon their agreement with his own view that the Church authorities should more definitely and more aggressively refute modern erroneous teachings instead of following a policy of ignoring them (though this negative attitude of the Church perhaps seemed more real to him than it actually was).[1] His own attitude at this time is reflected in a letter to Frederick Rogers (Lord Blachford):

"We are in a strange time. I have not a shadow of misgiving that the Catholic Church and her doctrines are direct from God —but then I know that there is in particular quarters a narrowness which is not of God. And I believe great changes before now have taken place in the direction of the Church's course, and that new aspects of her aboriginal doctrines have suddenly come forth, and all this coincidentally with changes in the world's history, such as are now in progress; so that I never shut up when new views are set before me, though I might not take them as a whole."

But now, and for years to come, a cloud would hang over him in Rome. Nor would much be done to lift that cloud by the several conspicuous converts already mentioned, who had preceded or followed him into the Catholic Church years before— Talbot, Faber, Ward, Manning and the rest. Not that there was any vindictiveness; but not one of these men really understood Newman.

When, in 1862, Sir John Acton, with the convert Richard Simpson, resuscitated the *Rambler* under the name of the *Home and Foreign Review*, there was more trouble for Newman. He had no connection with the *Review*, but as he was a friend of both Acton and Simpson and had expressed sympathetic interest in the new undertaking, he was bespattered by the mud when the *Home and Foreign* was condemned by Bishop Ullathorne as being heretical. The injustice of the accusation that he was involved in this made him very indignant, as we see from a letter he wrote Father St. John.

---

[1] This notion of Newman's that the Church was remiss in failing to face modern errors openly, was surely modified when Pope Pius gave to the world his famous *Syllabus of Errors* in 1864.

"I wrote Bellasis and Ward, and I am going to write Ornsby, Acton and Arnold. Don't think I am overdoing it,—but the bishop's charges against the *Home and Foreign* are precise. . . . and I cannot allow myself to seem indifferent to the chance of people connecting me with them. How one's time and energy are frittered away in these explanations!

"Well, we shall be carried through. I have ever been brought through;—I said I should when the Achilli matter began; but here my own anticipation *then* of what was likely to happen appals me. It appals me to think that I should so rightly have guessed what was to take place at the end of another ten years. I then said that, as when twenty I was cut off from the rising talent of the University by my failure in the schools; as when thirty I was caught off from distinction in the governing body by being deprived of my tutorship; as when forty, I was virtually cast out of the Church of England by the affair of Tract Ninety; as when fifty, I was cast out of what may be called society by the disgrace of the Achilli sentence; so when I should arrive at sixty years, I should be cast out of the good books of Catholics, and especially of ecclesiastical authorities.

"This appals me in this way: what is to happen if I live to be seventy? Am I to lose all of you and be left desolate? Or is our House to be burned to the ground? Or am I to be smitten with some afflicting disorder? These are questions which come before me, and don't be angry with me for mentioning them, for it is a great relief for me to speak and a pain to be silent.

"Well, I suppose it is all intended to keep me from being too happy. How happy I should be if let alone,—how fond of living! On the other hand, certainly, I have been carried through all those troubles which have come to me hitherto, and I believe I shall be to the end. . . . Now be good enough to say a Hail Mary for me instead of quarreling with me for saying all this."

CHAPTER TEN

PERIOD OF ECLIPSE

1

THERE NOW ENSUED FOR NEWMAN a period of frustration and eclipse which, on the whole, makes a sad story. After his return from Dublin he found that he had receded from the public view and had all but been forgotten by the world at large: even Catholics ignored him. Cardinal Wiseman displayed little interest in him or his activities; while that other notable convert, Henry Edward Manning, was forging to the front at the Cardinal's side and was more and more in the public eye.

Yet he was far from being a misanthrope, and what he called his "life of retirement" was lightened by many bright spots. Though he felt mistrusted by those in high authority who questioned his whole-hearted loyalty to the Church, he did not brood and had not lost his sense of humor. "They may have put me on the shelf," he said, "but they cannot prevent me from peeping out from it." And he did peep out, keeping in touch with current events, both religious and secular; and although his books were no longer in great demand, his pen was always busy.

Not long before he went to Ireland, he had begun to write another novel. Perhaps the success of *Loss and Gain* had encouraged him in the belief that he was capable, if he set his mind to it, of writing good fiction; fiction with a message. It was not to be an Oxford story this time but a tale of the third century—

Callista. But, like his other novel, *Loss and Gain,* it was a slice of his own life. As he had lived in Oxford in the flesh, he had lived in the early days of Christianity in spirit. The early Church was the door through which he discovered Catholic truth; here had been his battleground.

He had sketched the outline of *Callista* in 1852, then laid it aside. In 1855 his interest revived, and in the midst of the Irish University troubles, he completed the story. It was first published anonymously; only after a second edition was called for, did he openly acknowledge authorship. Then, as an antidote to the seeming failure of his Irish venture and the disappointing outcome of his dream of translating the Scriptures—not to mention his general loss of prestige both in Rome and at home—the unexpected success of this little book surely helped to bring surcease to his troubled soul.

Callista is a moving picture of persecuted Christianity in northern Africa in the third century. "It is an attempt," he says, "to imagine and express the feelings and mutual relations of Christians and heathens at the period to which it belongs, and it has been undertaken as the nearest approach which the author could make to a more important work suggested by a high ecclesiastical authority." What that "more important work" was to be is not in the record.

The story is little read today; but to me it has long had a special appeal as a true picture of third century life—far more so than Kingsley's *Hypatia.* Modern critics say it is less of a novel than a sermon. Perhaps the ideals it presents are too exalted for the modern mind. Yet there are dramatic incidents in it, with some chapters—such as that describing the locust invasion and that which describes the riot involving slaughter of the Christians—which are equal to the author's finest prose writings. The description of the madness which seizes Juba is also splendidly done. As for the discussions between the old heathen, Jucundus, and his nephews, as well as Callista's expressed doubts and convictions, they are all quite perfectly presented. However, when Callista talks, it is really Newman himself who is talking; when she reasons, it is Newman reasoning as he did during that unsettled period at Littlemore. In fact, like *Loss and Gain,* the story of Callista is fundamentally autobiographical.

The theme lies in the approach and conversion to Christianity of a beautiful young Grecian girl who has a passionate love for Greek idealism. The youth, Agellius, nephew of Jucundus, a lukewarm Christian, falls in love with her; but to win her he seems quite ready to ignore his faith if not to drop it entirely. She feels this and resents it, for although she knows nothing of Christianity, she greatly reveres a Christian woman called Chione, who has profoundly impressed her by her perfect Christian life. Consequently, when Agellius sues for her love but does not attempt to interest her in the Christian faith, she indignantly reproaches him:

" '. . . if, as you imply, my wants and aspirations are the same as yours, what have you done towards satisfying them? what have you done for that Master towards whom you now propose to lead me? No . . . you have watched those wants and aspirations for yourself, not for Him; you have taken interest in them, you have cherished them, as if you were the author, you the object of them. You profess to believe in One True God, and reject every other; and now you are implying that the Hand, the Shadow of that God, is in my mind and heart. Who is this God? Where, how, in what? Oh, Agellius, you have stood in the way of Him, ready to speak of yourself, using Him as a means to an end." To this he replies, "Oh, Callista, do my ears hear aright? do you really wish to be taught who the true God is?"

" 'No, mistake me not,' she cried passionately, 'I have no such wish. I could not be of your religion. . . . I thought every Christian was like Chione. I thought there could not be a cold Christian. Chione spoke as if a Christian's first thoughts were good will to others, as if his state were of such blessedness that his dearest heart's wish was to bring others into it. Here is a man who, so far from feeling himself blest, thinks I can bless him; comes to me, me, Callista, an herb of the field, a poor weed exposed to every wind of heaven and shrivelling before the fierce sun—to me he comes to repose his heart upon. But as for any blessedness he has to show me, why, since he does not feel any himself, no wonder he has none to give away. I thought a Christian was superior to time and place, but all is hollow. Alas, alas, I am young in life to feel the force of that saying with which sages go out of it, "Vanity and hollowness." Agellius, when I first heard you were a Christian, how my heart beat! I thought of her [Chione] who was gone; and at first I thought I saw her in you, as if there had been some magical sympathy between you and her; and I hoped that from you I might have learned more of that strange strength which my nature needs, and which she told me she possessed. Your words, your manner, your looks were altogether different from others who came near me. But so it was; you came and you went, and came again; I thought it reserve, I thought it timidity, I thought it the caution of a persecuted sect; but oh, my disappointment when first I saw in you indications that you were thinking of me only as others think, and felt towards me as others may feel; that you were aiming at me, not at your God; that you had much to tell of yourself, but nothing of Him. Time was I might have been led to worship you, Agellius; you have hindered it by worshipping *me*.' "

One more incident may be quoted. Callista has been imprisoned on suspicion of being a Christian. She is not yet one but is on the verge of conversion. She has refused—hardly knowing why—to burn incense to the Emperor. A pagan philosopher, Polemo, has been sent to her to try to persuade her to conform to the Roman pagan rite.

"After a time Callista said, 'Polemo, do you believe in one God?' 'Certainly,' he answered, 'I believe in one eternal, self-existing something.' 'Well,' she said, 'I feel that God within my heart, I feel myself in His Presence. He says to me, "Do this, don't do that." You may tell me that this dictate is a mere law of my nature, as to joy or to grieve. I cannot understand this. No, it is the echo of a person speaking to me. Nothing shall persuade me that it does not ultimately proceed from a person external to me. It carries with it its proof of its divine origin. My nature feels towards it as towards a person. When I obey it, I feel a satisfaction; when I disobey, a soreness,—just like that which I feel in pleasing or offending some revered friend. So you see, Polemo, I believe in what is more than a mere "something." I believe in what is more real to me than sun, moon, stars, and the fair earth, and the voice of friends. You will say, Who is He? Has He ever told you any thing about Himself? Alas, no! The more's the pity! But I will not give up what I have because I have not more. An echo implies a voice; a voice a speaker; that speaker I love and fear.' "

Here she is exhausted and overcome with her own emotions. " 'Oh that I could find Him,' she exclaimed, passionately. 'On the right hand and on the left I grope, but touch Him not. Why dost Thou fight against me, why dost Thou scare and perplex me, O First and Only Fair? I have Thee not, and I need Thee!' " Then she says to Polemo, " 'I am not a Christian, you see, or I should have found Him.' "

In the end, as she is about to go to her death, she receives the gift of faith and is baptized at the last moment by a persecuted bishop (who is really the great St. Cyprian). He steals his way into her cell. And then: "They got her out like a corpse [she had fainted from lack of food] and put her on the ground outside the prison . . . the instruments of torture preceding her. The fresh air of the morning revived her; she soon sat up. 'O beautiful Light,' she whispered. 'O lovely Light, my light and my life! O my Light and my Life, receive me!' "

Her conversations with both Agellius and Polemo surely reflect Newman's own mind and heart, with his profound sense, so marked throughout his entire life, of the Divine Indwelling. Many other passages in the story display powers of insight for picturing the struggles of weak humanity quite equal to those so characteristic of his Oxford discourses.

2

Newman's greatest consolation during these days of eclipse was the success of his boys' school at Edgbaston. In spite of the doubts expressed by many critics, who had not forgotten his administrative weakness in Dublin, his school prospered from the start. By 1859 it was attracting pupils from all England. With the cooperation of Ambrose St. John and the other Oratorians, he imparted to the school certain characteristics quite unknown to schools of the sort at this particular time. He favored a very informal atmosphere, and his personal relations with the students were always most intimate and friendly. Dr. Sparrow, one of his early students, wrote of this many years after. "Every month in my time," he said, "each form went up to the Father's room and was examined *viva voce* in the work done during the previous month. . . . Father was one of the most considerate and sympathetic of examiners. He was always most particular to urge upon the boys a high standard of honor and would never tolerate anything mean or shabby. His persistent kindness won all hearts. To the boys he was always the great hero."

In the school's third year an incident occurred which shows how forceful and independent Newman could be when occasion demanded. The teachers had protested against the authority given to Mrs. Wootten, the matron of the school, who was a convert and highly regarded by Newman. Most of the teachers quarrelled with her and finally demanded that she be dismissed, in default of which Father Darnell, the Head Master, said the entire staff would resign. Newman kept Mrs. Wootten at her post and let them resign. Then he sent Ambrose St. John on a flying trip to gather a new staff of teachers. It is interesting to note that one of the new teachers secured was Thomas Arnold, son of Dr. Thomas Arnold. Unlike his brother Matthew, young Thomas Arnold had not wandered into pantheism but had become a Catholic. Father Darnell's place as Head Master was filled by Father Ambrose, who continued in this position until his death in 1876.

Newman's interest in his school at this time is reflected in a letter to Dr. Russell of Maynooth College.

"I am overworked with various kinds of mental labor, and I cannot do as much as I once could. Yet it would be most ungrateful to complain, even if I were seriously incommoded, for my present overwork arises from the very success of a school which I began here shortly after I retired from the University. When we began, it was a simple experiment, and onlookers seemed surprised when they found we had in half a year a dozen; but at the end of our third year we now have seventy. St. Christopher took up a little child and he proved too heavy for him; and thus we in our simplicity allowed ourselves to profess to take boys, and are seriously alarmed at the responsibility which we have brought upon ourselves. As all other schools are increasing in number, it is a pleasant proof of the extension of Catholic education."

3

By far the greatest annoyance to him during these years was the persistent spread of false statements and malicious gossip. Stories were circulated that he was unhappy in the Catholic Church and was preparing to return to Anglicanism. In fact, there were gossips who already had him back—secretly! When rumors of this kind were finally brought to his attention, his indignation knew no bounds. Finally, a statement appeared in the *Globe* newspaper to the effect that as he had left the Brompton Oratory he would soon be leaving Birmingham, in preparation for his return to the Church of England. When he saw this, he instantly wrote to the editor:

"Sir,—A friend has sent me word of a paragraph about me which appeared in your paper of yesterday, to the effect that I have 'left, or am about to leave, my Oratory, of which I have, for several years, been the head, as a preliminary, in the expectation of my private friends, to my return to the Church of England.' . . . Accordingly I lose not an hour in addressing these lines to you, which I shall be obliged by your giving at once to the public:

"The paragraph is utterly unfounded in every portion of it. (1) For the last thirteen years I have been head of the Birmingham Oratory. I am head still; and I have no reason to suppose I shall cease to be head, unless advancing years should incapacitate me for the duties of my station. (2) On the other hand, from the time I founded the London Oratory now at Brompton, twelve years ago, I have had no jurisdiction over it whatever; and so far from being its head, it so happens that I have not been within its walls for the last seven years. (3) I have not had one moment's wavering of trust in the Catholic Church ever since I was received into her fold. I hold, and ever have held, that her Sovereign Pontiff is the center of unity and the Vicar of Christ; and I have ever had, and have still, an unclouded faith in her creed in all its articles; a supreme satisfaction in her worship, discipline, and teaching; and an eager longing, and a hope against hope, that the many dear friends whom I have left in Protestantism may be partakers of my happiness. (4) This being my state of mind, to add, as I hereby go on to do, that I have no intention, and never had any intention, of leaving the Catholic Church and becoming a Protestant again, would be superfluous, except that Protestants are always on the look-out for some loophole or evasion in a Catholic's statement of fact." Then he adds:

"I do hereby profess, *ex animo*, with an absolute internal assent and consent, that Protestantism is the dreariest of possible religions; that the thought of the Anglican service makes me shiver, and the thought of the Thirty Nine Articles makes me shudder. Return to the Church of England? No! 'The net is broken and we are delivered.' I should be a consummate fool (to use a mild term) if in my old age I left 'the land flowing with milk and honey,' for the city of confusion and the house of bondage."

Two years after this (in 1863) when commenting on the persistency with which people believed and circulated false stories about him and his intentions, he wrote to a friend:

"Catholics seem to me to have begun them, by their silly and mischievous statements about me. It was said I had preached in favor of Garibaldi, had subscribed to the Garibaldi fund, etc. Then Protestants, who have always shown a great readiness to take up the vaguest whisper of such an insinuation, boldly proclaimed that I was coming back to them. You do not know to what an extent this went, especially during the last two years. It is more than two years since a convert wrote to me to say that he was unsettled, and, as his defence, suggested that I was unsettled too. In spite of various strong written denials on my part, as far back as 1859, the report became invested with most plausibly minute details, and assumed a very positive tone. People were kept back from the Church by the distinct assurance I was becoming a Protestant. One Protestant clergyman, in position, wrote to me to smooth the way for return,—and, when in answer I begged him to lay aside the thought as inconsistent with what I might call the *rerum natura*, for my mind was so constituted as to make it impossible, I only got a second letter telling me he hoped I should overcome my 'pride' which was the only obstacle to my confession of a change! One person, a country gentleman, at length wrote to a county paper, saying that it was notorious that I had given up all definite religion, and was living in Paris!"

4

It is quite evident that these rumors and this reckless gossip came not from his real friends of the old Tractarian days. Friendly relations had continued without interruption between him and many of those who, though they may have disapproved of his course and would not follow him into the Catholic Church (nor indeed display very much sympathy), nevertheless respected and revered him. In these years, while he was seemingly in eclipse (though quite happily absorbed in his boys' school and the activities of his Oratory), there came friendly gestures from several of these old friends, including Church and Copeland and also Isaac Williams, who visited him at Edgbaston. At about the same time, he received a long letter from John Keble—the first for many years. It was awaiting him on his return from a short visit to the Continent. A passage from his reply shows how the old affection still lived.

"I returned from abroad last night and, among the letters on my table waiting my arrival, found yours. I answer it before any of the others. . . . I have not been abroad for pleasure till now, since I went with dear Hurrell. I went to St. Germains near Paris to see the Wilberforces. Then my dear and faithful friend who went with me—Ambrose St. John—insisted I should cut across to Treves, the place of sojourn of St. Athanasius, St. Ambrose and St. Jerome. . . . I have said all this, knowing it will interest you. Never have I doubted for one moment your affection for me, never have I been hurt at your silence. . . . It was not the silence of men, nor the forgetfulness of men, who can recollect about me and talk about me enough, when there is something to be said to my disparagement. You are always with me in thought of reverence and love, and there is nothing I love better than you, and Isaac, and Copeland, . . . except Him whom I ought to love best of all and supremely. May He Himself . . . give me His own Presence, and then I shall want nothing and desiderate nothing; but none *but* He, *can* make up for the loss of those old familiar faces which haunt me continually."

A rather wistful letter penned during these days to the sister of Frederick Bowles, his old colleague of Littlemore, who had long been dead, well illustrates his natural tendency towards introspection, as well as his sensitive temperament:

"Sometimes," he says, "I seem to myself inconsistent, in professing to love retirement, yet seeming impatient at doing so little; yet I trust I am not so in any very serious way. In my letter to the Bishop of Oxford, on occasion of No. Ninety, I said that I had come forward because no one else had done so, and that I rejoiced to return to that privacy which I valued more than anything else. When I became a Catholic, I considered I should never even write again, except on definite unexciting subjects, such as history and philosophy and criticism; and, if on controversial subjects, still not on theology proper. And when I came here, where I have been for fourteen years, I deliberately gave myself to a life of obscurity, which in my heart I loved best. And so it has been, and so it is now, that the routine work of each day is in fact more than enough for my thoughts and my time. I have no leisure. I have had to superintend the successive enlargements of our Church, to get the library in order, to devote a good deal of pains to our music, and a great deal more to our accounts. . . .

"And I am not only content, but really pleased that so things are. Yet there are those considerations which from time to time trouble me. First, lest my being where I am is my own doing in any measure, for then I say: 'perhaps I am hiding my talent in a napkin.' Next, people say to me: 'Why are you not doing more?

How much you could do.' And then, since I think I could do a great deal if I were let do it, I become uneasy. And lastly, willing as I am to observe St. Philip's dear rule that we 'should despise being despised,' yet when I find that scorn and contempt become the means of my Oratory being injured, as they have before now, then I get impatient."

Such was his state when the year 1863 drew to a close. His time was filled mainly with his work at the Oratory school and his spiritual duties, rounded out, of course, with his incessant letter writing. Here he was quite hidden from the public eye, and most of England seems to have all but forgotten that he was still alive. Seldom quoted in the press, seldom mentioned or thought of by the ruling powers of the Church in England or elsewhere: even in London, where Cardinal Wiseman was still carrying on and Dr. Manning was always in the newspapers, the name of John Henry Newman seemed only to live as a figure of the past whose sun had definitely set.

He was now approaching his sixty-fourth year and appears to have been much occupied with premonitions that his end was not far away. His mission in this life, he was quite sure, was now definitely over. But such thoughts, instead of depressing him, tended to brighten his days, as he turned his mind more and more to the "blessed vision of peace," so clear and unmistakable, which had maintained him now for many long years. He would soon, he firmly believed, be passing from "shadows and images to truth." Yet his health was as good as could be expected of a person of his years, and when, at this time, his doctor predicted for him a hale and hearty old age—provided he did not worry himself to death—he was (or pretended to be) greatly shocked.

He did very little writing during these quiet years, aside from occasional spiritual meditations and his voluminous correspondence; but now, in what he had come more and more to view as the evening hours of his sojourn on earth, we find him turning once again to the writing of verse. In the following lines, composed near the end of 1863, he was to express his mood. They are the well known verses "The Two Worlds."

> Unveil, O Lord, and on us shine,
>   In glory and in grace;
> This gaudy world grows pale before
>   The beauty of Thy face.
>
> Till Thou art seen it seems to be
>   A sort of fairy ground,
> Where suns unsetting light the sky,
>   And flowers and fruit abound.
>
> But when Thy keener, purer beam
>   Is poured upon our sight,
> It loses all its power to charm,
>   And what was day is night.
>
> Its noblest toils are then the scourge
>   Which made Thy blood to flow;
> Its joys are but the treacherous thorns
>   Which circle round Thy brow.
>
> And thus, when we renounce for Thee
>   Its restless aims and fears,
> The tender memories of the past,
>   The hopes of coming years,
>
> Poor is our sacrifice, whose eyes
>   Are lighted from above;
> We offer what we cannot keep,
>   What we have ceased to love.

Without doubt, as his sixty-fourth year approached, he was living daily more and more close to his God, feeling quite sure that he was soon to leave behind all "restless aims and fears," as he came out of the shadows into Reality.

Yet there were other moods. Though in looking back on his life he recognized many mistakes and failings, he knew that he had also experienced many triumphs. Although his actions as well as his views had often been criticised or misinterpreted—and would continue to be—he was confident that much would be justified in the future. The legacy of truth which he would leave to posterity would in time be more fully understood, as indeed it has been.

But were these days of obscurity and eclipse to crown his life and mark his final hour? No, it was not to be. For in this evening of his life he was to be suddenly awakened, as by a trumpet blast, to achieve a victory which would arouse the world that had forgotten him; he would awaken the Church, not merely at home but throughout the entire world, to a new realization that here indeed was a still-living champion and powerful defender of the Catholic Faith.

CHAPTER ELEVEN

APOLOGIA PRO VITA SUA

1

ONE OF THE conspicuous figures in the Anglican Church who had been "conditioned" by the rise of Liberalism during the first half of the nineteenth century was Dr. Charles Kingsley, a close friend and follower of Arthur Penrhyn Stanley, Dean of Westminster Abbey, of which Dr. Kingsley had become a Canon in 1863. At Oxford in Newman's time, Stanley had at first supported the Tractarian movement, but he had reverted completely by 1850, then proclaiming belief in two principles which he ever after adhered to, viz., "The so-called supremacy of the Crown in religious matters is in reality nothing but the supremacy of law; and, the Church of England, by the very condition of its being, is not High nor Low, but Broad, and has always included, and meant to include, opposite and contradictory opinions." He was now recognized, with Dr. Benjamin Jowett and others, as one of the leading exponents of the Broad Church school—which had really had its genesis a few decades before in the teachings of men like Dr. Thomas Arnold and Dr. Whately. Dr. Kingsley was one of this school.

I suggested in an earlier chapter that the tendencies displayed in Dr. Arnold's attitude would ultimately issue in the philosophy later reflected by his son Matthew's mature views. Matthew

Arnold came in time to the point where he defined God as simply "the stream of tendency by which all things fulfil the order of their being," summing up this vague definition by asserting that "God is the thing not ourselves which makes for righteousness." At the same time he expressed the opinion that belief in miracles among Protestants would become extinct within a generation—although among Catholics, on account of their mental inferiority, it might take two generations to evaporate completely!

The Broad Church school had not, by 1863, quite reached the point of negation voiced by Matthew Arnold a few years later; but it was definitely traveling in that direction. Traditional Christianity, as envisioned by earlier Anglicanism, High or Low, was being superseded by Liberalism. The progress of this trend was to be vividly pictured two decades later in the writings of the Broad Churchmen in both England and America.

Dr. Charles Kingsley, for many years Rector of Eversley, had become chaplain to Queen Victoria before he was made a canon of Westminster. An eloquent preacher and a man of culture, he was at the same time bitterly anti-Catholic. He is best remembered by the present generation as a writer of fiction—particularly of *Westward Ho,* an Elizabethan story in which he unmercifully castigated the Jesuits, and *Hypatia,* a tale of the third century wherein he found it difficult to say anything good about the Alexandrian Fathers and saints or the rise of Christian monasticism. Quite naturally, he had always looked askance at the Tractarian movement; and a man of John Henry Newman's cast of mind and convictions helped to keep his anti-Catholic prejudices and hates at white-heat.

Linked by marriage with Kingsley was James Anthony Froude (a younger brother of Hurrell Froude), who had lapsed from Tractarianism and was now the same type of Liberal as were Kingsley and Stanley. He had become a writer of history and had just brought out two volumes of his well known *History of England,* covering the reformation period of the sixteenth century. Froude went out of his way in these volumes to laud "Good Queen Bess" to the skies and to castigate the Catholics of the period in unmeasured terms. With great delight, Kingsley undertook the writing of a review for *Macmillan's Magazine* of January, 1864. The following excerpts are quoted from this review of Dr. Kingsley's.

"The Roman religion had, for some time past, been making men not better men, but worse. We must face, we must conceive honestly for ourselves, the deep demoralization which had been brought on in Europe by the dogma that the Pope of Rome had the power of creating right and wrong; that not only truth and falsehood, but morality and immorality, depended on his setting his seal to a bit of parchment. From the time that indulgences were hawked about in his name, which would insure pardon for any man . . . the world in general began to be of that opinion. But the mischief was older and deeper than those indulgences. It lay in the very notion of the dispensing power. A deed might be a crime, or no crime at all—like Henry VIII's marriage of his brother's widow—according to the will of the Pope. If it suited the interest or caprice of the old man of Rome *not* to say the word, the doer of a certain deed would be burned alive in hell forever. If it suited him, on the other hand, to say it, the doer of the same deed would go, sacramentis munitus, to endless bliss. What rule of morality, what eternal law of right and wrong, could remain in the hearts of men born and bred under the shadow of so hideous a deception? . . .

"So again of the virtue of truth. Truth for its own sake has never been a virtue with the Roman clergy. Father Newman informs us that it need not be, and on the whole ought not to be; —that cunning is the weapon which Heaven has given to the saints wherewith to withstand the brute male force of the wicked world which marries and is given in marriage. Whether his notion be doctrinally correct or not, it is, at least, historically so."

Having had these lines brought to his attention, Newman immediately wrote to the publishers of the magazine, protesting that it was a grave slander. They at once handed the letter to Dr. Kingsley, who wrote Newman as follows under the date of January 4, 1864.

"That my words were just, I believed from many passages of your writings; but the document to which I expressly referred was one of your sermons on 'Subjects of the Day,' No. XX in the volume published in 1844, and entitled 'Wisdom and Innocence.' It was in consequence of that sermon that I finally shook off the strong influence which your writings exerted on me, and for much of which I still owe you a deep debt of gratitude. I am most happy to hear from you that I mistook (as I understand from your letter) your meaning; and I shall be most happy, on your showing me that I have wronged you, to retract my accusation as publicly as I have made it."

Newman was quick to reply that the explanation was quite inadequate, in view of the charge Kingsley had made—merely to refer "generally to a Protestant sermon of mine, of seventeen pages, published by me as Vicar of St. Mary's, and treating of the bearing of the Christian towards the world; and also referring to my works *passim*; in justification of your statement, categorical and definite, that 'Father Newman informs us that truth for its own sake need not, and on the whole ought not to be, a virtue of the Roman clergy.' " Then he added some words of amazement that the eminent Dr. Kingsley should have been guilty of such a statement.

Here a friend of both (a Protestant) intervened and tried to calm the troubled waters; but Kingsley failed to supply any definite evidence to support his accusation and merely wrote to Newman: "As the tone of your letter, (even more than the language) makes me feel, to my very deep pleasure, that my opinion of your words was a mistaken one, I shall send at once to *Macmillan's Magazine*, the few lines I enclose." These were the lines:

"In your last number I made certain allegations against the teaching of the Rev. Dr. Newman, which were founded on a sermon of his, 'Wisdom and Innocence.' . . . Dr. Newman has, by letter, expressed in the strongest terms, his denial of the meaning which I have put upon his words. No man knows the use of words better than Dr. Newman; no man, therefore, has a better right to define what he does, or does not, mean by them. It only remains, therefore, for me to express my hearty regret at having so seriously mistaken him, and my hearty pleasure at finding him on the side of truth, in this, or any other matter."

This patronizing apology, with no attempt to indicate any definite basis for his charge, was wholly unsatisfactory to Newman; and he particularly resented the line, "No man knows the use of words better than Dr. Newman," et cetera. Kingsley withdrew that line but insisted that "by referring to the sermon on which my allegation was based, I have given not only you, but everyone, an opportunity of judging of their injustice. Having done this, and having frankly accepted your assertion that I was mistaken, I have done as much as one English gentleman can expect of another."

The "apology" appeared with the objectionable sentence deleted; but Newman declined to leave the matter in that state. He decided to publish all the correspondence, with comments of his own. He pointed out that the sermon in question was not preached when he was a Catholic; and by quoting the sermon he proved that there was nothing in it to justify Kingsley's charge; and that Kingsley, in his apology, had done no more than imply that he took the word of a liar who did not profess to lie—because they were both English gentlemen.

Kingsley was no doubt stung by this summing up; but he would have been wise to drop the matter there. Instead, he rashly launched a new attack on Newman in a forty-eight-page pamphlet labelled, "What Then Does Dr. Newman Mean?" In this he embarked on an abusive attack on the Catholic Church and her teachings, with caustic criticisms of her saints and her priesthood—as well as all her work in the world for eighteen centuries. It was crowded with false statements and abuse. Then, after having exhausted this theme, he turns to Newman and asks: "What does Dr. Newman mean? I am henceforth in doubt and fear as much as any honest man can be, concerning every word Dr. Newman may write. How can I tell that I shall not be the dupe of some cunning equivocation, of one of the three kinds laid down as permissible by Blessed Alfonso da Liguori and his pupils? . . . What proof have I, then, that by *mean* it, I never said it!' Dr. Newman does not signify, 'I did not say it: but I did mean it'?" He closes his intemperate pamphlet with a side-swipe at the Catholic priesthood as a whole, and particularly at what he styles the "hapless Irish Celts" who are ruled by them!

Newman took this torrent of abuse calmly enough, but he at once realized that the reckless Kingsley had delivered himself into his hands. He would answer Kingsley's question, "What does Dr. Newman mean?" And in doing so he saw an opportunity to fulfill a promise long in his mind—that in the event of his ever being openly and formally challenged regarding his Catholicity, it would be his duty openly to meet it. In Kingsley's attack such an opportunity had come. He would answer not only Kingsley, but the army of critics and doubters unknown to him throughout the world. He would plead his cause before all England. Kingsley's question would have an answer which all the world would hear.

"He asks what I mean?" writes Newman. "Not about my words, not about my arguments, not about my actions, as his ultimate point, but about that living intelligence by which I write and argue and act. He asks about my mind, and my beliefs, and

its sentiments; and he shall be answered. . . . I must now give
the true key to my whole life; I must show what I am, that it
may be seen what I am not, and that the phantom be extin-
guished which gibbers instead of me, . . . I will vanquish, not
my accuser, but my judges. . . . For twenty years and more I
have borne an imputation, of which I am at least as sensitive,
who am the object of it, as they can be, who are only the judges.
I have not set myself to remove it, first, because I have never had
an opening to speak, and next, because I never saw in them a
disposition to hear. I have wished to appeal from Philip drunk to
Philip sober. When shall I pronounce him to be himself again?
If I may judge from the tone of the public press, which represents
the public voice, I have great reason to take heart at this time.
I have been treated by contemporary critics in this controversy
with great fairness and gentleness, and I am grateful to them for
it. However, the decision of the time and mode of my defence
has been taken out of my hands; and I am thankful that it has
been so. I am bound now as a duty to myself, to the Catholic
priesthood, to give account of myself without any delay, when I
am so rudely and circumstantially charged with untruthfulness.
. . . I accept the challenge, and I shall be content when I have
done so."

The result was that there appeared, between April 11 and
June 2, 1864, in seven parts, one of the greatest religious Confessions of all time. As one non-Catholic and unsympathetic contemporary said of it at the time: "As a specimen of mental analysis, extended over a whole lifetime, the *Apologia* is probably without a rival. St. Augustine's *Confessions* is a purely religious retro-
spect; Rousseau's are philosophical; Dr. Newman's psychological.
. . . The mental power, the strange self-anatomy, the almost
cold, patient review of past affections, anxieties, and hopes, are
alike astonishing. The examination is not a *post-mortem*, for there
appear color, light, and consciousness in the subject; it is not a
vivisection, for there is no quivering, even of a nerve."

2

Many are familiar with the *Apologia* in modern editions but are not familiar with the circumstances under which it was written. Newman grasped a great opportunity, not only to answer Kingsley effectively, but to bring himself once more before the world that had forgotten him. He took full advantage of the opportunity. His sense of the dramatic is plainly evident in the method he adopted. Gone was his pensive mood of a few months before, with his premonitions about an early death. In times to come he will have his pensive moments; but his quarter-century still to be lived will never again bury him in obscurity.

It was necessary, first of all, to interest the public and win its sympathy. He could then relate his life-story with the confidence that it would be read. The first edition began with a chapter discussing "Dr. Kingsley's Method of Disputation," followed by another headed, "True Mode of Meeting Dr. Kingsley." Both chapters were devastating in their effect: witty, sarcastic and entertaining, they left Kingsley's statements without a leg to stand on. All this was to insure that the reader would follow the dispute until he reached the succeeding serious chapters. To issue the *Apologia* in weekly sections, thus awakening curiosity on what was to come, was also shrewd. Verily, the forgotten recluse in Birmingham was displaying objective practicality which might well make his friend Manning (who at first viewed the *Apologia* as a mere voice from the dead) look to his laurels.

This clever publicity was needed only for the first editions. All later editions abridged, and finally omitted, the opening chapters on Kingsley's charges; [1] their purpose had passed, for the victory had been won.

---

[1] There is an Oxford University Press Edition of 1913 (reprinted several times since) which restores these chapters and also prints the pamphlets which passed between Newman and Kingsley.

As we know it today, the *Apologia* embraces five sections or chapters: first, the story of Newman's religious development and evolution from his childhood until 1833; second, his experiences in the Oxford Movement from 1833 to 1839; then follows the storm and stress period from 1839 to 1841; and finally, the period of his gradual approach to full Catholic truth—from 1841 to 1845. Appended to this is a fifth section entitled "Position of My Mind Since 1845" (it was originally headed, "General Answer to Mr. Kingsley").

That it was a heart-breaking thing for this diffident, sensitive soul to expose his inner self to the world in this way is obvious enough. But with all his native timidity, he was no coward and no weakling. If he must fight in defence of himself and of his Church, he was the last man to hesitate. This is indicated by a touching passage in the preface, from which I quote:

"It is not at all pleasant for me to be egotistical; nor to be criticised for being so. It is not pleasant to reveal, to high and low, young and old, what has gone on within me from my early years. It is not pleasant to be giving to every shallow or flippant disputant the advantage over me of knowing my most private thoughts, I might even say the intercourse between myself and my Maker. But I do not like to be called to my face a liar and a knave; nor should I be doing my duty to my Faith or to my name, if I were to suffer it. I know I have done nothing to deserve such an insult; and if I prove this, as I hope to do, I must not care for such incidental annoyances as are involved in the process."

It is scarcely necessary to give space here to excerpts from the earlier parts of the *Apologia*, for I have already quoted frequently from it in the foregoing pages. But it will not be amiss to give a little attention to the last section of the book, which describes the "Position of My Mind Since 1845"—that is to say, his Catholic position. The section is replete with striking passages in defence of or in explanation of various phases of the Catholic Faith. I shall quote a few.

"From the time that I became a Catholic, of course I have no further history of my religious opinions to narrate. In saying this, I do not mean that my mind has been idle, or that I have given up thinking on theological subjects; but that I have had no variations to record, and have had no anxiety of heart whatever. I have been in perfect peace and contentment. I never have had one doubt. . . .

"Many persons are very sensitive of the difficulties of Religion; I am as sensitive of them as any one; but I have never been able to see a connection between apprehending those difficulties, however keenly, and multiplying them to any extent, and, on the other hand, doubting the doctrines to which they are attached. Ten thousand difficulties do not make one doubt, as I understand the subject; difficulty and doubt are incommensurate. There of course may be difficulties in the evidence; but I am speaking of difficulties intrinsic to the doctrines themselves, or to their relations with each other. A man may be annoyed that he cannot work out a mathematical problem, of which the answer is or is not given to him, without doubting that it admits of an answer, or that a certain particular answer is the true one. Of all points of faith, the being of a God is, to my own apprehension, encompassed with most difficulty, and yet borne in upon our minds with most power.

"People say that the doctrine of Transubstantiation is difficult to believe; I did not believe the doctrine till I was a Catholic. I had no difficulty in believing it as soon as I believed that the Catholic Roman Church was the oracle of God, and that she had declared this doctrine to be part of the original revelation. It is difficult, impossible, to imagine, I grant;—but how is it difficult to believe? Yet Macaulay thought it so difficult to believe, that he had need of a believer in it of talents as eminent as Sir Thomas More, before he could bring himself to conceive that Catholics of an enlightened age could resist 'the overwhelming force of the argument against it.' 'Sir Thomas More,' he says, 'is one of the choice specimens of wisdom and virtue, and the doctrine of Transubstantiation is a kind of proof charge. Any faith which stands that test, will stand any test.' But for myself, I cannot indeed prove it, I cannot tell *how* it is; but I say, 'Why should it not be? What's to hinder it? What do I know of substance or matter? Just as much as the greatest philosophers, and that is nothing at all.' So much is this the case, that there is a rising school of philosophy now, which considers phenomena to constitute the whole of our knowledge in physics. The Catholic doctrine leaves phenomena alone. It does not say that the phenomena go; on the contrary, it says that they remain; nor does it say that the same phenomena are in several places at once. It deals with what no one on earth knows anything about, the material substances themselves. And, in like manner, of that majestic Article of the Anglican as well as of the Catholic Creed—the doctrine of the Trinity in Unity. What do I know of the essence of the Divine Being? I know that my abstract idea of three is simply incompatible with my idea of one; but when I come to the question of concrete fact, I have no means of proving that there is not a sense in which one and three can equally be predicated of the Incommunicable God."

As a whole, this last section of the *Apologia* is a vivid explanation of his Faith as a Catholic, with discussion of a multitude of reasons for his beliefs—just as the earlier part was an exposition of the errors he fell into and the blind alleys from which he had extricated himself during his long search for the truth. Thus, for example, he devotes much space to explaining (incidentally for Dr. Kingsley's enlightenment, but primarily to enlighten the non-Catholic world) the mission of the Church in her attitude towards fallen humanity. A striking passage is the following:

"She [the Catholic Church] does not teach that human nature is irreclaimable, else wherefore should she be sent? Not that it is to be shattered and reversed, but to be extricated, purified and restored; not that it is a mere mass of hopeless evil, but that it has the promise upon it of great things, and even now, in its present state of disorder and excess, has a virtue and a praise proper to itself. But in the next place, she knows and she preaches that such a restoration as she aims at effecting in it, must be brought about, not simply through certain outward provisions of preaching and teaching, even though they be her own, but from an inward spiritual power or grace imparted directly from above, and of which she is the channel. She has it in charge to rescue human nature from its misery, not simply by restoring it on its own level, but by lifting it up to a higher level than its own. She recognizes in it real moral excellence, though degraded, but she cannot set it free from earth except by exalting it towards heaven. It was for this end that a renovating grace was put into her hands, and therefore from the nature of the gift, as well as from the reasonableness of the case, she goes on, as a further point, to insist, that all true conversion must begin with the first springs of thought, and to teach that each individual man must be in his own person one whole and perfect temple of God, while he is also one of the living stones which build up a visible religious community. And thus the distinctions between nature and grace, and between outward and inward religion, become two further articles in what I have called the preamble of her divine commission."

Other brilliant passages might well be quoted. While the controversial and personal portions of the book were painful to him to write, this constructive discussion of the Catholic Faith, as he now knew it, must have given him great joy.

He inserted at the end an affectionate passage about his beloved St. Philip Neri, who was always present in his thoughts. "St. Philip," he said, "had a particular dislike of affectation both in himself and others, in speaking, in dressing, or in any thing. He avoided all ceremony which savored of worldly compliment, and always showed himself a great stickler for Christian simplicity in everything; so that, when he had to deal with men of worldly prudence, he did not very readily accommodate himself to them. And he avoided, as much as possible, having anything to do with two-faced persons, who did not go simply and straight-forwardly to work in their transactions. As for liars, he could not endure them, and he was continually reminding his spiritual children to avoid them as they would a pestilence. . . . These are the principles on which I acted before I was a Catholic; these are the principles which, I trust, will be my stay and guidance to the end."

He could not lay down his pen, after bringing the book to a close, without paying loving tribute, and offering it as a memorial of his devotion, to those beloved companions of his Oratory, many of whom had shared his trials and disappointments as well as his triumphs. This he did in the following words:

"I have closed this history of myself with St. Philip's name upon St. Philip's Feast Day; and having done so, to whom can I more suitably offer it, as a memorial of affection and gratitude, than to St. Philip's sons, my dearest brothers of this House, the priests of the Birmingham Oratory,—Ambrose St. John, Henry Austin Mills, Henry Bittleston, Edward Caswall, William Paine Neville, and Henry Ignatius Dudley Ryder?—who have been so faithful to me; who have been so sensitive of my needs; who have been so indulgent to my failings; who have carried me through so many trials; who have grudged no sacrifice, if I asked for it; who have been so cheerful under discouragements of my causing; who have done so many good works, and let me have the credit of them;—with whom I have lived so long, with whom I hope to die.

"And to you especially, dear Ambrose St. John; whom God gave me, when He took every one else away; who are the link between my old life and my new; who have now for twenty-one years been so devoted to me, so patient, so zealous, so tender; who have let me lean so hard upon you; who have watched me so narrowly; who have never thought of yourself if I was in question.

"And in you I gather up and bear in memory those familiar affectionate companions and counsellors, who in Oxford were given to me, one after another, to be my daily solace and relief; and all those others, of great name and high example, who were my thorough friends, and showed me true attachment in times long past; and also those many younger men, whether I knew them or not, who have never been disloyal to me by word or deed; and of all these, thus various in their relations to me, those more especially who have since joined the Catholic Church.

"And I earnestly pray for this whole company, with a hope against hope, that all of us, who once were so united, and so happy in our union, may even now be brought at length, by the Power of the Divine Will, into One Fold and under One Shepherd."

Dated May 26, 1864; in *Festo Corp. Christi.*

3

The success of the *Apologia* in bringing from obscurity this personality who had been well-nigh forgotten by his countrymen was truly amazing. It was not only welcomed with joy and deep appreciation by the whole Catholic world but awakened old friendships, long quiescent, in the Anglican world. Nor was interest confined to religious circles. It was applauded in unmeasured terms by many secular journals and newspapers, notable among these being the London *Times*, the *Spectator* and the *Saturday Review*. This was to be expected of the *Spectator*, which under the editorship of Richard Holt Hutton, had long been sympathetic towards Newman. The *Saturday Review*, however, although itself definitely anti-Catholic, quite accurately reflected the view of the Protestant public as a whole, in the following comment: "A loose and off-hand, and we may venture to add, an unjustifiable imputation, cast on Dr. Newman by a popular writer, more remarkable for vigorous writing than for vigorous thought, has produced one of the most interesting works of the present literary age. Dr. Newman is one of the finest masters of language, his logical powers are almost unequalled, and in one way or another, he has influenced the course of English thought more perhaps than any of his contemporaries."

The different chapters of the *Apologia*, issued Thursday after Thursday for seven weeks, were being read by thousands in clubs, in homes, on the tops of buses and in railway trains; and they were extensively discussed in pulpits—even in Parliamentary and political circles. They awakened new interest in the Puseyites (whose fortunes had declined in these latter days, though later to be revived by new men like H. P. Liddon). And not only the Anglican body as a whole were discussing Newman's *Apologia*, but Protestant non-conformists were reading the instalments with avidity and learning much about the despised "Romanists" which they never knew before. Altogether, the *Apologia* induced a more tolerant attitude towards the Catholic Church than had been evident in England at any time since the religious upheavals of the sixteenth century.

Newman was naturally gratified at the reception given his *Apologia*; especially was he overjoyed at the response of the English Catholic bishops and clergy; from all over England he received congratulations, no fewer than five hundred and fifty-eight priests signing memorials and sending personal messages of good will. But perhaps of all the letters he received, none was more gratifying than that from his Ordinary in the Birmingham diocese, Bishop Ullathorne.

William Bernard Ullathorne, who had been made bishop in 1850, after having been a vicar-apostolic before the restoration of the hierarchy, was one of the blessings of Newman's Catholic life. Of a wholly different temperament, and far from being the intellectual genius that Newman was, Ullathorne understood and sympathized with him in all his troubles. He was a rough-and-ready Yorkshireman, who in early life had gone to sea in search of adventure and had been quite mature before he became a Benedictine monk. He spent many years in Australia, where he became vicar-apostolic, returning home in 1839. An extremely objective person and a shrewd judge of others, he understood Manning, Ward, Talbot and other of Newman's critics—their faults as well as their virtues. Indeed, it has been said that Ullathorne was the one English bishop who kept Manning worrying.

Immediately after the publication of the *Apologia*, Bishop Ullathorne wrote Newman in terms which gave him great satisfaction, particularly for the reason that any commendation from this distinguished bishop would surely impress less friendly prelates. A few passages must be quoted.

"We have now been personally acquainted, and much more than acquainted, for nineteen years, during more than sixteen of which we have stood in special relation of duty towards each other. This has been one of the singular blessings which God has given me amongst the cares of the Episcopal office. What my feelings of respect, of confidence, and of affection have been towards you, you know well, nor should I think of expressing them in words. But there is one thing that has struck me in this day of explanations, which you could not, and would not be disposed to do, and which no one could do so properly or so authentically as I could; and which it seems to me is not altogether uncalled for, if every kind of erroneous impression that some persons have entertained with no better evidence than conjecture, is to be removed.

"It is difficult to comprehend how, in the face of facts, the notion should ever have arisen that, during your Catholic life, you have been more occupied with your own thoughts than with the service of religion and the work of the Church. If we take no other work into consideration beyond the written productions which your Catholic pen has given to the world, they are enough

for the life's labor of another. [But] these works have been written
in the midst of labor and cares of another kind, and of which the
world knows very little. . . . I have read on this day of its publication the seventh part of the *Apologia*, and the touching allu-
sion in it to the devotedness of the Catholic clergy to the poor in
seasons of pestilence, reminds me that when the cholera raged so
dreadfully at Bilston, . . . I asked you to lend me two Fathers to
supply the place of other priests whom I wished to send as a
further aid. But you and Father St. John preferred to take the
place of danger which I had destined for others, and remained
at Bilston till the worst was over." Then he cites at length the
work through the years of the Birmingham Oratory, and the
great and increasing success of the Oratory School.

The unanimous applause throughout the English-speaking
world created wide interest in Rome. Everybody, from the Holy
Father down, joined in the acclaim. Even Monsignor Talbot now
seemed to climb on the bandwagon. Within the month (July
1864) Talbot visited England and went directly to Birmingham
to call on Newman. The latter happened to be away, but Talbot
then wrote him a letter inviting him to visit Rome the following
winter to deliver a series of Lenten lectures in Talbot's own
Church. This invitation was framed in these words:

"One of the reasons for which I called upon you [at the Ora-
tory] was to invite you to come to Rome for next Lent to preach
in my church in the Piazza del Popolo, where you would have a
more educated audience than could ever be the case in England,
and where they are more open to Catholic influences. When I
told the Holy Father that I intended to invite you, he highly
approved of my intention, and I think myself that you will derive
great benefit from revisiting Rome and again showing yourself
to the ecclesiastical authorities there, who are anxious to see you."

One may picture the glint in Newman's eyes when he read this
pompous invitation from the man who, he felt, had for years been
thwarting him and repeating stories which had injured him. He

made short work of the invitation, at once sending this brief and pungent reply:

"Dear Monsignor Talbot:—I have received your letter inviting me to preach next Lent in your church in Rome to 'an audience of Protestants more educated than could ever be the case in England,' etc. However, Birmingham people have souls; and I have neither the taste nor talent for the sort of work you cut out for me, and I beg to decline your offer. . . . I am, very truly, John H. Newman."

That was that. Here is where Newman displayed his objective side forcibly enough. But Talbot did not forget it.

4

After the issuing of the *Apologia* and the universal applause it engendered, nothing more was heard from Dr. Kingsley. Silence reigned in that quarter and, quite generally, among the Broad Church contingent. Newman really cherished no ill will towards Kingsley. They never met; but ten years later, when Dr. Kingsley died, Newman wrote a friend the following letter:

"The death of Mr. Kingsley—so premature—shocked me. I never from the first have felt any anger towards him. As I said in the first pages of the *Apologia*, it is very difficult to be angry with a man one has never seen. A casual reader would think my language denoted anger—but it did not. I have ever found from experience that no one would believe me in earnest if I spoke calmly. When, again and again, I denied the repeated report that I was on the point of coming back to the Church of England, I have uniformly found that, if I simply denied it, this only made newspapers repeat the report more confidently; but if I said something sharp, they abused me for scurrility against the Church I had left, but they believed me. Rightly or wrongly, this was the

reason why I felt it would not do to be tame and not to show indignation at Mr. Kingsley's charges. . . . Within the last few
years I have been obliged to adopt a similar course towards those
who said I could not receive the Vatican Decrees. I sent a sharp
letter to the *Guardian*, and, of course, the *Guardian* called me
names, but it believed me, and did not allow the offense of its cor-
respondent to be repeated.

"As for Mr. Kingsley, much less could I feel any resentment
against him, when he was accidentally the instrument, in the
good Providence of God, by whom I had an opportunity given
me, which otherwise I should not have had, of vindicating my
character and conduct in my *Apologia*.

"I heard too, only a few weeks back, from a friend, that she
chanced to go into the Chester Cathedral, and found Mr. Kingsley preaching about me, kindly, though of course with criticisms
of me. And it has rejoiced me to have observed lately that he was
defending the Athanasian Creed, and, as it seemed to me, generally nearing the Catholic view of things. I have always hoped
that by good luck I might have met him, feeling sure that there
would be no embarrassment on my part; and I said Mass for his
soul as soon as I heard of his death."

CHAPTER TWELVE

HENRY EDWARD MANNING

1

IT IS NECESSARY TO DEVOTE a few pages at this juncture to Henry Edward Manning, the noted convert from Anglicanism, who, after fourteen years in the Catholic Church, was to become Archbishop of Westminster as the successor of Cardinal Wiseman. Ten years later he was himself to be a cardinal.

Born in Totteridge, Hertfordshire, July 15, 1808, he was Newman's junior by about seven years. His early education was at Harrow, and in 1827 he matriculated at Balliol College, Oxford. His father, a London banker who had been at one time Governor of the Bank of England, planned a commercial career for him; but young Henry dreamed of a political career leading into Parliament. Business reverses of the father cut short his stay at Oxford, and he was placed in a clerkship in the Colonial Office. Here he convinced himself that he had a vocation for the ministry, and he later returned to Oxford, where he was graduated in 1832 and was then ordained to the Anglican diaconate. Shortly thereafter he was given the curacy of Lavington parish, where the rector, Dr. John Sargent, had been stricken with a fatal illness and very soon passed away. On his death in 1833, young Manning succeeded him as rector.

In the meanwhile he had fallen in love with one of Dr. Sargent's daughters—Caroline. They were married November 17,

1833 by Bishop Samuel Wilberforce. It is interesting to note that of the other three daughters of Dr. Sargent, one was the wife of Bishop Wilberforce, another married Newman's great friend, Henry Wilberforce, and the third married George Dudley Ryder. The latter two were ultimately received, with their husbands, into the Catholic Church.

This Wilberforce family, with which young Manning was to have close relationship through his marriage to one of the "sylph-like Sargents"—as these four daughters were styled in certain Victorian memoirs—was outstanding in the religious world of its day. Of the four sons of the famous William Wilberforce, the leader of the anti-slavery movement in Parliament and the intimate friend and adviser of William Pitt, three—Henry, Robert and William—became Catholics. The other son, Samuel Wilberforce, who became Anglican Bishop of Oxford, remained a rigid Evangelical Protestant all his days. And as a result of the conversion of his brothers to Catholicism, there was a lifetime estrangement—so typical of so many in the days of the Oxford movement.

Samuel Wilberforce alone seems not to have been influenced by Newman at Oxford, where the four brothers were educated. Henry, the eldest, who became Newman's lifelong friend, was profoundly influenced by Newman and, as we have seen, ultimately followed him into the Catholic Church with his wife. He was the father of the well known Dominican Bernard Wilberforce, and one of his daughters married Hurrell Froude, a nephew of Newman's dear friend of Tractarian days, Richard Hurrell Froude, who so profoundly influenced Newman in his evolution in the direction of High Churchmanship. Robert Wilberforce, who also worked with Newman during Tractarian days, became a Catholic and then went to Rome to study for the priesthood but died before ordination and is buried in Santa Maria Sopra Minerva opposite the Academia, where he had studied.

Of the Lavington circle of Wilberforces (including George

Dudley Ryder, whose son Father Ignatius Ryder was a notable Oratorian) and the Sargent sisters, a great many of their descendants have been Catholics, including eight who became priests or nuns.

Manning's married life was brief; his beautiful young wife was a victim of tuberculosis and passed away within less than four years. It was a tragic event for him; his memory of her never faded. A touching proof of this was disclosed after his death in 1892, when Herbert (later Cardinal) Vaughan said to Baron Friedrich von Hügel:

"You know what we all thought about the Cardinal and Mrs. Manning. Well, this is what happened shortly before his death. I was by his bedside; he looked around to see that we were alone; he fumbled under his pillow for something; he drew out a battered little pocketbook full of a woman's fine handwriting. He said, 'For years you have been as a son to me, Herbert. I know not to whom to leave this—I leave it to you. Into this little book my dearest wife wrote her prayers and meditations. Not a day has passed, since her death, on which I have not prayed and meditated from this book. All the good I may have done, all the good I may have been, I owe to her. Take precious care of it.' He ceased speaking, and soon afterwards unconsciousness came on." [1]

From the time of his wife's death Manning dedicated his life wholly to religion; but memories of his wife were always with him. When, fifteen years later, he became a Catholic, we find him writing: "Fifteen years ago a crucifix stood in sight of her dying bed, which taught me the article of Communion of Saints. And I have never been without one." When he set out for Rome after his ordination to the Catholic priesthood, her miniature was in his pocket. As he entered the Roman Academia it happened to be her birthday, and he wrote in his diary, "Nativity of Caroline, most lamented."

---

[1] Shane Leslie, *Henry Edward Manning: His Life and Labours.*

On the resignation of Archdeacon Webber in 1841, he became Archdeacon of Chichester, with residence at Lavington. Here his progress was marked; he became famous as an effective preacher, and it was obvious that he was destined for an exceptional career. He made many friends among the influential, one of the most notable being W. E. Gladstone, with whom he would have many passages-at-arms during the years to come.

His early years in the Anglican ministry were not marked by pronounced High Church views, and he remained outside the Oxford Movement. He disliked the Tracts for the Times and criticised Newman's Tract Ninety as not being a sound interpretation of the meaning of the Thirty-Nine Articles. In 1842 he wrote to Gladstone: "In some ways I thoroughly agree with Newman, in some things partially, in some not at all." But half a dozen years later he had adopted practically all of Newman's "Anglo-Catholic" principles. After Newman's exit to the Catholic Church in 1845 he is seen leaning more and more to the position of Pusey and Keble, and well before 1850 is classed as one of the most aggressive Puseyites. Actually, he seemed to be going beyond them in a friendly attitude towards the Catholic Church—which began to make Pusey very uncomfortable.

Back in 1834 Manning had subscribed to Luther's view of Baptism; but by 1842, when he wrote the essay called "The Unity of the Church," he had even accepted the theory of Apostolic succession. A still greater change occurred in 1848, when he visited Rome for the second time. This was when Newman was also there, studying for the priesthood. By chance they met in a Roman street. Newman says of this incident: "As for dear Manning, I thought him looking very ill. He ran up to me as I was getting into a carrozza—and I must fairly say that for the first instant I did not know him. And when I saw him again and again, his old face did not come out to me, nor did I get over, as one so often does, my first impression."

Manning was charmed with Pope Pius IX, to whom he was

first presented in April, 1848. He at this time writes to his friend Dodsworth: "Don't tell any soul what I add now, but there is something which brought you and other days to my mind, and that is the evening Benediction. . . . It is impossible not to love Pius IX. His is the most truly English countenance that I have seen in Italy."

When he got home that summer he found rumors afloat of his leanings toward Rome, and that both Pusey and Gladstone were worried about him. But to his friend Moberly he wrote, "My opinions are what they were when I wrote you from Rome. My charge is the case for the Church of England." Yet he wrote to Dodsworth shortly after, in reference to the appointment of the heretical Dr. Hampden to a bishopric: "I cannot serve what I cannot defend, and if I had failed to find a just defence I am afraid to think what must have followed." When talking with Gladstone at this time he assured him that his Roman visit had not weakened his devotion to the Anglican Church; but he also said to Dodsworth, "I feel clearer and more ready for all hazards. I have had things to cheer me, great depth and devotion in individuals, with no tinge of Anglicanism or any such sham." He surely was now unsettled—or muddled!

What finally brought matters to a head was the famous Gorham decision. Rev. G. C. Gorham, an unorthodox Anglican who denied the sacramental character of Baptism, was, to the horror of the Puseyites, appointed to a Living. A mighty protest went to the Archbishop of Canterbury—but to no purpose. Gorham's own bishop declined to install him, and wrote to Manning: "Yesterday afternoon, in virtue of the *fiat* of the Archbishop of Canterbury, Mr. Gorham was instituted in the Vicarage of Brampford Speke by H. J. Fust. His Grace's complicity in this awful work is thus constituted, and I cannot hold communion with him. I cannot communicate *in sacris* with him." Once more the civil power overruled the spiritual in connection with an orthodox doctrine of the Church of England.

Manning had already protested vigorously, insisting that this was the test whether the Church of England be a divine or human society. "The Gorham decision is enough for one day," he had said, "and the peril of this decision, whether for the truth or against it, is very great. I dread the day when such a subject as the other Holy Sacrament [the Eucharist] shall be brought not into a Council or Synod, not before the Church in any form in which we may believe the Holy Spirit may guide and preserve us, but into a wrangling Court before an incompetent judge."

At the same time Gladstone, who was equally alarmed, had written to Manning: "If Mr. Gorham be carried through, and that upon the merits, I say not only is there no doctrine of Baptismal Regeneration in the Church of England as State-interpreted, but there is no doctrine at all." Yet Gladstone, although calling himself an orthodox High Churchman, would not sign the protest which Manning circulated. Was he a politician first and a Churchman afterwards? When Manning hinted that if the Gorham decision stood he would leave the Church, Gladstone hinted that he would retire from politics. Yet when Manning did leave, Gladstone stayed in politics. And when, in June 1850, Manning told him, "I dare not say that my conscience will not submit itself to the Church which has its circuits throughout the world, and its center by accident in Rome," Gladstone set up a great wail.

Yet Manning still hesitated. He took definite action only when it was demanded that he, as Archdeacon, protest against the establishment of the Catholic hierarchy in England—the so-called Papal Aggression. To Dodsworth he now wrote: "I have seen the bishop and offered to resign my office, or to convene and express my dissent and resignation. Events have greatly brought this to its issue in the way I waited for. I wish to play it out on a field until the last move of duty is done. Then I shall lay down my weapons."

He laid them down then and there. Within a few weeks he had

left Lavington and was in London, where he talked at length with his friend Gladstone regarding his intentions. Finally, they went to an Anglican Church together—the last time for Manning. During the Communion service he said to Gladstone, "I can no longer take Communion in the Church of England," and then, as he arose to go, added, "Come!" But Gladstone turned indignantly away. Their friendship from that hour was frozen. When the day came for his reception into the Catholic Church, Manning sent this line to his friend: "Bear me in mind in your prayers tomorrow. And may God be with you always."

Gladstone was broken-hearted; he said he felt as though Manning "had murdered his mother." He never got over it. Although they made many contacts in the years to come, sometimes friendly and sometimes not, it was quite in vain that a decade later than this Manning extended the olive branch in these words: "When I laid down all I had, including your friendship, precious to me beyond wealth or prosperity, it was that I might cast the weight I had into the scale of positive truth—that is, my whole life and soul, with all its past and all its future." But Gladstone's cold heart was not warmed.

Manning had lost Gladstone's friendship, but many of his other cherished friends stood by him. Among these were James Hope-Scott and Dodsworth, who were also about to "cross over." It was with Hope-Scott that Manning called on Cardinal Wiseman at this time; and with him he was received into the Catholic Church at Farm Street by Father Brownbill, S.J., on Passion Sunday, April 9, 1851. "Now my career is ended," he said.

2

On Manning's conversion, congratulations poured in from many quarters, one of the first being Newman's. Within a few weeks he was confirmed by Cardinal Wiseman, and after some coaching by Father Frederick Faber, he was ordained to the priesthood by the Cardinal. He soon left for Rome, where he spent some months in study; and before he returned to England, Pope Pius conferred on him the Doctorate of Divinity.

His rise from that time was very rapid. He became invaluable to Cardinal Wiseman as a practical assistant. In the course of time he was made Provost, and during the ensuing years his influence was marked. As Newman had become a devotee of St. Philip Neri and been inspired to found the English Community of Oratorians, so Manning had been attracted by the personality of St. Charles Borromeo and had visited the Oblates of St. Charles at Milan, with the result that he founded, in 1857, at his parish church in Bayswater, St. Mary of the Angels, the Congregation of the Oblates of St. Charles. Well before Cardinal Wiseman's death, as well as after it, it was he who was largely responsible for the establishing of new Catholic schools, hospitals and many missionary activities among the poor. He also aggressively promoted missionary work among those who had fallen away from the Faith.

He was preaching with increasing power and made many converts. He converted Protestants even in casual conversation—or, as Ruskin said, "by fascination." During his first month in the Church, he converted seven; before he returned from Rome in 1852, he had converted fifteen; and while traveling home, he converted several more. He always kept a careful record of his conversions; this record shows that up to 1865 he had personally converted no fewer than 346 persons in England alone. Many were of the cultured—which was a matter of observation among his critics—but there were many of the poor and unprivileged in his list. His greatest interest during his long Catholic life was consecrated to efforts to alleviate the sufferings and poverty of the downtrodden slum-dwellers of London. Not the least of the acts that have made his name famous was his work in connection with the settlement of the London Dock strike in 1889—when he was in his eighty-first year!

In the earlier years it was common gossip among Protestants that it was dangerous to talk with Dr. Manning on religion, for before he had finished with you, he would have you in the Church. He failed, however, in one notable instance; that of Florence Nightingale. He led her to the door of the Church, but she was lost to him on the threshold.

His friendship with Miss Nightingale extended back to 1847, and he had done much to encourage her in the nursing vocation she sought, at a time when her family and friends opposed it. Brought up in the Anglican Church, she was torn between that Church and the Catholic. After Manning crossed over, she said to him: "I dislike and despise the Church of England. She received me into her bosom, but what has she ever done for me? She never gave me work to do for her, nor training to do it if I found it for myself. . . . If you knew what a home the Catholic Church would be to me! All that I want I should find in her. All my difficulties would be removed. . . . She would give me daily bread. The daughters of St. Vincent would open their arms to me."

It is beyond the scope of this work to include the story of Florence Nightingale's later years. One might have thought, in view of her earlier attitude, that Manning would have her in the Church *instanter*. But it was not to be. Though he was primarily responsible for starting her great career in the Crimean War, she never crossed the threshold of the Faith.

Manning had better luck, however, with a friend and confidante of Florence Nightingale—Miss Stanley, sister of the famous Dean of Westminster. Her conversion was one of the most notable of his achievements in this field.

As this narrative will show, Newman and Manning will have many differences and disputes after the latter becomes an archbishop. Indeed, they had often misunderstood each other from early days; it was temperament that divided them, perhaps, more than anything else. Shane Leslie, in his biography of Manning, appraised the situation thus:

"Of Newman and Manning religious history will ever treat. That two wills so strong, two minds so choice, and yet so diverse, have united on one Creed remains a matter of pride rather than distress to Catholics. . . . Out of their rivalry and suffering the strength and progress of the Church was moulded in England." Yet Manning and Newman were never, in intention, very far apart; there were differences of emphasis and of policy which drove Newman to exasperation on the one hand, and the more objective and less imaginative Manning to resentment and temper on the other; but at the height of their estrangement in 1866, Manning was to write a friend: "It is strange what efforts they [Protestants] make to believe that we are divided—above all, Dr. Newman and myself. I should be ready to let him write down my faith and I would sign it without reading it. So would he." [1]

3

Nicholas Cardinal Wiseman, who for some years had been declining in health, died in February 1865. For a number of years he had been losing his grip on things, as he passed the burden more and more to the shoulders of Provost Manning. No doubt his greatest achievement had been accomplished when he was building up and expanding the Church during and after the Oxford movement, with the stream of Oxford converts flowing in. Perhaps the Provincial Synod at Oscott in 1852, where Newman delivered his "Second Spring" address, registered Cardinal Wiseman's finest hour. After that, his days were crowded with rou-

---

[1] *Henry Edward Manning: His Life and Labours.*

tine duties, with his struggles to harmonize conflicting opinions upon policy among the old-school English Catholics—such as the controversy over his coadjutor, Dr. Errington—and, all the while, with slowly declining health. An impulsive soul, not possessing outstanding qualities for administrative duties, he frequently made mistakes and was often subject to criticism. But without the practical traits of a Manning or an Ullathorne, he was at the same time a great scholar, a brilliant writer and preacher, with exceptional intellectual depth and great personal sanctity. One might venture to say that in his general make-up he was more of a Newman than a Manning.

Abbot Cuthbert Butler, in his life of Ullathorne,[1] has appraised Cardinal Wiseman accurately: "In the combination of richly endowed nature, and attractive, loving personality, and well-balanced and all round character, and many sided intellectual attainment and successful achievement of a great life-work—he was indeed unique." But that life-work was practically completed well before he passed away.

At the time of the Cardinal's death, Newman preached a sermon full of memories of Dr. Wiseman's early kindnesses to him and of Dr. Wiseman's achievements in those earlier years. Yet Newman could not overlook the fact that the Cardinal, in his last years, had seemed to have lost interest in him, and that he had done little or nothing to shield him from unjust criticism. In a letter written at this time to Dr. Russell of Maynooth, he discloses his attitude.

"The Cardinal has done a great work—and I think has finished it. It is not often that this can be said of a man. Personally I have not much to thank him for *since* I became a Catholic. He always meant kindly, but his impulses, kind as they were, were evanescent, and he was naturally influenced by those who got around

---

[1] Cuthbert Butler, *Life and Times of Archbishop Ullathorne.*

him—and occupied his ear. . . . I have not seen him alone six or seven times in the last thirteen years." As Newman well knew (though he did not then specify), it was Dr. Manning who had "occupied his ear."

As to a successor to the archbishopric, there was at first some uncertainty. The chapter sent the name of Archbishop Errington to Rome with other names but not Manning's. Manning himself, in a letter to Monsignor Talbot in Rome, recommended either Bishop Ullathorne or Bishop Cornthwaite. Obviously, he did not expect his own appointment; but perhaps he and his close friends were not too surprised when the Holy See chose him. He was consecrated at St. Mary's, Moorfield, on June 8, 1865, by Bishop Ullathorne and a few months later went to Rome, where he received the pallium and was formally enthroned.

Newman would have preferred Bishop Ullathorne, but his comment on Manning's appointment was not ungenerous. "As to the new Archbishop," he wrote to a friend, "the appointment at least has the effect of making Protestants see, to their surprise, that Rome is not distrustful of converts, as such. On the other hand, it must be a great trial to the old priesthood to have a neophyte set over them all. Some will bear it very well—I think our own Bishop will—but I cannot prophesy what turn things will take on the whole. He [Manning] has great power of winning men where he chooses. Witness the fact of his appointment,—but whether he will care to win inferiors, or whether his talent extends to the case of inferiors as well as superiors, I do not know. . . . One man has one talent, one another. You speak of me. I have generally got on well with juniors but not with superiors."

Newman began by being affable to Manning; the latter began by being affable towards Newman—as indeed he was towards everyone. No sooner was he appointed than he wished to obtain for Newman a titular bishopric—in fact, he had suggested this to Wiseman two years before—but Newman promptly and wisely declined. He had become more wary than of yore; besides, he was more confident of his own position in the Church, having achieved so astounding a success with his *Apologia*. "He wants to put me in the House of Lords and muzzle me," was his thought. He wrote to the new archbishop, in acknowledging his invitation to be present and take part in his consecration:

"I will readily attend your consecration on one condition. . . . The condition I make is this:—A year or two back I heard you were doing your best to get me made a bishop *in partibus*. I heard this from two or three quarters, and I don't see how I can be mistaken. If so, your feeling toward me is not unlikely to make you attempt the same thing now. I risk the chance of your telling me you have no such intention, to entreat you not to entertain it. If such an honor were offered to me, I should persistently decline it, very positively, and I do not wish to pain the Holy Father, who has always been so kind to me, if such pain can be avoided."

The new archbishop of course acceded to Newman's request. Nothing more was said about the matter (perhaps a relief to both, though for different reasons).

4

Despite the friendly gestures between Manning and Newman at this time, a new storm was brewing for the latter. Cardinal Wiseman, in the days before his ill health set in, had made strenuous efforts to attempt the building-up of a real Catholic university in England, which would provide Catholic youth with educational facilities from which they had been shut out at Oxford and Cambridge because of the requirement that all students sign the Thirty-Nine Articles of religion. He had even hoped that Oscott might be developed to reach this position. And William George Ward, teaching theology for many years at Old Hall, St. Edmund's College, was strongly in favor of developing a real

Catholic university in England. This was also the attitude of
Father Frederick Faber, the head of the Brompton Oratory in
London, and of Dr. Manning. All these men were opposed to
the idea of Catholic youth being sent to Oxford or Cambridge,
even if the bars were let down. These famous converts were
definitely opposed to their own *alma mater*, Oxford University.

But now the Universities had been thrown open to Catholics by
the abolition of the requirement to sign the Thirty-Nine Articles,
and Catholic parents were beginning to send their sons to both
Oxford and Cambridge. Newman, surely more "practical" in
this matter than Manning, Ward and Faber, immediately suggested that a Catholic center be established in Oxford to protect
the faith of the Catholic students there. He well knew what was
happening in Oxford. It was no longer the center of traditional
religion, as in his own time, but was becoming more and more
infiltrated with the scepticism of the utilitarian school of John
Stuart Mill and his followers. He did not believe that Oxford
itself could be indoctrinated with Catholic beliefs: but at least,
the Catholic students should be shielded from these devastating
materialistic influences.

Shortly before the death of the Cardinal, he discussed this situation with Bishop Ullathorne. The Bishop suggested that the
Birmingham Oratorians take over the small Catholic mission already in Oxford and send one or two resident priests there without delay. Newman at once agreed, and with a group of his
friends, accumulated a fund and purchased some excellent land
near the University, on which to erect a building to be used for
an Oratory and general Catholic center.

That Newman did this with some trepidation (for he instinctively felt that Manning and Ward would try to prevent his going
to Oxford) is evident from a letter he wrote Hope-Scott at this
time:

"The Bishop has offered us the Mission—and he is collecting
money for Church and priest's house. They would become *pro*

tempore the Church and House of the Oratory. . . . So far, as far as the plan goes, is fair sailing . . . but can the Oratory, that is, I, when once set up, without saying a word to anyone, make the Oratory a Hall? The Oratory is confessedly out of my Bishop's jurisdiction. Propaganda might at once interfere—perhaps would. Our Bishop left to himself would be for an Oxford Catholic College or Hall, but Propaganda would be against him, and my only defence would be the support of the Catholic gentry."

His prognostications were correct. Propaganda *was* against the whole scheme. And why? Briefly, because Manning, without doubt greatly influenced by Ward and Faber (though the latter had recently died), was definitely opposed to Catholic youth being sent to *any* non-Catholic College, and particularly to Oxford or Cambridge. This attitude was precisely the same as that of the Irish bishops in relation to the Queen's Colleges. Manning's views were submitted without delay to Propaganda, where our friend Monsignor Talbot was all-powerful. And at Manning's behest, at a meeting of the English bishops at Eastertide, a resolution was drafted discouraging Catholic parents from sending their sons to Oxford. When this happened, Newman wrote Hope-Scott once more:

"At present, I am simply off the rails. I do not know how to doubt that the sudden meeting of the Bishops has been ordered apropos of my going to Oxford. If I can understand our Bishop, the notion is to forbid young Catholics to go to Oxford—and to set up a University elsewhere. If so, what have I to do with Oxford? What call have I, at the end of twenty years, apropos of nothing, to open theological trenches against the Doctors and Professors of the University?"

He was now told by his bishop to drop the idea—which probably was no shock to him, despite the earlier encouragement of the same bishop. The latter now explained the attitude in the seats of the mighty. The upshot of the affair was that Newman and his friends were left high and dry with the Oxford property on their hands. It had to be sold later on at a substantial loss.

In fairness to Newman, it should be emphasized that he never considered his Oxford plan an ideal solution of the problem. Always, he was in favor of the establishing of an English Catholic university on the lines of that in Louvain, Belgium. Such had been his dream in connection with the Dublin university. But he well knew—what some of the more "practical" minds did not seem to realize—that under the conditions then prevailing in England, there was little hope of success in building up such a university at that time. Nor was he unmindful of the fact that, regardless of all official protests, many Catholic parents would continue to send their sons to Oxford or Cambridge.

So the scheme was dropped. But not for good. Let us jump ahead a little. About two years later (in the spring of 1866) Bishop Ullathorne thought the time had arrived when the plan for an Oratory in Oxford under Newman's jurisdiction could be successfully carried through. He assured Newman that there would now be no opposition from Propaganda.

This change of front came as a surprise to Newman, and he was inclined to be incredulous. But after persistent urging from the Bishop, he went ahead and purchased a new plot of ground for an Oxford chapel. Yet, despite Ullathorne's confident assurances, he feared that there would be a hitch: that Propaganda would forbid the project as before. In the event, there was not merely a hitch; there was definite opposition. It would seem that here Archbishop Manning surely "scored over" Bishop Ullathorne—perhaps with glee, for Ullathorne, with his practical objectivity, had more than once made him nervous.

Cardinal Reisach came to England at this time to ascertain the feelings of English Catholics on the Oxford question. But he did not talk with Newman. The Archbishop guided him as to whom he should talk to; and Newman was not on his list. William George Ward was of course on the list. This convinced Newman at once that despite Bishop Ullathorne's backing, his plans were being blocked by the Archbishop. Though he had been actively appealing for financial support by sending out a circular-letter signed by a group of laymen, he now decided to await developments.

At this very time Archbishop Manning was writing Monsignor Talbot a long letter, from which I quote this passage:

"You will see in the *Tablet* an address by Father Newman signed by most of our chief laymen. (1) The address carefully omits all reference to Oxford. (2) It is signed also by men most opposed to our youth going there, e.g., Lord Petre. (3) But it will be used, and by some is so intended, as a means of pushing Dr. Newman's going to Oxford, and ultimately the University scheme. I only wish you to be guarded against supposing the Address to prove that the signers are in favor of the Oxford scheme. Do not let Propaganda alarm itself. If it will only be firm and clear we shall get through all this and more."

It seems evident that, despite these reassurances, Talbot was dissatisfied with Manning; that he thought the latter not aggressive enough in opposing Newman's plans; for we find a long letter from him to the Archbishop. His irritation is most marked in the following passage:

"Dr. Newman is the most dangerous man in England, and you will see that he will make use of the laity against your Grace. You must not be afraid of him. It will require much prudence, but you must be firm, as the Holy Father still places confidence in you; but if you yield and do not fight the battle of the Holy See against the detestable spirit growing up in England, he will begin to regret Cardinal Wiseman, who knew how to keep the laity in order. . . . Dr. Ullathorne has been the cause of the whole mischief. If he had only obeyed the letter of Propaganda and communicated to Dr. Newman the inhibition placed on his going to Oxford, he could not have sent forth a circular saying that the whole Oxford project had the approbation of the Holy See."

After this, Manning seems to have been more aggressive in his opposition. Ullathorne had to retreat, and Newman to abandon his plans—just as he had feared. Then he drew up a memorandum outlining his exact views on the subject of Oxford, which Father St. John and Father Bittleston took to Rome. It was a brilliant defence of his attitude, but it seems to have accomplished little in clarifying matters with the Holy Father. Monsignor Talbot saw to that, quoting to the Pope several passages from Newman's *Rambler* article of years before, to remind the Pope that Newman had then spoken too well of the Catholic laity who were supporting him now! Perhaps the Pope gave slight attention to Talbot, but at least Newman was not helped.

It is unnecessary to detail the long discussions between Father St. John and Monsignor Talbot; but although the Oxford plan was abandoned this second time (leaving Newman with the real estate on his hands as before), it is evident that Father St. John did good work in weakening Talbot's prejudices against Newman. For on St. Philip's Day, May 26, 1867, we find Newman writing to Talbot as follows:

"Dear Monsignor Talbot: I have received with much satisfaction the report which Father St. John has given me of your conversations with him. I know you have a good heart; and I know you did me good service in the Achilli matter, and you got me a relic of St. Athanasius from Venice, which I account a great treasure; and for these reasons I have been more bewildered at your having of late years taken so strong a part against me, without (I may say) any real grounds whatever; or rather, I *should* have been bewildered, were it not that, for now as many as thirty-four years, it has been my lot to be misrepresented and opposed without any intermission by one set of persons or another. Certainly, I have desiderated in you, as in many others, that charity which thinketh no evil, and have looked in vain for that considerateness and sympathy which is due to a man who has passed his life in attempting to serve the cause and interests of religion, and who, for the very reason he has written so much, must, from the frailty of our common nature, have said things which had better not have been said, or left out complements and explanations of what he has said, which had better have been added. . . . I am now an old man, perhaps within a few years of my death, and you can neither do me good nor harm. I have never been otherwise than well disposed towards you. When you first entered the Holy Father's immediate service, I used to say Mass for you the first day of every month, that you might be prospered at your important post; and now I shall say Mass for you seven times, beginning with this week, when we are keeping the Feast of St. Philip, begging him at the same time to gain for you a more equitable judgment of us, and a kinder feeling towards us on the part of our friends, than we have of late years experienced."

A friendly acknowledgment from Talbot, with an attempt to explain his past misjudgments, reached Newman in due course. Not long after this, Talbot's health declined, his nervous system collapsed and his mind gave way. He lingered on for some time in this state, in which he finally died. Newman cherished no more animosity against him than he did against Charles Kingsley —nor against any others who had thwarted him. If he found it difficult to forget injuries, he could always forgive them.

5

The failure of his plans for protecting the faith of Catholic students at Oxford now seemed final to him—at least for the duration of his own lifetime. But he felt confident that some time in the future his view of the matter would be accepted by the Church. In this he was more far-seeing than his critics. Though he did not live to witness it, a few years after his death in 1890,

Pope Leo XIII reversed the policy which had been so persistently defended by Manning, adopting precisely what Newman had been advocating as a practical solution of the problem. Thus the final verdict of the Holy See was that he had been right after all.

The collapse of his Oxford dreams did not react on Newman as it might have a few years before; he was not unduly depressed. The success of his *Apologia* had brought a new lease of life and vitality to this sensitive man who had thought at the end of 1863 that his life-work was at its end. A passage from his journal at this period reflects his new attitude of serenity:

"I have just now looked over what I wrote in January, 1863. I have got hardened against the opposition made to me, and have not the soreness at my ill treatment on the part of certain influential Catholics which I had then . . . On all these accounts, though I still feel keenly the way in which I am kept doing nothing, I am not so much pained at it,—both because by means of my *Apologia* I am indirectly doing a work, and because its success has put me in spirits to look out for other means of doing good, whether Propaganda cares about it or not. . . . Faber being taken away, Ward and Manning take his place. Through them, especially Manning . . . the Oxford scheme has been for the present thwarted—for me probably for good—and this morning I have been signing an agreement by which I shall sell my land to the University. And now I am thrown back again on my do-nothing life—how marvellous! Yet, as I have drawn out above, from habit, from recklessness, and from my late success, my feeling of despondency and irritation seems to have gone."

Perhaps the most interesting personal event of this period was his visit at Hursley to John Keble, whom he had not met for more than twenty years. And there he rather unexpectedly met Dr. Pusey, also after a separation of twenty years. A letter to Father Ambrose describes the occasion.

"I had forgotten the country, and was not prepared for its woodland beauty. Keble was at the door. He did not know me, nor I him. How mysterious that first sight of friends is, for, when I came to contemplate him, it was the old face and manner, but the first effect or impression was different. He then said, 'I must go and prepare Pusey.' He did so, and then took me into the house where Pusey was.

"I went in rapidly, and it is strange how action overcomes pain. Pusey, being passive, was evidently shrinking back into the corner of the room, as I should have done, had he rushed in upon me. He could not help contemplating the look of me narrowly and long. 'Ah,' I thought, 'you are thinking how old I have grown, and I see myself in you,—though you, I do think, are more altered than I.' Indeed, the alteration in him startled, I will add, pained and grieved me. I should have known him anywhere; his face is not changed, it is as if you looked at him through a prodigious magnifier. I recollect him short and small, with a round head and smallish features, flaxen curly hair; huddled up together from his shoulders downward, and walking fast. This as a young man; but comparing him even as he was when I last saw him in 1846, when he was slow in his motions and staid in his figure, there was a wonderful change in him. His head and features are half as large again; his chest is very broad and he is altogether large, and (don't say all this to anyone) he has a strange condescending way when he speaks. His voice is the same; were my eyes shut, I should not be sensible of any alteration.

"As we sat together at table, I had a painful thought, not acute pain, but heavy. Here were three old men, who had worked together vigorously in their prime. This is what they have come to—poor human nature! After twenty years they meet together round a table, but without a common cause of free outspoken thought; kind indeed, but subdued and antagonistic in their language to each other, and all of them with broken prospects, yet each viewing in his own way, the world in which those prospects lay. . . . Pusey is full of his book, the *Eirenicon*, which is

to be published, against Manning, and full of his speech on the
relations of physical science with the Bible, which he is to deliver
at the Church Congress at Norwich; full of polemics and hope.
Keble is quite different; he is as delightful as ever, and it seemed
to me as if he felt a sympathy and intimacy with me which he
did not show towards Pusey. I judge by the way and tone he
spoke to me of him. I took an early dinner with them; and when
the bell chimed at four o'clock for service, I got into my gig, and
so from Bishopstoke to Ryde, getting there between six and
seven."

Keble died within the year, and then followed the death of
Mrs. Keble, who had long been very ill and bedridden. Keble at
that time had passed his seventy-third year. Newman describes
his death in a letter written in April 1866.

"Keble was told that his wife could not live many hours. He
had borne up in spite of his great infirmities, longer than I had
supposed possible. He was seized with fainting fits. His friends
took him from her room. When he got into his own room, he
fancied it a church. He knelt down and said the Lord's Prayer.
Then he began a Latin hymn—we could not make out what.
Then he ended with the prayer which he first said on his knees as
a little child. These were his last words."

Newman was very indignant when, shortly after Keble's death,
certain ex-Anglicans—some now sceptics but some of them
Catholics—made some unkind remarks about Keble's failure to
become a Roman Catholic years before, implying that he had
been hypocritical. "It is grievous that people are so hard," he
wrote to his old friend Coleridge. "In converts it is inexcusable.
It is a miserable spirit in them. How strange it is;—Keble seems
to have received all doctrine except the necessity of being in communion with the Holy See. To continue what I said the other
day, it seems to me no difficulty to suppose a person in good faith
on such a point as the necessity of communion with Rome. Till
he saw that (or that he was not in the Church), he was bound

to remain as he was, and it was in that way that he always put it."

Thus it was that John Keble, his closest friend of Tractarian days after the death of Hurrell Froude, passed out of Newman's life; but tender memories lingered and never faded.

As for Dr. Pusey, the old friendship persisted; in fact, down to the latter's death, after the meeting with Keble in 1865, they kept in touch with each other, always on friendly terms and frequently indulging in extended letters. In this very year they were to engage in controversy anew after the publication of Pusey's book, *Eirenicon*, which contained an unfair attack on the Catholic Church's teaching of devotion to the Blessed Virgin Mary and, obliquely, a castigation of Archbishop Manning. Newman's *Letter to E. B. Pusey* (later published) was a masterpiece. Despite the fact that Manning had, in his view, been recently harassing him, Newman now rushed to the defence of both the Church and the Archbishop.

CHAPTER THIRTEEN

"HEART SPEAKETH UNTO HEART"

1

COR AD COR LOQUITUR—heart speaketh unto heart—adopted by Newman as the motto on his shield when he became a cardinal, was indeed appropriate for him—for he spoke to *all* hearts. It was during the half-dozen years following the publication of the *Apologia* that he produced three of the most notable works of his career—his greatest poem, his brilliant reply to Dr. Pusey in refutation of the latter's charges regarding the so-called "Mariolatry" in the Catholic Church, and the *Grammar of Assent*. Many-sided as he was, he achieved new distinction in all three fields. His lifelong preoccupation with the Unseen, the realm of the supernatural life, is reflected in *The Dream of Gerontius*; his beautiful conception of the Mother of God and her attributes is given to us in unequalled language in his reply to Dr. Pusey; and in the *Grammar of Assent* we have the finest example of that side of his mind which was always fascinated by the potentialities of Reason as related to Faith.

Thus we find that during a time when violent agitation was being carried on by outstanding Catholics like Manning, Ward and so on, regarding the pending Vatican Council, at which the infallibility of the Pope would be formally defined; and when Newman himself was once more being suspected of less than whole-hearted loyalty to the Church, he was quietly producing several of the greatest works of his career. Not that he was at all indifferent to these practical ecclesiastical questions; he was in the thick of the fight, as we shall see. But the remarkable thing is that in a time of so much commotion he could have produced some of his best intellectual and spiritual work. It was, of course, possible only because of his preoccupation with the spiritual aspects of life, these outweighing, in his view, the mundane entanglements of the hour—for to him the latter "were as so much dust, when weighed in the balance."

In these years, the peaceful round of duties at his Oratory and school invited a quiet and holy personal life and kept at a distance —for a time—the outer world of restlessness and clamor. We find him writing in his journal in October 1867:

"I was never in such happy circumstances as now, and I do not know how I can fancy I shall continue without some or other real cross. I am my own master—I have my time my own—I am surrounded with comforts and conveniences—I am in easy circumstances—I have no cares, I have good health—I have no pain of mind or body, I enjoy life only too well. The weight of years falls on me as snow, gently though surely, but I do not feel it yet. I am surrounded with dear friends—my reputation has been cleared up by the *Apologia*. What can I want but greater gratitude and love towards the Giver of all good things? There is no state of life I prefer to my own—I would not change my position for that of anyone I know—I am simply content—there is nothing I desire—I should be puzzled to know what to ask, if I were free to ask. I should say perhaps that I wish the financial matters of the Oratory and School to be in better state—but for myself I am covered with blessings, and as full of God's gifts as is conceivable. I have nothing to ask for but pardon and Grace and a happy death."

It was during this period of peace that he revisited Littlemore with Father St. John—his first return there after twenty-two years. To see once more the old familiar scenes of long ago touched him deeply. The story is told that a passer-by saw an old man, poorly dressed, leaning over the lych-gate of the church-yard that surrounds the Littlemore church, which Newman had built thirty years before; and that the old man was crying. "He was dressed," the observer said, "in an old gray coat with the collar turned up, and his hat was pulled down over his face, as if he wished to hide his features."

The old man leaning over the lych-gate was Newman. Some have thought that he was crying because he had left Anglicanism behind him at Littlemore. No, it was not Anglicanism that he missed; it was his beloved retreat at Littlemore, with its associations of friends and companions of past years, so many of whom had passed away or wandered off into other fields.

There was another—more amusing—incident which occurred a few years later. Dean Church, with whom the old Oxford intimacy had had a rebirth, sent him a news item clipped from a Somersetshire paper, asking him if there was anything in the story. The item was as follows:

"St. Paul's Cathedral. A few weeks since one of the Vergers of the Cathedral accosted a poorly clad, threadbare looking individual, who stood at the entrance scanning the alterations of the sacred edifice, with a 'Now then, move on, we don't want any of your sort here.' It was Dr. Newman."

Dean Church was naturally curious to get Newman's opinion of this report. This was the reply the latter sent:

"Yes, I was morally turned out and I told you so at the time. I did nothing but what you might have done in Chester or Carlisle, where you are not known. I stood just inside the door listening to the chant of the Psalms, of which I am very fond. First came Verger one, a respectable person, enquiring if I wanted a seat in the choir, half a mile away. No, I said,—I was content where I was. Then came the second, not respectable, with a voice of men-

ace. I still said No. Then came a third, I don't recollect much
about him, except that he said he could provide me with a seat.
Then came number two again in a compulsory mood,—and I
vanished. I am sure if I were a Dissenter, or again one of Mr.
Bradlaugh's people, nothing would attract me more to the
Church of England than to be allowed to stand at the door of a
Cathedral. Did not St. Augustine, when still a Manichee, stand
and watch St. Ambrose? No verger turned him out!"

That seemed enough; but rereading the clipping later, he was
disturbed by the word "threadbare." The state of his clothes was
always a touchy subject. He hastily wrote Church: "On the contrary it was a brand new suit, which I had never put on until I
went on that visit to you—and which I did not wear twice even
at Abbotsford—I thought it due to London. Indeed, all my visiting clothes are new, for I do not wear them here, and I am almost tempted, like a footman of my father's when a boy, to leave
home, in order to have an opportunity of wearing them."

2

The Dream of Gerontius, the writing of which belongs to this
period, was written on a sudden impulse, put aside before being
shown to anyone, and then forgotten. Later, the editor of *The
Month*, the Jesuit magazine, called and asked Newman for a
contribution. He rummaged among his papers to find something
already written, stumbled on these verses and told the editor he
might have them if he cared for them.

The editor of *The Month* did care. They appeared in the two
issues following and immediately caused a sensation. Widely read,
they were highly praised by Swinburne and other critics, both
Catholic and non-Catholic. It is said that Newman wrote them
in 1865, and the theme, which is a description of the passage

of a soul (your soul, my soul, anybody's soul) from earthly life through purgatory to the Beatific Vision, was perhaps inspired by the sudden death at that time of the Oratorian Father Gordon, who had been very close to him.

It is only possible to give the briefest outline of this famous poem; and this is best done by quoting a few of the most beautiful lines. The poem begins with Gerontius on his deathbed; the "dread visitant is knocking his dire summons at his door" : he is frightened and exclaims:

> 'Tis death,—O loving friends, your prayers!—'tis he!
> As though my very being had given way,
> As though I was no more a substance now,
> And could fall back on naught to be my stay.
> (Help, loving Lord! Thou my sole refuge, **Thou**)
> And turn no whither, but must needs decay
> And drop from out the universal frame
> Into that shapeless, scopeless, black abyss,
> That utter nothingness of which I came.

He hears the low voices of those in the room, chanting the Litany of the Dying, dimly, as though at a distance, for he is scarcely conscious. But he tries to cling to life, makes a declaration of Faith, while the prayers of those in the room soothe him as he all but slips away. Then he seems to go into a refreshing sleep and there comes to him a "heart subduing melody," the song of his guardian angel. He wonders now that he has no fear; but the angel tells him that it is a presage "as a ray, straight from the Judge, expressive of thy lot." At the same time he is conscious of evil spirits trying to clutch him, but this ceases as Gerontius seems soaring through choirs of angels singing hymns of praise of the Redemption. The final purification of his soul is now to come "in the fiery lake of Purgatory"; and Gerontius gives voice to one of the most beautiful lyrics that Newman ever wrote:

Take me away, and in the lowest deep
*   There let me be.*
And there in hope the lone night watches keep,
*   Told out for me.*
There, motionless and happy in my pain,
*   Lone, not forlorn,—*
There will I sing my sad perpetual strain
*   Until the morn.*
There will I sing and soothe my stricken breast,
*   Which ne'er can cease*
To throb, and pine, and languish, till possest
*   Of its Sole Peace.*
There will I sing my absent Lord and Love;—
*   Take me away,*
That sooner I may rise and go above,
*   And see Him in the truth of everlasting day.*

The voice of Gerontius ends now, but the words of his guardian angel are heard as his soul is immersed in the cleansing lake of purgation, bidding him farewell:

Softly and gently, dearly ransomed soul,
*   In my most loving arms I now enfold thee,*
And, o'er the penal waters as they roll,
*   I poise thee, and I lower thee, and hold thee.*

And carefully, I dip thee in the lake,
*   And thou, without a sob or a resistance,*
Dost through the flood thy rapid passage take,
*   Sinking deep, deeper into the dim distance.*

Angels, to whom the willing task is given,
*   Shall tend, and nurse, and lull thee, as thou liest;*
And Masses on the earth, and prayers in Heaven,
*   Shall aid thee at the Throne of the Most Highest.*

Farewell, but not forever, brother dear,
  Be brave and patient on thy bed of sorrow;
Swiftly shall pass thy night of trial here,
  And I will come and wake thee on the morrow.

These few quotations do not of course fully indicate the scope of this great poem. Only a full reading can do that. One should not miss the description of the scene where the priest begins by reciting the *Asperges*:—"Thou shalt sprinkle me with hyssop, and I shall be cleansed: Thou shalt wash me, and I shall be whiter than snow." The passing of the soul may be a matter of a mere second, but the priest's *"Subvenite, Sancti Dei,"* and in fact, all the prayers, seem to be heard by Gerontius as he falls asleep and then, awakened and refreshed, hears the voice of his guardian angel.

Literary critics point out flaws in this poem. It is far beyond my capacity to question this; but I insert a comment with regard to its significance made in 1890 by R. H. Hutton, editor of the London *Spectator*:

"None of his writings engraves more vividly on his readers the significance of the intensely practical convictions which shaped his career. And especially it impresses on us one of the great secrets of his influence. For Newman has been a sign to this generation that unless there is a great deal of the loneliness of death in life, there can hardly be much of the higher equanimity of life in death. To my mind the *Dream of Gerontius* is a poem of a man to whom the vision of the Christian Revelation has at all times been most real, more potent to influence action, and more powerful to preoccupy the imagination, than all worldly interests put together." [1]

---

[1] *Cardinal Newman.*

3

If the *Dream of Gerontius* emphasized Newman's lifelong pre-occupation with the reality of the supernatural, and conveyed to the world his conception of the loveliness of the life to come, to which God calls suffering humanity—in no less degree did he, in his famous "Reply to Dr. Pusey" (who had charged that the Catholic Church views the Blessed Virgin as equal to God Himself), demonstrate his understanding of and devotion to the Mother of God. In words of great beauty he pictured her true status and also her glories.

Many Protestants said hard things about Newman for his ardent devotion to the Blessed Virgin Mary, pointing out that he had claimed when an Anglican that the "Mariolatry" of the Catholic Church repelled him. It has been said that when, after he became a Catholic, he glorified Mary in his sermons, his new attitude "bewilders the Protestant imagination in his willingness to accept vague tradition of the most distant and uncertain origin, as evidence for historic fact, as that in which he deals with the death of the Mother of Christ."

Such bewilderment is due to ignorance of the Church's teaching of the supernatural. When Newman once understood this, he of course glorified Mary. He was not a mere visionary; his beliefs were based on objective realities: supernatural realities. For instance, he says of the Catholic Church: "Her sacraments and her hierarchical appointments will remain, even to the end of the world, after all but a symbol of the heavenly facts which fill eternity. Her mysteries are but the expression in human language of truths to which the human mind is unequal." In the operation of natural law he did not fail to recognize the supernatural agencies beyond. "Every breath of air and every ray of light and heat, every beautiful prospect is, as it were, the skirts of their garments, the waving of the robes of those who see God."

The occasion of Pusey's book was this. Pusey had been for some time disputing with Dr. Manning regarding the latter's view that the Anglican Church, even in its Puseyite section, was not truly Catholic; and hence there could not be that unity between the two Churches of which Pusey dreamed. Manning had recently sent an open letter to Pusey in which he dwelt on such differences as recognition of the Pope and veneration of the Blessed Virgin and the saints. Pusey's *Eirenicon* was a reply to Manning, in which he so grossly misinterpreted the Catholic teaching regarding the Mother of God that Newman, who had a high regard for Pusey and deeply respected his lifelong sincerity, felt impelled to write him an open letter refuting his charges and explaining the true teaching of the Church.

Basing his charges on some extravagant Italian forms of devotion and a few emotional writers, Pusey had asserted that the Catholic Church teaches that "the Blessed Virgin is superior to God; that Our Lord is subject to her command"; that she "takes His place as an Advocate with Father and Son; . . . that Mary alone can obtain a Protestant's conversion [this line to shock Protestants?]; . . . that as He is Priest, in a like sense is she Priestess; that His Body and Blood in the Eucharist are truly hers and appertain to her; that as He is present and received therein, so is she present and received therein"—and so on and so on.

That the famous Dr. Pusey, eminent as a scholar and a student of Catholic theology, seriously believed that the Catholic Church taught all this, utterly astonished Newman. He wrote to him: "Sentiments such as these I freely surrender to your animadversion; I never knew of them till I read your book. . . . I could not have conceived them to be said. . . . There is nothing of them in the Missal, in the Roman Catechism, in the Roman Raccolta, in the 'Imitation of Christ,' in Gother, Challoner, Milner, or Wiseman, as far as I am aware." He then proceeds to explain the true belief of Catholics concerning the Blessed Mother, as authorized by the Church. I insert a few outstanding passages:

"Did not the All-wise know the human heart when He took to Himself a Mother? Did He not anticipate our emotion at the sight of such an exaltation in one so simple and so lowly? If He had not meant her to exert that wonderful influence in His Church, which she has in the event exerted, I will use a bold word, He it is who has prevented her. If she is not to attract our homage, why did He make her solitary in her greatness amid His vast Creation? If it be idolatry in us to let our affections respond to our faith, He would not have made her what she is, or He would not have told us that He had so made her; but, far from this, He has sent His Prophet to announce to us, 'A Virgin shall conceive and bear a Son, and they shall call His name Emmanuel'; and we have the same warrant for hailing her as God's Mother, as we have for adoring Him as God."

He explains at great length the recognized position of the Church from the earliest times regarding the Blessed Mother, supplying a multitude of historical references; and then, after reminding Pusey of his (Pusey's) professed belief in her as the Virgin Mother, he says to him:

"What fullness of sanctity, what fullness and redundance of Grace, what exuberance of merits must have been hers, when once we admit the supposition, which the Fathers justify, that her Maker really did regard her merits and take them into account, when He condescended 'not to abhor the Virgin's womb.' Is it surprising then, that on the one hand she should be immaculate in her conception? Or that on the other she should be honored with an Assumption, and exalted as a queen with a crown of seven stars, with the rulers of day and night to do her service? Men sometimes wonder that we call her Mother of life, of mercy, of salvation; what are these titles compared to that one name, the Mother of God?"

Newman ends this long, fully documented letter to Pusey, with the following beautiful passage:

"So far concerning the Blessed Virgin; the chief, but not the only subject of your volume. And now, when I could wish to proceed, she seems to stop all controversy, for the Feast of the Immaculate Conception is upon us; and close upon its Octave, which is kept with special solemnities in the Churches in this town, come the great Antiphons, the heralds of Christmas. That joyful season,—joyful for all of us,—while it centres in Him Who then came on earth, also brings before us in peculiar prominence that Virgin Mother who bore and nursed Him. Here she is not in the background, as at Eastertide, but she brings Him to us in her arms. Two great Festivals, dedicated to her honor,—to-morrow's and the Purification,—mark out and keep the ground, and, like the towers of David, open the way to and fro, for the high holiday season of the Prince of Peace. And all along it her image is upon it, such as we see it in the typical representation of the Catacombs. May the sacred influences of this tide bring us all together in unity. May it destroy all bitterness on your side and ours! May it quench all jealous, sour, proud, fierce, antagonism on our side; and dissipate all captious, carping, fastidious, refinements of reasoning on yours! May that bright and gentle Lady, the Blessed Virgin Mary, overcome you with her sweetness, and revenge herself on her foes by interceding effectually for their conversion."

4

This letter to Pusey was greeted with enthusiasm by the Catholic world. Nor was it lost on the authorities at Rome, now more convinced than ever of Newman's power as a defender of the Faith. But William George Ward (now editor of the *Dublin*

Review) took exception to certain phrases Newman had used. With Manning's approval, he decided to attack it in the *Review*. But his article never appeared; Bishop Ullathorne called Archbishop Manning's attention to the fact that Ward would be overstepping his rights as a layman in censuring a member of the priesthood. So Manning called Ward off. But Newman, who had first received two congratulatory letters from Manning, learning that nevertheless he had approved Ward's planned attack, was furious with him. Manning tried to be conciliatory, but it was a long while before Newman could bring himself to forgive and forget. He wrote Bishop Ullathorne a heated letter about Manning. Manning, hearing of it, condemned it as "Temper! Temper!" It included this stinging passage:

"I will say to your Lordship that I cannot trust the Archbishop. Last spring he wrote to me flattering letters upon my letter to Pusey; and then he followed them up by privately sending to your Lordship for approval an article intended for the *Dublin Review,* in which I was severely handled for certain passages in it. I think that, as a matter of prudence, I never shall trust him till he has gone through Purgatory, and has no infirmities upon him."

That Newman knew his position on this matter to be stronger than Manning's is shown by a letter to his friend Miss Bowles: "When I published my letter to Pusey, he [Manning] sent two letters praising—but a little while after he sent two Bishops an article [Ward's] which was to appear in the *Dublin* against portions of it, asking their sanction to it. The one [Bishop Clifford] replied that, so far from agreeing with the article, he heartily agreed with me,—the other [Bishop Ullathorne] that, since he was my natural judge he would not commit himself by any previous extra-judicial opinion, and on the contrary, if the article was published, he should recommend me to commence ecclesiastical proceedings against the editor, in that he, [Ward] a layman, had ventured seriously to censure a priest. . . ."

Obviously there was plenty of fight in the resuscitated New-man. He would show more of it later on.

5

Before closing this chapter a few pages must be devoted to Newman's third fine achievement of this period, the completion of his famous work on Faith and Reason, the *Grammar of Assent*. For years he had been preoccupied with the subject, but put off work on it again and again. But while he was on a holiday in Switzerland in the summer of 1865, the theme gripped him anew. It was, he said, "a subject which had teased me for these twenty or thirty years. I felt I had something to say upon it, yet, whenever I attempted, the sight I saw vanished, plunged into a thicket, curled itself up like a hedgehog, or changed colors like a chameleon. . . . At last . . . when I was up at Glion, over the Lake of Geneva, a thought came into my head as the clue, the 'open sesame,' of the whole subject, and I at once wrote it down, and I pursued it about the Lake of Lucerne. Then, when I came home I began in earnest and have slowly got through it."

I shall not attempt a full analysis of this remarkable book; but it may be well to indicate a few high-lights of his theme. Depart-ing somewhat—though not in essentials—from the scholastics, he holds that Reason alone, in view of the limitations of our human nature, is not enough, with its usual logical abstractions, to account wholly for our certitudes. Hence he insists that a man believes, not alone with his mind or intellect, but with his whole being—heart, mind and soul as indissolubly one. This thesis leads him to emphasize the difference between what he calls *notional* assent and *real* assent.

By "notional assent" he means the sort of assent we give to any abstract proposition through the operation of the mind alone.

"Real assent," on the other hand, is that which grows out of our own personal experience and in response to our entire being. He then discusses these two distinct attitudes of the mind. If the proposition is accepted merely as a result of abstract reasoning, it is classed by him as *inference*. If, however, the proposition is at once accepted without reservation, then it is *assent*. When the assent involves a particular concrete fact, it is *real* assent; when it involves some abstract or general idea it is *notional* assent.

He is careful to explain his definitions, that there may be no confusion. And then he emphasizes the fact that whereas both types of assent are equally valid, *real* assent, by reason of its direct, intuitive character, is a living thing which results in action and conduct, while *notional* assent is inert and remains sterile in the mind.

Except for the close student accustomed to logical reasoning, the book is difficult. Indeed, it gives evidence of his own struggles to elucidate his subject clearly. But when (as he often does) he illuminates his thesis by concrete examples, his ideas come home to us vividly. There are many passages in the book (as there are in his *Development of Christian Doctrine*) which make it fascinating reading for the common man. One is an illustration he employs to indicate the difference between notional and real assents.

"Let us consider, too, how differently young and old are affected by the words of some classic author, such as Homer or Horace. Passages, which to a boy are but rhetorical commonplaces, neither better nor worse than a hundred others which any clever writer might supply, which he gets by heart and thinks very fine, and imitates, as he thinks, successfully, in his own flowing versification, at length come home to him, when long years have passed and he has had experience of life, and pierce him, as if he had never before known them, with their sad earnestness and vivid exactness. Then he comes to understand how it is that lines, the birth of some chance morning or evening at an Ionian

Festival, or among the Sabine hills, have lasted generation after generation, for thousands of years, with a power over the mind, and a charm, which the current literature of his own day, with all its obvious advantages, is utterly unable to rival. Perhaps this is the reason of the medieval opinion about Virgil, as if a prophet or magician; his single words and phrases, his pathetic half-lines, giving utterance, as the voice of Nature herself, to that pain and weariness, yet hope of better things, which is the experience of her children in every time."

That he was conscious of the difficulties of his attempt to elucidate his subject, is indicated by letters to friends. One to Henry Wilberforce regarding the relative status of Faith and Reason between a Catholic and a freethinker, will bear quoting:

"As to what I have done [the writing of the book], I cannot tell if it is a Truism, a Paradox, or a Mare's nest. Since it certainly *may* be any one of the three, the chance of its being anything better is not encouraging. I consider that there is no such thing as a perfect logical demonstration; that there is always a margin of objection even in Mathematics, except in the case of short proofs, as the propositions of Euclid. Yet on the other hand it is a paradox to say there is not such a state of mind as certitude. It is as well ascertained a state of mind, as doubt—to say that such a phenomenon in the human mind is a mere extravagance or weakness is a monstrous assertion which I cannot swallow. Of course there may be abuses and mistakes in particular cases of certitude, but that is another matter. *It is a law of our nature*, then, that we are certain on premises which do not reach demonstration. This seems to me undeniable. . . .

"Now I know to say all this and no more, is to open the door to endless disputes. . . . The key, however, of the position, in the controversy which is before us, is this—and to gain that on either side is the victory—whether you may or may not rationally keep your mind *open* to change on a point on which your convictions have already told you to decide one way. Here I say there is a difference between science and religion. . . . Ought I to be as open to listen to objections brought to me against the honor, fidelity, love towards me of a friend, as against the received belief that the earth is 95 million miles from the sun? Again, there is a truth which no natural reason can gain, *revealed*. God may put his own *conditions* on the development of that truth,—and (though at first sight paradoxical) He may make one of those conditions to be a slowness to receive more truth—(I don't mean of course a slowness to be taught, but a slowness to see that He is teaching). This condition may be necessary on conservative reasons, from the extreme difficulty to human nature of retaining what is supernatural, so that, if we took in new truths too quickly, we might lose the old. . . . When I am asked why I *cautiously and promptly* exclude doubts, I answer I do so because they *are* doubts; I don't see the need of excluding objections. . . . How could God exist without beginning? In reason this is no objection, for reason tells us that *something* must have been without beginning. But to the imagination it is an overpowering difficulty. To a half educated man I should say, strangle the doubt—don't read the book which so affects you. This is not bidding him not to listen to reasons, but to insufficient reasons, to false reasons, which are a temptation to him. The rule, 'strangle doubts,' is a rule of the Confessional, not a point of dogmatic theology. And as to prayer, *usum non tollit abusus*. God has given His friends a privilege—that of gaining favors from Him. A father says to his child going to school, 'Now mind you write to me once a week.' And he rewards him in various ways, if he is obedient in this respect—we are God's children—we are not grown men—Saints would worship God solely because He is God—we all love Him for Himself, but, considering what we are, it is merciful that He has made hope as well as faith and love, a theological virtue. But this is but a poor and scanty exposure of a wonderful paradox. . . ."

For Newman, the key to truth is found in personality; whereas most metaphysicians reason from universals to arrive at particulars, he reverses the process. "Let concretes come first," he said, "and so-called universals second." Not for nothing had he in earlier days saturated himself with the Alexandrian Fathers, with their discussions of the Incarnation and matters like the mystery of the Holy Trinity; for on their great teaching he had built his own religion. In many ways he was unique, making admissions which to some appeared to be characterized by scepticism; and introducing ideas which were novel indeed. As Canon Barry said, in his study of Cardinal Newman:

"It would be difficult to name a controversial divine who had ever made these admissions in this way before; to the unphilosophical, of which Kingsley and J. A. Froude were a type, they would seem to border on scepticism, to conceal infinite reserve, and to furnish bigotry with weapons of defence. Newman was engaged upon two inquiries, for which the shallow enlightenment of an age when Bentham was a prophet and Macaulay a teacher, could not be prepared. He was grappling with the idea of evolution and the fact of the unconscious. So have they been termed since; in his language we call the one 'development,' the other 'implicit reason.' His claim to be original in philosophy rests on discoveries to which the zeal for theology impelled him." [1]

6

The *Grammar of Assent*, when it appeared in 1870, was applauded in some Catholic circles, criticised in others. Certain Jesuits claimed that it was contradictory, in some particulars, to the scholastic viewpoint. This led to a controversy between Newman and Father Thomas Harper, S.J., which Newman welcomed,

---

[1] William Barry, *Cardinal Newman, a Study*.

for he had claimed no infallibility for his reasoning; but he had the last triumphant word. The book was, of course, criticised by Dr. Orestes Brownson; but by this time Newman had become immune to the latter's missiles. On the other hand, wonder of wonders (to Newman), William George Ward highly praised the book; and the "estrangement" between these two converts extending over many years now began to break down. Ward wrote to Newman that he was sure the book would form the basis for a new and important phase of Catholic philosophy; his congratulations were enthusiastic; and he proceeded to write a series of articles for the *Dublin Review*, strongly praising it.

That this gesture of Ward's delighted Newman is shown by a letter to Ward at this time. "It is a great pleasure to me to receive your letter, both as expressing a favorable opinion of my book and recording a point of agreement between us on an important subject. . . . It would be strange indeed if I were not quite aware, as I am, that there are portions of my theory which require finishing and revising. I expect it to be my last work; meaning by work labor and toil."

Perhaps a few lines will fit in here regarding the long estrangement between Ward and Newman. There is an amusing side to Ward's "estrangements." He was possessed of a conscience which told him that it was his *duty* to break with his family and intimate friends who differed with him on religion and refused to be converted. His estrangement with Newman was of this nature. Newman refused to see things through Ward's eyes. But it is evident that Ward never felt any personal resentment, whether Newman did or not. And so when they did finally find themselves in agreement on an important matter, as with Newman's new book, there was evidently no need of burying hatchets. They bowed to each other with unruffled cordiality—though I think Newman still kept a weather eye on Ward.

Ward's notion of estrangements is well illustrated by his relations with his brother Henry. This brother strongly disapproved of his becoming a Catholic; they seem to have differed on most other subjects also. But instead of quarreling, W. G. Ward decided, after his conversion to Catholicism, to ignore his brother, treating him as a stranger and having no contact with him. It is evident that Henry had the same cast of mind, for he readily agreed to this arrangement.

The amusing side of this matter is emphasized by an incident cited by Ward's son Wilfrid. It happened that one night the two brothers accidentally met at the Haymarket Theatre. Both forgot their "estrangement" and entered into friendly conversation. But the next morning a note arrived from Henry: "Dear William, in the hurry of the moment tonight I quite forgot that we agreed to meet as strangers, and I write this lest you misunderstand me, to say I think we had better adhere to our arrangement, and I remain, dear William, your affectionate brother, Henry Ward." William immediately replied: "Dear Henry, I too had forgotten our arrangement. I agree with you that we had better keep it up; and I remain, your affectionate brother, W. G. Ward."

But this rule of insisting that relatives or intimate friends be treated as strangers, should they differ with him on the subject of religion, did not apply to others who *were* strangers or mere casual acquaintances. He was ready at all times to dispute with such on any subject under the sun, and especially with those whose views on religion were the reverse of his own. But he always stated his own views with unqualified bluntness, regardless of consequences.

An illustration relates to his first meeting with Thomas Henry Huxley (an equally blunt person). He had joined the Metaphysical Society, an organization made up of a number of distinguished men, mostly of very sceptical views. Typical of their class was Huxley, a man of no religious beliefs whatever. He called himself an agnostic; in fact, he claims to have invented the term. At the first meeting, when Ward was to join in a debate, it was ruled that no charges of moral reprobation, or personal attacks of any kind, could be indulged in by the debaters. In reference to this ruling, Mr. Ward arose and said:

"While acquiescing in this condition as a general rule, I think it cannot be expected that Christian thinkers shall give no sign whatever of the horror with which they would view the spread of such extreme opinions as those advocated by Mr. Huxley."

This quite naturally brought Huxley to his feet with this remark: "As Dr. Ward has spoken I must in fairness say that it will be very difficult for me to conceal my feelings as to the intellectual degradation which would come of the general acceptance of such views as Dr. Ward holds." [1] After that, the chairman must have had to work hard to restore order.

But despite this antagonistic beginning, his speaking acquaintance with Huxley, whose ideas he loathed, continued indefinitely —while his family arrangement of non-intercourse was carefully respected.

A unique but utterly sincere character was William George Ward. He surely made the dust fly in the intellectual atmosphere of English Catholicism, more so than all the other Oxford converts bundled together.

---

[1] Wilfrid Ward, *William George Ward and the Catholic Revival.*

CHAPTER FOURTEEN

THE LAST STORM

1

NEARLY FORTY YEARS had gone by since the beginning of the Whig ascendancy in Parliament, when the Benthamite philosophy of utilitarianism, with its antagonism toward traditional Christianity, had first alarmed men like John Keble, who had inspired the Oxford awakening in which Newman had so outstanding a part. In that earlier time the effect on modern thought of men like John Stuart Mill (the most conspicuous of those who were to "perfect and refine" the cruder ideas of Jeremy Bentham) was but beginning. But by 1870, the teachings of this brilliant utilitarian in the science of political economy and theory were quite paramount; and, in the domain of religious thought, his views had done not a little to qualify the beliefs of practically every Christian communion except the Catholic. In both Oxford and Cambridge utilitarian philosophy was now being given far more attention than any form of Christian teaching.

John Stuart Mill was a younger contemporary of John Henry Newman. Born in 1806 he lived on until 1875. The eldest son of James Mill (a freethinker and associate of Bentham), he went far beyond his father as a champion of materialism, but closely followed him in his views on religious belief. In the younger Mill's autobiography, written near the close of his life, he says:

"My father, educated in the creed of Scotch Presbyterianism, had by his own studies and reflections been early led to reject not only the belief in Revelation, but in the foundations of what is commonly called Natural Religion. . . . I was thus one of the very few examples in this country, of one who has not thrown off religious belief, but never had it; I grew up in a negative state with regard to it. I looked upon modern exactly as I did ancient religion, as something which in no way concerned me. This point in my early education, however, had one bad consequence deserving notice. In giving an opinion contrary to the religious world, my father thought it necessary to give it as one which could not prudently be avowed to the world. This lesson of keeping my thoughts to myself, at that early age, was attended with some moral disadvantages; though my limited intercourse with strangers, especially such as were likely to speak to me on religion, prevented me from being placed in the alternative of avowal or hypocrisy."

Then Mill goes on to say: "The world would be astonished if it knew how great a proportion of its brightest ornaments—of those most distinguished in popular estimation for religion and virtue—are complete sceptics in religion; many of them refraining from avowal, less from personal considerations, than from a conscientious, though now in my opinion a most mistaken apprehension, lest by speaking out what would tend to weaken existing beliefs, and by consequence (as they suppose) of existing restraints, they should do more harm than good."

When John Stuart Mill gave expression to the opinion that "those most distinguished in popular estimation for religion and virtue are complete sceptics in religion," he was describing a condition which, in the last half of the nineteenth century, had spread widely throughout Great Britain as well as on the European Continent. It was a time of increasing scepticism; Darwinism, as promoted by Thomas Huxley, the apostle of agnosticism, was undermining orthodox faith among the educated classes, while

John Tyndall and Herbert Spencer were busily at work helping along this new era of "enlightenment," and the famous French writer Ernest Renan, with his *Vie de Jésus* (now translated into English), was undermining the faith of thousands of English men and women in the Divinity of Christ.

In this same period, the leaders of the Anglican Broad Church school were trying to harmonize their beliefs with this sceptical trend—mainly by dropping or qualifying literal interpretations of Christian dogmas and introducing symbolical meanings. Dean Stanley and Dr. Benjamin Jowett were conspicuous exponents of this school; and among the cultured laity, Matthew Arnold was becoming their prophet. These were of those whom John Stuart Mill classed as "most distinguished in popular estimation for religion and virtue."

Of course England still comprised large groups who adhered to old religious traditions, though increasing portions of all Protestant sects were accepting the new opinions, and more "liberal" sects were springing up. Also frank unbelievers, like Charles Bradlaugh, were getting a wide hearing. As for the Puseyites, with their outstanding leaders, Dr. Pusey, R. W. Church and Canon H. P. Liddon, they were struggling mightily against this dissolving trend in their own communion. But their way was hard, and they suffered much persecution from the more popular liberalizers, who were steadily infiltrating into their Church the sceptical philosophies of Mill, Huxley and Spencer.

This wave of nineteenth century scepticism did its best to shake the foundations of the Catholic Church, but with no success. It is one more demonstration of the stability of the Rock of Peter, that at this time she proclaimed to the sceptical and cynical world several great pronouncements which contradicted this materialism. In the year 1854, the dogma of the Immaculate Conception was defined; in 1864 Pope Pius IX issued his famous *Syllabus,* condemning all the errors of the modern materialistic school;

and at the Vatican Council in 1870—the first ecumenical council since the Council of Trent in the sixteenth century—the dogma of the Infallibility of the Pope in *ex cathedra* pronouncements was defined.

All three of these acts were of course derided by those "most distinguished in popular estimation for religion and virtue" in England, as well as by all full-blown sceptics. They were also greeted with ridicule by many of those non-Catholics who still adhered to much orthodox Christianity—like the Puseyites in the Church of England. The latter rejoiced that the Roman Church was now headed by a reactionary Pontiff, who, they said, was weakening his Church among the thoughtful; and they expected to profit by an influx of more "liberal" Catholics coming into their camp—an expectation which was not realized however: for there was no lapsing of Catholics to Anglicanism. In fact, conversions of Anglicans to the Catholic Church during these years were as numerous as at any time since the 1840's.

2

The pontificate of Pius IX, extending from 1846 to 1878, was not only the longest of any occupant of the Papal chair but was the stormiest of any Pope since the days of Innocent III in the thirteenth century. He was ever confronted with tragic circumstances. Yet he came through it all with flying colors, and when, at the age of eighty-five, he departed this life, the news of his death came as a distinct shock to the entire world—Catholic and non-Catholic.

When he became Pope in 1846, all Italy was in a political turmoil and on the threshold of wars which would last many years. Mazzini was then becoming a power, as was Garibaldi, not to mention Count Cavour. These leaders differed in many things but were always united on one thing—the overthrow of the temporal power of the Papacy.

The new Pope began by inaugurating many reforms; but while his program of reform was approved by these politicians, they had no intention of modifying their plans for undermining the Church. All the revolutionary leaders in Italy were definitely anti-clerical and strong champions of the modern philosophy of materialism.

War shortly broke out between Sardinia and Austria; the Sardinians invaded Papal territory, drawing the Papal States against their will into the Austrian war. The Pope opposed this but was powerless to prevent it; then his chief minister, Count Rossi, was murdered and the Pope made a prisoner. But luckily he was able to escape from Rome, going to Gaeta, near Naples, where he was to remain until early in 1850. Then the ill-starred Roman Republic set up by Garibaldi fell (owing to the intervention of the French) and Pope Pius was able to return to Rome.

Despite all these tumultuous events, the Pope carried on in Gaeta in traditional fashion. And after he had returned to Rome he proclaimed 1850 a Jubilee year. At the same time he issued the bull which restored the Catholic hierarchy in England; he appointed Bishop Wiseman the new Archbishop of Westminster and bestowed upon him the cardinalate.

From this time on the Pope remained in Rome; but unsettlement on the Italian peninsula persisted, with but temporary lulls, until the new kingdom of Italy came into being in 1870. The Papacy then suffered the loss of all its "temporalities," and the long distressing period ensued, with the Pope a voluntary "prisoner" in the Vatican. This situation was not brought to an end until the days of Pope Pius XI, when the Lateran Treaty of 1929 was signed, a compromise with the kingdom of Italy which resulted in the creation of the small section in the heart of the

city of Rome known as Vatican City, under exclusive ownership
and control of the Church.

This long period of turmoil spread over John Henry Newman's
entire life in the Catholic Church until 1870. When, in 1847, he
was in Rome, studying for the priesthood, the Italian disturb-
ances had already begun. In 1849, when he was building up his
Oratory at Birmingham, Pope Pius had fled to Gaeta. A year
later, at the time of the so-called "Papal Aggression," Newman
was under fire like all other English Catholics. In 1854, when
Pope Pius formally defined the dogma of the Immaculate Conception, Newman had already delivered his great sermon on "The
Glories of Mary for the Sake of Her Son," [1] and was being derided, as the Pope was derided in 1854, not only by sceptics but
by the leading Puseyites—who did not dream that their lineal
descendants in our time would be celebrating both the Feast of
the Assumption and the Feast of the Immaculate Conception!
And in the year 1864, when Pope Pius gave his great *Syllabus* to
the world, condemning the materialistic teachings of modern
thinkers like Mill, Huxley and Spencer, Newman was publishing
his *Apologia*, in which, among other things, he said:

". . . in these latter days . . . outside the Catholic Church,
things are tending . . . to atheism in one shape or other. What
a scene, what a prospect, does the whole of Europe present at
this day: and not only Europe, but every government and every
civilization through the world which is under the influence of the
European mind. Especially, for it most concerns us, how sorrowful, in the view of religion, even taken in its most elementary,
most attenuated form, is the spectacle presented to us by the
educated intellect of England, France and Germany. Lovers of
their country, and of their race, religious men, external to the
Catholic Church, have attempted various expedients to arrest

---

[1] This is one of the most beautiful discourses of Newman's career. It was delivered in 1849 and is found in the volume entitled, *Discourses to Mixed
Congregations.*

fierce, wilful human nature in its onward course, and to bring it
into subjection. . . . Thirty years ago, education was relied
upon; ten years ago there was a hope [in England] that wars
would cease forever, under the influence of commercial enterprise
and the reign of the useful and fine arts; but will any one venture
to say that there is anything anywhere on this earth, which will
afford a fulcrum for us, whereby to keep the earth from moving
onwards?"

In these words Newman was indicting the very errors that
Pope Pius condemned in his famous *Syllabus*, which was greeted
by the non-Catholic world as hopelessly reactionary. Many critics
of Newman (and even some admirers) have expressed the view
that this "literary recluse" was never alive to the social trends of
his day; that he displayed no interest in or understanding of the
momentous happenings of his time, which were leading the world
on its "march of progress to a higher social and material civilization." Just the reverse of this was true. He was as fully alive to
the dire effects of the views that Pope Pius condemned in his
Syllabus as any man of his time. In his old age, in writing to a
friend, he says:

"My apprehensions are not new, but above fifty years standing. I have all that time thought that a time of widespread infidelity was coming, and all through those years the waters have
in fact been rising as a deluge. I look for the time after my life,
when only the tops of the mountains will be seen like islands in
the waste of waters. I speak principally of the Protestant world—
but great actions and successes must be achieved by the Catholic
leaders, great wisdom as well as courage must be given them from
on high, if Holy Church is to be kept safe from this awful
calamity, and though any trial which came upon her would be
temporary, it may be fierce in the extreme while it lasts." [1]

---

[1] These words of Newman were prophetic. Have we not, in the present world
debacle, reached that time "when only the tops of the mountains [are] seen
like islands in the waste of waters"?

3

What was the nature and purpose of this *Syllabus of Errors*? It was a list of eighty "erroneous propositions," each with citations to support the condemnations of the errors listed. All of the erroneous doctrines which were condemned were being held, more or less, by that modern world of secularism, which was turning its back on the teachings of Christ.

The general purpose was, of course, to emphasize once again the Church's age-long opposition to man-made panaceas and nostrums as remedies for evils and to reiterate her teaching that this new Liberal view of man's person as a soul-less, earthbound creature, all-sufficient unto himself, independent of God, was a false and devastating philosophy. Just as the dogma of the Immaculate Conception, defined in 1854, signified that the Mother of God came into this world free from original sin, and so emphasized the Church's belief in the Supernatural and the Divine mysteries; so did the *Syllabus of Errors* condemn all teachings, which denied, directly or indirectly, the true nature of man as a child of God with an immortal destiny; which denied the Christian Creed as interpreted by Christ's Church; and, in short, denied the fact of Divine Revelation—that God had spoken and through His Son had offered redemption to a fallen humanity.

It is beyond the scope of this chapter to detail the numerous errors anathematized by Pope Pius, but they were all antichristian.

Probably the most furious resentment of the "enlightened" modern prophets of progress was of the Pope's basic contention that mankind is a fallen race as the result of "original sin"; for of course that doctrine had been one of the first to be abandoned by the Protestant world when men like John Locke began to preach the "perfectibility" of the natural man. Original sin had been distorted into a detestable doctrine by John Calvin, and now even his followers had begun to reject it; and all through the nineteenth century other Protestant sects were abandoning it entirely, as they took on the more pleasing teaching of the modern sceptical pundits.

Yet here again we find that Newman, writing his *Apologia* in the same year that Pope Pius anathematized the theory of man's perfectibility without supernatural aid, was the author of a striking paragraph on the doctrine of the Fall of Man which has become famous.

"To consider the world in its length and breadth, its various history, the many races of men, their starts, their fortunes, their mutual alienation, their conflicts; and then their ways, habits, governments, forms of worship; their enterprises, their aimless courses, their random achievements and acquirements, the impotent conclusion of long-standing facts; the tokens, so faint and broken, of a superintending design, the blind evolution of what turn out to be great powers or truths, the progress of things, as if from unreasoning elements, not towards final causes, the greatness and littleness of man, his far-reaching aims, his short duration, the curtain hung over his futurity, the disappointments of life, the defeat of good, the success of evil, physical pain, mental anguish, the prevalence and intensity of sin, the pervading idolatries, the corruptions, the dreary hopeless irreligion, that condition of the whole race, so fearfully yet exactly described in the Apostle's words, '. . . having no hope and without God in the world'—all this is a vision to dizzy and appal; and inflicts upon the mind the sense of a profound mystery, which is absolutely beyond human solution.

"What shall be said to this heart-piercing, reason-bewildering fact? I can only answer, that either there is no Creator, or this living society of men is in a true sense discarded from His pres-

ence. Did I see a boy of good make and mind, with the tokens
on him of a refined nature, cast upon the world without provi-
sion, unable to say whence he came, his birth-place or his family
connections, I should conclude that there was some mystery connected with his history, and that he was one, of whom, for one
cause or another, his parents were ashamed. Thus only should I
be able to account for the contrast between the promise and condition of his being. And so I argue about the world;—*if* there be
a God, *since* there is a God, the human race is implicated in some
terrible aboriginal calamity. It is out of joint with the purposes of
its Creator. This is a fact, a fact as true as the fact of its existence; and thus the doctrine of what is theologically called 'original sin,' becomes to me as certain as that the world exists, and as
the existence of God."

I have inserted these somewhat extensive quotations from his
writings to indicate Newman's true attitude to the Papal Definition of the Immaculate Conception and to the Encyclical of
Pius IX in 1864, with his *Syllabus of Errors*, condemning contemporary non-Catholic teachings. It will be seen how closely in
harmony with the thought of the Church Newman was at that
time. It would scarcely be necessary to point this out were it not
that the notion still enjoys wide currency that Newman was not
in sympathy either with the defining of the dogma of the Immaculate Conception, or with the issuing of the *Syllabus*—though, as
an obedient son of the Church, he conformed!

But what of his attitude to the third declaration, during the
Pontificate of Pius IX—Papal Infallibility, which was defined as
a dogma at the Vatican Council of 1870? This is the instance in
which, his critics have said, he failed to conform to the mind of
the Church—at least, in which he did not interiorly conform.
But let us see.

4

For twenty years or more, debate bearing on the question of formally defining this dogma had been going on between groups within the Church, one group strongly advocating the view that the definition would be timely, the other maintaining a negative stand. Not that any group in the Church denied the *fact* of Papal Infallibility any more than they denied the Divine Authority of the Church. But there was division of opinion as to the limitations of the Infallibility—and as to the timeliness of the proposed definition.

A powerful factor in favor of bringing the matter up at this time was the growing menace of modern scepticism, which seemed to be sweeping all before it. And just as the issuing of the *Syllabus* in 1864 had been in the nature of a rebuke to the sceptical world, so was it felt by many that it would be most timely to emphasize the dogma of Infallibility—not only to the outside world but to Catholics also—by a formal definition; for this fundamental truth seemed in some quarters to be obscured because, though held by the Church from the earliest times, it had never been *formally* defined as an article of faith.[1]

Doubtless another factor which created popular enthusiasm for the definition in large sections of the Church was the spectacle of the heroic Pope, Pius IX, in strife all his days but with a striking consciousness of his divine mission. He, personally, was definitely in favor of defining the Infallibility at this time.

Archbishop Manning, with his intellectual and equally aggressive friend William George Ward, took a strong stand with

---

[1] The Vatican Council, which convened in December 1869 and adjourned in October 1870, was not convened primarily to debate the question of the definition, as is often assumed. This was only one of many questions to be decided. Though there was some opposition, the dogma was favored by a very large majority and when promulgated was accepted by all the bishops.

the powerful group of Continental prelates who definitely favored the definition, exerting his best talents to line up the Catholics in England, not to mention hesitant ones elsewhere. William George Ward, being a layman, could not be a part of the Council, but at least he could make the fur fly in the columns of the *Dublin Review*. Needless to say, he did!

As for Newman, his attitude was quite characteristic. He approached this question precisely as, all his life long, he had approached every important religious problem that involved a decision and a conclusion. He who had required four or more years to clarify his own mind on the problem of becoming a Catholic (even though he had already accepted most Catholic truth), approached the question of defining the Infallibility in the same cautious, careful way. He felt that the noisy advocates of the definition, like Manning, were in too much of a hurry and were going too fast; that this "development of dogma," like many other of the dogmas in the Church, should be given its full time for flowering. This had not been his attitude toward the definition of the Immaculate Conception in 1854, for he had felt that that definition was really long overdue.

Consequently he ranged himself with those who were opposed to defining the dogma at that particular time. There were many such, though most of them were not *opposed* beyond holding that it would be better to delay matters to some more opportune time. Newman was of this type; he was not at any time in the position of men like the well known Dr. Döllinger of Munich, who altogether rejected belief in the dogma of Papal infallibility. Again and again, while the controversy was raging, and when he rather recklessly spoke of Manning's group as "an insolent and aggressive faction," Newman asserted that since becoming a Catholic he had of course believed in the Pope's infallibility in *ex cathedra* pronouncements, and, should the Council adopt a definition officially, he would be among the first to conform. But Manning and his following were agitating for a form of definition which, he feared, would imply that the Pope was personally impeccable, as well as infallible in all his judgments, regardless of their scope. It was his fear that this might prevail that caused the cautious Newman to use intemperate language.

When the Vatican Council was about to be convened, Pope Pius personally invited Newman to attend its sessions and take part. But it was typical of him that he asked to be excused. He was not a bishop and would have no official status at the Council. But while he did not attend, he did much to help Bishop Ullathorne, Bishop Clifford of Clifton and Bishop Dupanloup of Orleans, whose views were much like his own. His counsel and advice were of much help to these friends. A characteristic letter, bearing on his reluctance to plunge into the turmoil, written to Sister Maria Pia (the former Maria Rosena Giberne, a friend and admirer of many years) will bear quoting.

"Don't be annoyed," he wrote, "I am more happy as I am [remaining home] than in any other way. I can't bear the kind of trouble I should have, if I were brought forward in any public way. Recollect, I could not be *in* the Council unless I were a bishop—and really and truly I am *not* a theologian. A theologian is one who has mastered theology—one who can say how many opinions there are on every point, what authors have taken which, and which is the best—who can discriminate exactly between proposition and proposition, argument and argument, who can pronounce which are safe, which allowable, which dangerous —who can trace the history of doctrines in successive centuries, and apply the principles of former times to the conditions of the present. This is to be a theologian—this and a hundred things besides—which I am not, and never shall be. Like Saint Gregory Nazianzen, I like going my own way, and having my time my own, living without pomp or state, or pressing engagements. Put me in official garb, and I am worth nothing; leave me to myself, and every now and then I shall do something. Dress me up, and you will soon have to make my shroud—leave me alone, and I shall live the appointed time. Now take this in, as a sensible nun."

One would venture to say that in describing in the above letter the qualifications necessary for a theologian, Newman was coming pretty close to describing himself. But his inherent modesty and humility would never allow him to admit this.

When the definition was finally proclaimed in the summer of 1870, it turned out to be exactly what Newman had always believed as to the limitations of Papal Infallibility, not the extreme form which Archbishop Manning and William George Ward and their followers had been advocating. That Newman was surprised at the outcome as well as gratified, there is no denying. But he was greatly relieved and immediately undertook to defend it; his letters at this time fully confirm this fact. Though he had felt that the pronouncement of any definition at this time was hardly necessary and that, in any event, the matter should be approached more deliberately (for he feared that any definition such as Manning and Ward wanted would cause hesitation on the part of non-Catholics who were otherwise attracted to the Church), he was now to rejoice that the Council had simply defined a dogma of the Faith in the form which had been held implicitly from ancient times and in which he had believed ever since he became a Catholic.[1]

---

[1] To indicate the precise character of the definition adopted regarding the *Infallibility,* the following words in which the Vatican Counsel stated it are here quoted: "Faithfully adhering to the tradition handed down from the beginning of the Christian Faith for the Glory of God, our Saviour, the exaltation of the Catholic religion, and the salvation of Christian peoples, with the approval of the Holy Council, we teach and define it to be a Divinely revealed dogma, that the Roman Pontiff when he speaks *ex cathedra,* that is, when in discharge of his office as Pastor and teacher of all Christians, he defines in virtue of his supreme Apostolic authority a doctrine concerning Faith or Morals to be held by the Universal Church, is, through the Divine assistance, promised to him in Blessed Peter, possessed of that infallibility with which the Divine Redeemer willed His Church to be endowed, in defining doctrines concerning Faith and Morals; and therefore such definitions of the Roman Pontiff are of themselves, and not through the consent of the Church, irre-

As a result of this outcome, he was now in a better position to defend the dogma than was either Manning or Ward—who had really wanted something quite different. And when the opportunity came a few years later to defend it eloquently, he succeeded beyond the expectations of himself or his friends.

The definition was, of course, sweepingly criticised and ridiculed by the Liberals; and one of the most conspicuous lay members of the Anglican Church, who was classed as a Puseyite—William Ewart Gladstone—now saw fit to launch an aggressive attack on the dogma and on the Catholic Church as a whole. In this attack he doubtless voiced the views of most English Protestants.

Archbishop Manning undertook to reply to Gladstone's attack, but this seemed not to impress Gladstone to any marked extent. Then Newman was urged to take up the cudgels. He did so in his famous *Letter to the Duke of Norfolk*, a sweeping logical defence of the dogma and of the Catholic Church. It was a very scholarly defence and was a great triumph for Newman. But it was not, at the moment, an unalloyed triumph. Although Manning gave it unstinted praise and William George Ward reviewed it approvingly in the *Dublin Review*, trouble arose in Rome. The translation of the *Letter* sent to Propaganda was poorly done, and Cardinal Franchi at Rome thought he detected in it some passages which were questionable. He asked Archbishop Manning to have Newman make some corrections. But Manning now came out strongly in Newman's defence, writing Cardinal Franchi as follows:

"I warmly implore your Eminence to take no public steps as regards Father Newman's pamphlet, for the following reasons: The heart of Father Newman is as straight and Catholic as it

---

formable." Thus this power of the Pope to define infallibly must be confined to Faith and Morals as contained in the Revelation given to the Apostles; revealed once and for all, unchangeable and irreformable.

ever was. His pamphlet has a most powerful influence over the non-Catholics of this country. It makes a wholesome impression, especially on various Catholics of a difficult nature and unsatisfied ideas. The aforesaid Father has never, up to the present, so openly defended the prerogatives and infallible authority of the Roman Pontiff, though he has always believed and preached this truth. . . . Under the circumstances, I warmly implore you to leave what is well alone. It is not only the petition of a true friendship and old, but the counsel of prudence."

That this letter of Manning's went far to increase Newman's prestige in Rome is unquestioned. And from this time on, the long estrangement between the two men, due mainly to misunderstandings and to temperament on the part of both, disappeared from the picture. Never again did they quarrel; and although they would still differ at times on minor matters, Newman buried his hatchet, and Manning did his uttermost to be cordial to the man of whose intellect he had perhaps always been a little jealous. When Manning came home from Rome with the cardinal's hat, their friendship was such that Newman could write a bantering letter, reminding him of "the contrast between the circumstances under which you return invested with this dignity, and twenty-five years ago."

As for William George Ward, this period seems to have marked a further easing of their mutual "estrangement." Doubtless Ward rejoiced at this, for he had really always revered Newman; the Oxford memories had never died out. He used to say that in Oxford his heart beat fast if he heard Newman's step on the staircase; and with all their differences of later years, his feeling of reverence and affection was still alive. The story is told by his son Wilfrid Ward, that his father told him, shortly before he died, of a dream he had had one night in which he found himself at a dinner party seated next to a veiled lady with whom he got into animated conversation. Her voice and manner charmed him, and at last he said to her, "I have never felt such charm in any conversation since I used to talk with John Henry Newman at Oxford." The lady replied, "I am John Henry Newman," and raising her veil showed him the well known face.

5

After the excitement resulting from the agitation connected with the Vatican Council, and Newman's share in it, little happened to upset the serenity of his life—except that which is always a trial to the elderly: the loss of old friends and companions. Those who died in these years included not only members of his own family and relatives. In 1873 his old friend James Hope-Scott and that closer friend of many years, Henry Wilberforce, died. Then soon followed the death of the Duchess of Argyle and also two of the Sisters of the Dominican convent at Stone, with whom he had long been intimate through correspondence. Old friends like Pusey and Church were ill, which also worried him greatly. "What a year it has been for deaths," he wrote to Sister Mary Gabriel near the end of 1873. "The shafts have been flying incessantly and unexpectedly on all sides and strewing the ground with friends. It makes one understand St. John's dreary penance in living to be ninety. Well might he say, 'Amen, veni Domine Jesu.' "

But his greatest trial of all was in the year 1875, with the death of his very close friend and constant companion, Ambrose St. John. His intimacy with Father St. John extended back to Oxford and Littlemore days; he had been his closest companion and his one confidant during the years at Littlemore when Newman was on his "Anglican deathbed"; he had entered the Catholic Church with him and was his companion in Rome in 1846 and

1847; and together they had formed the English Oratory of St. Philip Neri. In all the years of Newman's Catholic life, Ambrose St. John had been at his side. For many years, he had been the Headmaster of the Edgbaston school.

How tragic to him was St. John's passing is vividly pictured in a long letter to his old friend Frederick Rogers (then Lord Blachford). He describes in great detail the events which led up to this sad ending. A few passages must be quoted.

"From the first he loved me with an intensity of love which was unaccountable. At Rome twenty-eight years ago he was always so working for and relieving me of all trouble, that being young and Saxon-looking, the Romans called him my Angel Guardian. As far as this world was concerned, I was his first and last. He has not intermitted this love for an hour up to his last breath. At the beginning of his illness he showed in various ways that he was thinking of and for me. . . . I had no suspicion of this overwork of course, but which reminds me that, at that time, startled at the great and unexpected success of my pamphlet, I said to him, 'We shall have some great penance to balance this good fortune.'

"There was on April 28 a special High Mass at the Passionists two miles from this. He thought he ought to be there, and walked in a scorching sun to be there in time. He got a sort of stroke. He never was himself afterwards. A brain fever came on. After the crisis, the doctor said he was recovering—he got better every day —we all saw this. On his last morning he parted with great impressiveness from an old friend, once one of our lay brothers, who had been with him through the night. The latter tells us that he had in former years watched, while with us, before the Blessed Sacrament, but he had never felt Our Lord so near him, as during that night. He says that his (Ambrose's) face was so beautiful. Both William Neville and myself had noticed that at different times; and his eyes, when he looked straight at us, were brilliant as jewels. It was the *expression*, which was so sweet, tender and beseeching. When his friend left him in the morning, Ambrose smiled on him and kissed his forehead, as if he was taking leave of him. Mind, we all of us thought him getting better every day. When the doctor came, he said the improvement was far beyond his expectation. . . .

"I have not time to go through that day, when we were so jubilant. In the course of it, when he was sitting on the side of his bed, he got hold of me and threw his arm over my shoulder and brought me to him so closely, that I said in joke, 'He will give me a stiff neck.' So he held me for some minutes, I at length releasing myself from not understanding, as *he* did, why he so clung to me. Then he got hold of my hand and clasped it so tightly as really to frighten me, for he had done so once before when he was not himself. I had to get one of the others present to unlock his fingers, ah! little thinking what he meant. At seven p.m. when I rose to go, and said, 'Good-bye, I shall find you much better tomorrow,' he smiled on me with an expression I could not and cannot understand. It was sweet and sad and perhaps perplexed, I cannot interpret it. But it was our parting.

"About midnight I was awakened at the Oratory, with a loud rapping at the door, and the tidings that a great change had taken place in him. We hurried off at once, but he had died almost as soon as the messenger started. He had been placed or rather had placed himself with great deliberation and self-respect in his bed—they had tucked him up, and William Neville was just going to give him some arrowroot when he rose upon his elbow, fell back and died. . . ."

Though sympathy poured in from all directions, Newman was for a long time inconsolable. To a friend he wrote: "This is the greatest affliction of my life, and so sudden. Pray for me!" To another he said, "I do not expect ever to get over the loss I have had. It is an open wound which in old men cannot be healed."

6

The loss of Ambrose St. John cast a shadow over him for the rest of his days; but it weighed more heavily the first year or two. What, he constantly asked himself, had he now to look forward to? His years were piling up, and the thought that he would soon follow those who had gone, or were almost daily going, was never absent from his mind.

There were, however, also brighter moments which helped to keep his interest alive and to cheer him in these troubled days. One of his great comforts was the intimacy, which had undergone a revival, with his Anglican friend, R. W. Church, now Dean of St. Paul's—and also with that friend of later years, Richard Holt Hutton. Hutton had first come into his life at the time of the *Apologia* in 1864. He was then editor of the *Spectator* but personally unknown to Newman. After his defence of Newman in the controversy with Kingsley, a friendship sprang up between them which grew with the years. Originally a nominal Unitarian, Hutton had later in life joined the Anglican Church, though he still seemed inclined to a moderate or "liberal" view of Christianity rather than complete orthodoxy.

While Hutton often criticised Newman on his interpretations of Christian doctrine, they came to love and revere each other for the sterling qualities of both. At about the time of Newman's death a decade later, Hutton wrote a sympathetic biography of the Cardinal, summing up his judgment of him in the following passage:

"In a century in which physical discovery and material well-being have warped and almost absorbed the admiration of mankind, such a life as that of Cardinal Newman stands out in strange and almost majestic, though singularly graceful and unpretending contrast, to the eager and agitated turmoil of confused passions, hesitating ideals, tentative virtues, and groping philanthropies, amidst which he has lived." [1]

Hutton tried to induce Newman to join the Metaphysical Society, where debates were carried on from all points of view on the foundations of religious belief. Aside from Anglicans like Church and Hutton, and Gladstone, with Cardinal Manning and William George Ward, the society (as we have already said) was mainly made up of Liberals, including Huxley and Tyndall, and other agnostics and freethinkers. Newman declined to join, though the invitation was several times renewed. He did not approve of the Metaphysical Society—at least for himself. In 1876 he is writing Dean Church: "I hear that you and the Archbishop of York (to say nothing of Cardinal Manning) are going to let Professor Huxley read in your presence an argument in refutation of our Lord's Resurrection. How can this possibly come under the scope of a Metaphysical Society? I thank my stars that, when asked to accept the honor of belonging to it, I declined. Aren't you in a false position? . . ."

Nothing more clearly emphasizes the difference in temperament between Newman and men like Manning and Ward than his attitude in this matter. They loved disputation in every form; it was their life; to shoot their shrapnel into the ranks of the enemy or to take part in noisy quarrels was second nature to them. On the other hand, Newman always shrank from the controversial atmosphere. Though he was doomed, throughout his long life, frequently to become involved in controversy, it was never to his taste. Not only was his nature such that he dreaded turmoil, but his deep sympathy and charity towards all, of whatever creed, was always a factor. His heart went out to opponents, even though his head reprobated their views.

An outstanding example of his lifelong attitude is shown when he delivered, years before, his lectures on "Difficulties of Angli-

[1] *Cardinal Newman.*

cans"—probably the most controversial series of his whole life.
It was a distasteful job; but he tried at the beginning to emphasize the fact that he had a sympathetic, rather than a caustic, understanding of the doubts and difficulties and disagreements of
his Anglican audiences. "Others," he said, "have scoffed at you,
but I never; others may have made light of your principles or
your sincerity; others may have predicted evil of you. I have only
felt vexed at the prediction."

It was perhaps true also, as indicated in his note to Dean
Church, that the views of Professor Huxley were so abhorrent to
him that he shrank from any contact with a man who was doing
more to de-Christianize England at that time than any other one
personality. Huxley was brilliant but sarcastic, intolerant of
minds like Newman's. He was to say, in the last year of Newman's
life, "If I were called upon to compile a Primer of Infidelity, I
think I should save myself trouble by making a selection from his
[Newman's] works." He referred particularly to Newman's *Essay
on Miracles* and his *Essay on Development.* Huxley's deductions
were shallow and absurd. Perhaps if Newman at that time had
not been at the end of his life, he might have replied to this
vicious but silly attack; as it was, he ignored it.

As old age closed down on him more and more, we find that
his mind often runs back in tender recollection of the years spent
in the Anglican communion and of those Anglican friends of
earlier days. We find an interesting passage in his journal dated
November 1877.

"Do you love, my dear Self, or don't you, your active abidance
time in the Church of England? E.g. you have a photograph of
Trinity Chapel before your eyes daily, and you love to look at it.
Yes—and it is in a great measure an abstraction. It is not the
Church of England that I love—but it is that very assemblage, in
its individuals concrete, which I remember so well—the times and
places—the scenes, occurrences—my own thoughts, feelings and
acts. I look at that communion table, and recollect with what

feelings I went up to it in November 1817 for my first communion—how I was in mourning for the Princess Charlotte, and had black silk gloves—and the glove would not come off when I had to receive the Bread, and I had to tear it off and spoil it in my flurry. But the Church of England, as such, does not come into my tender memories."

It was at the end of 1877 that Trinity College, Oxford, his old *alma mater,* invited him to become an Honorary Fellow. This was a gesture which brought great joy to him; not only as a token of recognition at Oxford of his life of devotion to religion, but because the new generation there had not completely forgotten him. He wrote Bishop Ullathorne when announcing the invitation: "Trinity College has been the one and only seat of my affections at Oxford, and to see once more, before I am taken away, what I never thought I should see again, the place where I began the battle of life with my good angel by my side, is a prospect almost too much for me to bear."

In February 1878 the Trinity Fellows invited him to visit the college. His visit was very affecting to all. His former associates had all passed away except Dr. Thomas Short, his first tutor, who was now in his eighty-ninth year. After sixty years their meeting was touching.

They gave him an anniversary dinner, at which he made a charming little address replete with reminiscences of his college days. James Bryce (later Lord Bryce) presided. Long after, he wrote these lines in describing the occasion:

"There was something tenderly pathetic to us younger people in seeing the old man come again, after so many eventful years, to the hall where he had been wont to sit as a youth, the voice so often heard in St. Mary's retaining, faint though it had grown, the sweet modulations Oxford knew so well, and the aged face worn deep with the lines of thought, struggle and sorrow. . . . What struck us most was the mixture of sadness and pleasure with which he came among us and recalled his early days."

But as the year 1878 ended and his eightieth year was not far away, events such as the reception at Trinity College seemed to him to mark his valedictory. He had reached the age when he no more dwelt on thoughts of a future in this life, living from day to day with an inward peace. The year before, he had finished re-editing his many volumes of sermons and other works, such as the *Essay on Development* and the old volumes on the *Via Media* (with annotations), and had at last finished his volumes on St. Athanasius. The only other writing he had done since his *Letter to the Duke of Norfolk,* were some verses and a series of meditations and prayers—some of which, with their exquisite beauty, still live among the faithful.

Yet, despite his weight of years, he was fairly vigorous physically. Canon Scott Holland has told us of a visit to the Oratory at about this time. "I recall," he says, "the swift sudden way in which I found him beside me as I was being led through the upper room to my friend; I turned at the sound of the soft, quick voice, and there he was, white, frail and wistful, for all the ruggedness of the actual features."

But an event of far-reaching importance was in the making, which would once more arouse him and change his attitude toward the future, even as he had been aroused fifteen years before when the controversy with Kingsley gave him a new lease of life. In April 1878 the aged Pope Pius died and was succeeded by Leo XIII. This event seems to have had for him a providential significance. It was quite like him to connect it with something he had said in his Duke of Norfolk letter—that at the Council of Ephesus, Leo the Great had opposed exaggerations of the definition then proclaimed; and if, in connection with the definition adopted at the Vatican Council, exaggerated interpretations of its meaning should become current, "another Leo will be given for the occasion"—to set things right.

Moreover, an incident which seemed to fit the occasion and which greatly cheered him was that the new Pope Leo, shortly

after his installation, wrote to him personally, sending his blessing
and enclosing a picture from his own breviary. Pius IX had also
sent Newman his special blessing at the time he entered the
Church, and he had revered this Holy Father throughout all the
years of his pontificate, despite many misunderstandings. He had
nevertheless felt that he had always been under a cloud in Vatican circles (at least until very recently) while Pope Pius was on
the throne.

But with the installation of Leo XIII his view underwent a
marked change. We find him at this time writing Dr. Pusey:

"If the common reports are true, the present Pope, when in
his high place as cardinal, was in the same ill odour at Rome as
I was. Here then a fellow feeling and sympathy with him colours
to my mind his act towards me. He seems to say:—

" 'Non ignara mali, miseris succurrere disco.' "

CHAPTER FIFTEEN

CARDINAL OF SAINT GEORGE

1

ONE COLD WINTER MORNING in February 1879, when Newman was confined to his bed with a heavy cold, a message arrived from Bishop Ullathorne requesting his immediate attendance at Oscott on a matter of supreme importance. Word was sent to the Bishop regarding Newman's indisposition; upon which the Bishop urged that some trustworthy representative be sent to him without delay. Forthwith, one of the Oratorians, Father T. A. Pope, was despatched to Oscott to wait on the Bishop. Here he received the startling news that Cardinal Nina, the Pope's Secretary of State, had sent a letter to Cardinal Manning, in which he stated that the Holy Father wished to confer on Newman the cardinal's hat, as a recognition of and reward for his great services and loyalty to the Church throughout the long years of his priesthood. And the Pope desired to know, if the offer were formally made, would Newman feel that he could accept the honor?

One may imagine the scene when this news was brought to the aged Oratorian on his sick-bed, already prepared to pass to the Great Beyond at any hour. He was being invited by the Vicar of Christ to become a Prince of the Church. Words cannot describe his astonishment—and his joy. It was like a shaft of bright sunshine breaking through the twilight of an ending day. "The cloud has been lifted from me forever!" he exclaimed. One who was present has told us: "He felt as though the Heavens had opened and the Divine Voice had spoken its approval of him before the whole world."

What brought about this surprising event? It is an interesting story. Quite unknown to Newman, certain of his English Catholic admirers felt very strongly that he should receive from Rome some formal recognition of his many years of constructive work for the Church in England. And the Duke of Norfolk, who commanded great influence in Rome, was chosen, with Lord Petre and Lord Ripon, to suggest to Cardinal Manning the idea of inducing the new Pope, Leo XIII, to offer Newman the cardinalate. Manning fully agreed; he brought the question up with the ecclesiastical authorities in Rome, where he found much sympathy for the proposal; but nothing was then actually done to bring the subject before the Pope. In the meantime the Duke of Norfolk went to Rome to discuss the matter with the authorities. His views were communicated to Pope Leo, and then he was given an opportunity to interview the Pontiff and explain to him how popular the idea was among Newman's English admirers. Years later, in a statement to Wilfrid Ward, the Duke outlined his motives for making the appeal and the Pope's response to it. From this statement I quote a few excerpts:

"I was moved very much by the feeling that it was due to Newman himself that his long life of marvellous and successful labour for religion should receive the highest mark of recognition which the Holy See could give him. . . . But my chief reason for moving in the matter was based on more general grounds. I do not think that any Catholic has been listened to by those who are not Catholics with so much attention, respect and, to a great extent, sympathy as Newman. But while numbers were brought by him to see and to accept the truth, I felt very strongly that the full outcome of his labours was most unhappily limited by the impression which was made to prevail by a certain school of well intentioned people that he did not really speak the mind of the Church or represent the beliefs which the Church called upon her children to accept. . . . They in their turn persuaded themselves that the arguments and example of Newman could be admired by them as showing what a grand and beautiful and divinely authoritative institution the Catholic Church might be, but that they were not called upon to obey that authority because the opinion held of Newman by many Catholics showed that the Catholic Church was not really what Newman said it was. It appeared to me therefore that in the cause both of justice and of truth it was of the utmost importance that the Church should put her seal on Newman's work.

". . . Again it was sometimes urged that in Newman intellectual qualities were allowed somewhat to overcloud the simplicity of Catholic faith. But it would be difficult indeed to gather from any other writer than Newman such sublime conceptions of devotion to the Mother of God or of our kindred with the saints; and in all this the high intellectual insight is blended with the most childlike tenderness. I feel very strongly that the action of the Holy See in making Newman a Cardinal brought out this great side of his character, this great lasting teaching of his life, and that in this act our Country received yet another pledge of 'Rome's unwearied love.' "

Pope Leo was greatly impressed with the Duke's explanation and immediately acceded to the request that Newman be made a cardinal. All this occurred, of course, some time before Newman or the world in general knew anything about what was going on.

2

But now, alas, after the first rush of joy at the news, this feeble old man of nearly four score years realized that cardinals who are not bishops of dioceses, are always required to reside in Rome. How could he, with his growing feebleness and at this last stage of his life, uproot himself from his well-loved home and his precious Oratory, where he had lived for so many years and where he hoped to die?

So he immediately wrote to Bishop Ullathorne to express his gratitude but pointed out the impossibility at his age of accepting the honor unless he could remain at his Oratory—which, he assumed, was something that could not be allowed.

"I trust that his Holiness," he wrote, "and the most eminent Cardinal Nina, will not think me a thoroughly discourteous and unfeeling man, who is not touched by the commendation of superiors, or a sense of gratitude, or the splendour of dignity, when I say to you, my Bishop, who know me so well, that I regard as altogether above me the great honor which the Holy Father proposes, with wonderful kindness, to confer on one so insignificant, an honour quite transcendant and unparalleled, than which His Holiness has none greater to bestow.

"For I am, indeed, old and distrustful of myself; I have lived now thirty years *in nidulo meo* in my much loved Oratory, sheltered and happy, and would therefore entreat His Holiness not to take me from St. Philip, my Father and Patron.

"By the love and reverence with which a long succession of Popes have regarded and trusted St. Philip, I pray and entreat His Holiness in compassion of my diffidence of mind, in consideration of my feeble health, my nearly eighty years, the retired course of my life from my youth, my ignorance of foreign languages, and my lack of experience in business, to let me die where I have so long lived. Since I know now and henceforth that His Holiness thinks kindly of me, what more can I desire?"

On its face, this letter might seem to read rather like a refusal of the Cardinalate. But his real meaning was that he wished to accept, provided he be allowed to remain in his Oratory. He should have so stated in plain words; but his delicate temperament shrank from seeming to wish to bargain with the Holy See. However, the next day he went to Oscott to talk with the Bishop and make his meaning clear. Ullathorne forwarded Newman's letter to Manning together with the following letter of his own:

"I had no time yesterday to write you a more private letter after seeing Dr. Newman yesterday. He is very much aged, and softened with age and the trials he has had, especially by the loss of his two brethren, St. John and Caswall; he can never refer to these losses without weeping and becoming speechless for the time. He is very much affected by the Pope's kindness, would, I know, like to receive the great honor offered him, but feels the whole difficulty at his age of changing his life, or having to leave the Oratory, which I am sure he could not do. If the Holy Father thinks well to confer on him the dignity, leaving him where he is, I know how immensely he would be gratified, and you well know how generally the conferring on him of the Cardinalate will be applauded . . ."

This explanation should have convinced Manning, especially as Ullathorne followed it up with a private letter to the same effect; but his practical mind may have induced him to brush aside the suggestion as only Ullathorne's and not Newman's. He may easily have assumed, also, that the suggestion that Newman remain in his Oratory would not be allowed. At any rate, he still took it for granted that Newman wished to decline the offer (thus ignoring Ullathorne's expressed opinion).

In the meantime Newman had written to the Duke of Norfolk, who forwarded his letter to Manning, who had gone to Rome. Upon receipt of it, Manning did go at once to the Holy

Father and explain Newman's wish to remain at his Oratory. The Pope readily acceded to the request, and on March 2 Manning telegraphed and wrote to Ullathorne that all was settled. Pope Leo, having a precedent in the case of Cardinal de Berulle, founder of the French Oratory in the seventeenth century, gladly followed this precedent in Newman's case.

It seems possible, too, if not probable, that Manning had indulged in a little gossip; for a rumor spread and was featured in the English newspapers that Newman had positively declined. He was more than embarrassed when he received congratulations that he had done so, from a few old Anglican friends. One of these was Dr. Pusey, who still cherished his lifelong anti-Papal attitude. But Newman made short work of these unwelcome congratulations.

On receiving the definite news of the Pope's decision through Bishop Ullathorne, Newman wrote at length to Manning at Rome. Several letters were exchanged, Manning explaining in detail why he had misunderstood him. The disturbing gossip now ceased. At about the middle of March, when Cardinal Nina sent to Manning the official notice that the Cardinalate was to be conferred at the next consistory, Manning wrote to Newman as follows:

"The enclosed letter of Cardinal Nina has just reached me. I forward it to you with great joy. I hope you may have yet many years to serve the Church in this most intimate relation to the Holy See. From the expressions used by many of the Sacred College to me I can assure you of the joy with which they will receive you. I remember in 1854, I think, writing from Rome to wish you joy on another event. I have still greater pleasure in conveying to you this greater completion of your many labours."

After all the confusion had cleared up and it was officially announced that Newman was to receive the honor, and shortly go to Rome, congratulations poured in from all England and abroad, the first of all coming from the Irish members of Parliament. They jointly united in a great reception for him at the home of T. W. Allies. This frightened him. He exclaimed to Father Neville: "It has all come too late; I am unused to public speeches. I am old and broken; it is too late to begin. I fear I shall break down." But when the day arrived for him to go to London, he found that despite his infirmity he could "go through with it." He delivered a splendid address. After stepping off the train on his return home, he strode to the Oratory with firm steps, and as he entered the house, exultantly exclaimed, "All is right! I did splendidly!"

It was indeed another lease of life—though not of course the overcoming of his physical weakness—and he would feel, for a long time to come, that it was *not* "too late." His mind and heart were still as young as ever; and he retained energy enough to make new marks upon his time.

3

It was, of course, necessary for him to go to Rome for the reception of the honor. He left the Oratory on Wednesday of Easter Week, April 12, accompanied by Father Neville. Fathers Pope and Eaglesim had gone on ahead to meet him on his arrival at Rome. I will let Newman himself describe the journey and his reception by the Holy Father, quoting from two letters which he sent home. There is a very human touch here.

"We went at one go from Boulogne to Turin without any discomfort, getting to the latter place by Saturday night. We heard Mass next morning and went to Genoa, where the weather was not good, and I found myself wet and cold. Unable to take wine the journey was too much for me, and I had to remain two days at Pisa—else, we should have been at Rome on Tuesday night; but we staid an idle day at Pisa, and another day went no further than Siena—and so got here half past four p.m. yesterday, Thursday. . . . Everyone has been surpassingly kind. William, perhaps Thomas, is to see Cardinal Nina tonight. It is not very warm, yet thunders. We have not settled where to pitch our tent. I make a bad hand at Italian, the easiest of languages. After all, we left behind my coat of arms. Do you recollect in the Vulgate or in A'Kempis, the words 'Cor ad cor loquitur'? Look into the concordance of the Vulgate, among the books of reference in the library, and find out if there is any such text in Scripture.

"I have been laid up with a bad cold ever since I have been here. Yesterday and today I have been in bed. It has seized my throat and continues hard. The weather is so bad. It pulls me down sadly. Here great days are passing, and I am a prisoner in the house.

"The Holy Father received me most affectionately—keeping my hand in his. He asked me, 'Do you intend to continue head of the Birmingham House?' I answered, 'That depends on the Holy Father.' He then said, 'Well, then, I wish you to continue head,' and he went on to speak of this at length, saying there is a precedent for it in one of Gregory XVI's Cardinals. . . . He asked me various questions—was our house a good one? How many were we? Of what age? When I said we had lost some, he put his hand on my head and said, 'Don't cry.' When I was leaving he accepted a copy of my four Latin Dissertations, in the Roman edition. I certainly didn't think his mouth large until he smiled, and then the ends turned up, but not unpleasantly—he has a clear white complexion. He speaks very slowly and clearly and in an Italian manner."

From the time of this audience and the Consistory on May 12, his doctor insisted that he remain indoors, as his heavy bronchial cold was stubborn. Indeed, the ill old man found it impossible to offer Mass except at rare intervals. But when the great day arrived he was a little better and was able to go to the Palazzo della Pigna, the residence of Cardinal Howard (who had loaned his apartment for the ceremony). Here he received from the Vatican the *biglietto,* informing him that at a secret Consistory held that morning, His Holiness had raised him to the rank of Cardinal, with the title of Saint George. He was further informed that His Holiness would receive him the next morning to confer the biretta.

It was next in order for the new Cardinal to deliver his acceptance speech. He did so before the assembled throng, which consisted of many ecclesiastics and lay people, including English and Americans. It was a splendid address which, first of all, displayed his inherent humility; but it more particularly demonstrated the fact that he was still greatly preoccupied with the menace and dangers to Christians from the modern trend towards Liberalism—materialist philosophy, which, throughout his entire career, had been having and still was having such devastating effects upon society. Fifty years before, he had begun his fight against this evil thing; he still wished to fight it as aggressively as ever. This seemed to him a signal opportunity to emphasize it.

The address is too long to quote in full, but it will not be amiss to quote a few passages. He first spoke of the wonder and gratitude which came to him and was with him still, at the condescension and love of the Holy Father in singling him out for the great honor, and particularly in permitting him to live and end his days in his beloved Oratory. Then he proceeded with the address.

"In a long course of years I have made many mistakes. I have nothing of that high perfection which belongs to the writings of the saints, viz., that error cannot be found in them; but what I trust that I may claim, all through what I have written, is this—an honest intention, a willingness to be corrected, a dread of error, a desire to serve Holy Church, and, through God's mercy, a fair measure of success."

After requesting the privilege of speaking in his native tongue rather than in Italian, his facility in which was limited, he at once launched into the main theme of his address, which was to point out the devastating effect on society of the spirit of scepticism in religion—that growing menace so dire in its effects that the next generation of men would suffer untold agony: for by that time, "the tops of the mountains would only be seen like islands in the waste of waters."

"Liberalism in religion," he said, "is the doctrine that there is no positive truth in religion, but that one creed is as good as another, and this is the teaching which is gaining substance and force daily. It is inconsistent with any recognition of any religion, as true. It teaches that all are to be tolerated, for all are matters of opinion. . . . Revealed religion (it is said) is not a truth, but a sentiment and a taste; not an objective fact, not miraculous; and it is the right of each individual to make it say just what strikes his fancy. Devotion is not necessarily founded on Faith. Men may go to Protestant Churches and to Catholic, may get good from both and belong to neither. They may fraternize together in spiritual thoughts and feelings, without having any views at all in common, or seeing the need of them. Since, then, religion is so personal a peculiarity and so private a possession, we must of necessity ignore it in the intercourse of man with man. If a man puts on a new religion every morning, what is that to you? It is as impertinent to think about a man's religion as about his sources of income or the management of his family. Religion is in no sense [they imply] the bond of society. . . .

". . . For myself, I would rather speak of it in my own country which I know. . . . It must be recollected that the religious sects, which sprang up in England three centuries ago, and which are all-powerful now, have ever been fiercely opposed to the Union of Church and State, and would advocate the un-Christianizing of the monarchy and all that belongs to it, under the notion that such a catastrophe would make Christianity much more pure and much more powerful. . . . Consider what follows from the very fact of these many sects. They constitute the religion, it is supposed, of half the population; and, recollect, our mode of government is popular. Every dozen men taken at random whom you meet in the streets have a share in political power —when you inquire into their forms of belief, perhaps they represent one or other of as many as seven religions; how can they possibly act together in municipal or in national matters, if each insists on the recognition of his own religious denomination? All action would be at a deadlock unless the subject of religion was ignored. . . .

"Such is the state of things in England, and it is well that it should be realized by all of us; but it must not be supposed for a moment that I am afraid of it. I lament it deeply because I foresee that it may be the ruin of many souls; but I have no fear at all that it really can do aught of serious harm to the Word of God, to Holy Church, to our Almighty King, the Lion of the tribe of Judah, Faithful and True, or His Vicar on earth. Christianity has been too often in what seemed deadly peril, that we should fear for it any new trial now. So far is certain; on the other hand, what is uncertain, and in these great contests commonly is uncertain, and what is commonly a great surprise, when it is witnessed, is the particular mode by which, in the event, Providence rescues and saves His elect inheritance. Sometimes our enemy is turned into a friend; sometimes he is despoiled of that special virulence of evil which was so threatening; sometimes he falls to pieces of himself; sometimes he does just as much as is beneficial, and then is removed. Commonly the Church has nothing more to do than to go on in her own proper duties, in confidence and peace; to stand still and see the salvation of God."

All his friends rejoiced that he went through this address without faltering, though so ill. An old Protestant friend who was present said: "Dr. Newman looked ill and faint, but he read the address in a beautiful clear voice, and it was a very touching one, in some respects, to listen to. I have written a line to Dr. Pusey to tell him of it, as I thought he would like to hear something of one whom he loved so much. Dr. Newman's face looked like that of a saint." And Father Pope wrote home, "I am now easy about the Father—I have been at times uneasy. The cough is obstinate and the weakness great, but he seems today quite himself."

But the many celebrations which he now had to attend exhausted him, especially as he was expected to make frequent addresses, and he was rushed back to his bed. An affection of the lungs set in which greatly worried the doctors. He had hoped to spend time visiting all the Holy Places in Rome, making friends of other members of the Sacred College of cardinals, and also seeing much of the Pope. But all had to be abandoned. Only twice was he well enough to see and talk with the Holy Father before he was hastily taken home.

In the second week of June his doctors considered it safe to risk this home journey; but they forbade him making the side trips which he had planned, one to see his old friend, Sister Maria Pia in Autun, and another to Munich to visit Dr. Döllinger, whom he fancied he might win back to the Church.

On the first day of July, 1879, he arrived, without serious mishap, at his beloved Oratory, weary with the strain of travel but with a feeling of great joy. He was affectionately welcomed by his companions of the Oratory and by a great concourse of the laity of the city.

4

A big reception had been arranged for him before his arrival. It seemed as if all Birmingham was participating in the welcome. He was first met on the road by a group of Oratorians, who boarded his carriage, and on the way home he was dressed by Father Henry Bittleston in his red cassock, cloak and biretta, and cardinal's cap. A procession formed and marched to the Church —the Cardinal under a canopy—and first proceeded to St. Philip's chapel, where the Blessed Sacrament was kept. There were prayers; and then the procession returned to the high altar and the Cardinal knelt on a prie-dieu in the center of the sanctuary. After a fervent prayer of thanksgiving, he went to the throne, where all present came and kissed his ring. After that was over, the throne was moved to the center of the sanctuary. He sat down, and then began a deeply touching but very informal address to his "dear children."

The elaborate pomp and ceremony arranged for the occasion meant little or nothing compared to his joy and solace at reaching home at last. Says Father Ryder: "He was wonderful to look at as he sat facing the congregation, his face was as the face of an Angel—the features that were so familiar to us, refined and spiritualized by illness, and the delicate complexion and silver hair touched by the rose tints of his bright unaccustomed dress. Leaning his head upon his hand, be began to talk to us and must have spoken for twenty minutes or more. . . . If I remember right, he began by exclaiming, 'O it is *such* a happiness to get home!' " A few excerpts from this talk will help to visualize this happiness:

"My dear children," he said, "I am desirous of thanking you for the great sympathy you have shown towards me, for your congratulations, for your welcome, and for your good prayers;

but I feel so very weak—for I have not recovered yet from a long illness—that I hardly know how I can be able to say ever so few words, or to express in any degree the great pleasure and gratitude to you which I feel.

"To come home again! In that word 'home' how much is included. I know well there is a more heroic life than a home life. We know the blessed Apostles—how they went about, and we listen to St. Paul's words—those touching words—in which he speaks of himself and says he was an outcast. Then, we know, too, our Blessed Lord—that He 'had not where to lay His head.' Therefore, of course, there is a higher life, a more heroic life, than that of home. But still, that is given to few. The home life —the idea of home—is consecrated to us by our patron and founder St. Philip, for he made the idea of home the very essence of his religion and institute. We have even a great example in Our Lord Himself; for though in His public ministry He had not where to lay His head, yet we know that for the first thirty years of His life He had a home, and He therefore consecrated, in a special way, the life of home. And as, indeed, Almighty God has been pleased to continue the world, not, as angels, by a separate creation of each, but by means of the Family, so it was fitting that the congregation of St. Philip should be the ideal, the realization of the Family in its perfection, and a pattern to every family in the parish, in the town, and throughout Christendom.

"Therefore I do indeed feel pleasure to come home again. Although I am not insensible of the great grace of being in the Holy City, which is the centre of grace, nor of the immense honour which has been conferred upon me, nor of the exceeding kindness and affection to me personally of the Holy Father—I may say more than affection, for he was to me as though he had been all my life my father—to see the grace which shone from his face and spoke in his voice; yet I feel I may rejoice in coming home again—as if it were to my long home—to that home which extends to heaven, 'the home of our eternity.' And although there has been much of sickness, and much sadness in being prevented from enjoying the privileges of being in the Holy City, yet Almighty God has brought me home again in spite of all difficulties, fears, obstacles, troubles and trials. I almost feared I should never come back, but God in His mercy has ordered it otherwise.

"And now I will ask you, my dear friends, to pray for me, that I may be as the presence of the Holy Father amongst you, and that the Holy Spirit of God may be upon this Church, upon this great city, upon its Bishop, upon all its priests, upon all its inhabitants, men, women and children, and as a pledge and a beginning of it I give you my benediction."

Gradually, after a long rest in his home surroundings, he recovered his strength and then resumed his active duties in the affairs of the Oratory and School. He received visits from friends from far and wide—old friends, new friends—and, as in the past, his letter writing went on voluminously. Father Neville says, "His strength, which had been severely tried in Rome, was rapidly regained, his health was good, and he had the happiness of being conscious that the readiness and vigor of his mind were undiminished. But fatigue during exertion came upon him more quickly than heretofore. It was a warning to him that he would have less opportunity to make up for loss of time."

That his mind was as vigorous as ever is shown by a letter to Miss Bowles, who had been telling him of a mutual friend who had drifted away from the Church and ceased to be a Christian, being influenced by the sceptical thought of the day.

"I think those shocking imaginations against everything supernatural and sacred, are as really diseases of the soul as complaints of the body are, and become catching and epidemic, by contact of neighborhood or company. . . . were I deliberately to frequent the society, the parties of clever infidels, I should expect all sorts of imaginations contrary to Revealed Truth, not based on reason, but fascinating or distressing, unsettling visions, to take possession of me. . . . This does not apply to intercourse with hereditary and religious Protestants, but to our heresiarchs, to the preachers of infidel science, and to our infidel literati and philosophers. This leads me on to recur in thought to the fierce protests and shuddering aversion with which St. John, St. Polycarp and Origen are recorded to have met such as Marcion and his fellows—and, though it may be impossible to take their conduct as a pattern to copy literally, yet I think we should avoid familiar intercourse with infidel poets, essayists, historians, men of science, as much as ever we can lawfully. I am speaking of course of such instruments of evil as really propagate evil.

"As to your very distressing intelligence, which has led to the above, I should hope and pray, hoping with great hope, and praying with great anxiety, that like a bodily complaint it will at length run its course, though the course may be long."

CHAPTER SIXTEEN

"OUT OF THE SHADOWS INTO REALITY"

1

DURING THE MONTHS immediately following his elevation to the cardinalate, the new Cardinal was plied with invitations to attend receptions of one sort or another. His enfeebled condition prevented him from attending very many, but he felt obliged to accept the more important ones. Perhaps the most notable reception of all was that given him at Norfolk House, where many distinguished figures, including Cardinal Manning and most of the British and Irish bishops, as well as the Prime Minister, Lord Salisbury, W. E. Gladstone, and many government officials and a host of the laity, did him honor.

He was also lavishly entertained by his brother Oratorians at the Brompton Oratory, where he delivered a touching address. One of the Oratorian Fathers has given us an interesting sidelight on this Brompton celebration—which I quote.

"The Cardinal assisted at Vespers and gave his Benediction at the London Oratory, and assisted us afterwards in the Little Oratory. It was very touching. Lord Emly broke down. James Anthony Froude [long a wanderer from his youthful convictions] wrote a mournful, affecting letter to the Duke, asking if he might come to the Little Oratory to hear the Cardinal. 'Since last I heard that musical voice,' he wrote, 'my faith is all but shattered. Perhaps if I might hear him again it would at least awaken in me some echoes of those old days.' "

However, this impulse of Froude's once again to hear the old Tractarian leader had no lasting effect on him; for when he died, fourteen years later, he had shown no signs of a return to any definite form of traditional Christianity.

James Anthony Froude, who married Dr. Charles Kingsley's sister and was the youngest brother of Hurrell Froude, was an ardent Tractarian during his years at Oxford and was very active. He assisted Newman at that time in the writing of the *Lives of English Saints*. Ordained a deacon in 1845, he soon thereafter left the Church, coming under the influence of Thomas Carlyle, and was obliged to give up his Fellowship at Oxford. Then he turned to the writing of history. The first two volumes of his *History of England*, covering the sixteenth century, appeared, it will be recalled, just prior to Kingsley's attack on Newman. Later, he wrote a life of Carlyle, and he was for many years editor of *Fraser's Magazine*. Two years before his death he was appointed Regius Professor of Modern History at Oxford, the university from which he had been ejected for his abandonment of Anglicanism in 1847!

The younger Froude was gifted as a writer, picturesque and romantic. His famous history of England has all the engaging qualities of a fascinating novel; but it is not history. Full of inaccuracies and distorted interpretations of events, it is considered utterly unreliable by all competent judges. But because of its literary quality, it was widely accepted in the 1860's as an accurate history of the Protestant religious revolt of the sixteenth century. His later historical writings were equally romantic and unreliable. Before he died in 1894, basking in the sunshine of Liberalism, chronic historical inaccuracy such as his had acquired among scholars the nickname of "Froude's disease." His career vividly reflected the devastating effect of that philosophy of

Liberalism which Newman for so many years had been inveighing against and had outlined so eloquently in his address at Rome when accepting the dignity of the cardinalate.

That a number of the old Tractarians had wandered off into sceptical fields, becoming caught up in modern materialistic philosophy, had always weighed heavily on Newman's mind; and that the younger brother of Hurrell Froude should have wandered off in that direction must surely have been keenly felt. Newman had always kept in touch with the Froude family, and he did have the happiness of converting the wife of the third brother, William Froude. He had high hopes of converting William also (who had followed James Anthony into the sceptical camp); but William, when seeming on the verge of conversion, had died suddenly in a foreign land.

Newman watched closely the careers of these men who had lapsed from Puseyism to Broad Church or sceptical fields. There had been many, the numbers increasing as the years went by. When he became a cardinal and saw one after another of these old friends of his youth dying outside *any* Church, he left no stone unturned to get in touch with those still living, with the hope (which never failed with him) that perhaps an opportunity might come to influence or befriend them.

A notable case of this sort was that of Mark Pattison. He had been, in the days of the Oxford movement, one of the most ardent of his younger followers. Ordained to the Anglican ministry in 1843, he was up to that time a strong supporter of the Tractarian movement and worked closely with Newman and Pusey. But after 1845 he drifted away and for the remainder of his life had little religion. Going to Germany for study and becoming fascinated with German philosophy of the Kantian and Hegelian vintages, he reached the point where he freely criticised his old master, Newman, as "a man with a singularly bigoted outlook on life."

At the time Newman became a cardinal, he had not seen Pat-

tison for many years; they were in effect strangers, living in different worlds. But Newman had not forgotten him and for all
the years had been remembering him in his prayers. And now,
near the close of 1883, learning that Pattison was very ill, probably on his deathbed, and in a desperate mental state, he determined to go to him. The Cardinal himself was also ill at this time
and confined to *his* bed. The doctor strenuously protested against
his going out. But he exclaimed, "Is the little life left in me to be
weighed against the chance of good in a case like this? Let the
doctors say what they will, I shall go."

Although he had not seen Pattison for nearly forty years, he
had loved him in the old days, and he loved him still. He first
wrote him a letter: "My very dear Pattison, I grieve to hear that
you are very unwell. How is it that I, who am so old, am carried
on in years beyond my juniors? This makes me look back in my
thoughts forty years, when you, with Dalgairns, and so many
others now gone, were entering into life. For the sake of those
dear old days, I cannot help writing to you. Is there any way in
which I can serve you? At least I can give you my prayers, such
as they are. Yours affectionately."

The scholarly Pattison, who had long been a tutor at Lincoln
College, Oxford, was greatly surprised at the receipt of this
friendly letter from the man he had for many years been criticising and accusing of shallow and superstitious views. But he was
himself now near life's end and in agony of spirit. He replied to
Newman the next day:

"My dear Master:—When your letter, dear master, was
brought to my bedside this morning, and I saw the wellknown
handwriting, my eyes filled with tears. And when I found in what
affectionate terms you addressed me, I felt guilty, for I thought,
would he do so if he knew how far I had traveled on the path
which leads away from those ideas which I once shared with him?
Or is your toleration so large, that though you know me to be in
grievous error, you could still embrace me as a son? If I have not

dared to approach you in any way of recent years, it has been only from the fear that you might be regarding me as coming to you under false colors. The veneration and affection I felt for you at the time you left us, are in no way diminished, and however remote my intellectual standpoint may be from that which I may presume to be your own, I can still truly say that I have learnt more from you than from anyone else with whom I ever have been in contact. . . . Your affectionate son and pupil."

These letters opened the way for further exchanges. Newman wrote a few days later: "I find it a duty to answer your question to me about toleration. I am then obliged to say that what Catholics hold upon it, I hold with them. That God, who knows the heart, may bless you now and ever is the fervent prayer of your affectionate friend, J.H.N." This was followed by a line saying he would visit him; and though Pattison protested, he went anyway.

Father Ryder, who reported this incident, said: "They passed some hours together. Each knew that neither the other nor himself could live long. Neither could say which was the likely one to be first called away. The result of the visit will no doubt be asked for, but it will be in vain; for the Cardinal was not the sort of person to say much on what was so grave, so anxious, so private as this, the result of which must be in the hands of God. Nevertheless, what he did say was expressive of satisfaction and hope. The journey, far from exhausting him, apparently quite set him up. Mr. Pattison died in the spring."

2

The Cardinal's life during these ripened years of his ninth decade was, of course, in striking contrast to the life of that other English Cardinal, Henry Edward Manning. The latter, being

Archbishop of Westminster and active head of the Catholic hierarchy in England, had his official duties to perform. Newman, on the other hand, though a cardinal priest, was not a bishop, and he had no duties of an administrative character; only those which he might impose upon himself, such as the guidance of his Oratory and school. His life as an ecclesiastic was in no way changed from what it had been before—except, of course, that his new dignity enabled him to speak with greater authority and to be listened to with greater respect by the entire world of Catholics and non-Catholics.

These were the years when Cardinal Manning, conspicuous though he had been in Catholic circles for thirty years and more, was to add greatly to his prestige and gain the good will, not only of all English Catholics (even those who had been suspicious of him as an "upstart convert"), but of the entire English nation, Catholic and Protestant. His great solicitude for the poor, which expressed itself in a very concrete and constructive way, called for the admiration of all England.

For example. It was suggested that a fitting permanent memorial of Cardinal Wiseman would be the erection of a great Catholic cathedral in Westminster. He was heartily in favor of the building of a cathedral and did much to promote the plan. But he insisted that first things should come first; and the first thing for London Catholics was the care and education of the poor and underprivileged Catholic children. As we know, he achieved wonderful results in this connection. The establishment of scores of free schools for the children of the Catholic poor was viewed by him as a far greater memorial to the memory of Cardinal Wiseman (who had ever been preoccupied with this same problem) than the erection of a new cathedral, much as this was needed.

He was always deeply interested in educational problems, as he was in other social and economic questions. If his career had been that of a statesman, he would have made his mark in that field. With his practical, objective personality, he associated himself with all classes, cultivated as close relations with the government as he could, and influenced constructive legislation in England to a considerable extent. In short, he was a man who "got things done."

An eloquent preacher, a great ecclesiastic, and a man of action, Manning also possessed other talents. While not in the same class as Newman in intellectual capacity, he did display unusual ability as a writer and clear thinker. His essay on *The Eternal Priesthood* was a masterpiece, though it is practically unknown to the present generation of Catholics. And some of his meditations, like *Towards Evening* and *Thoughts for Those Who Mourn*, also prove his talent as a spiritual writer. Many volumes of his sermons and addresses were later published; they are, as a whole, of high quality, though little read today. In fact, while not at all Newman's equal as a man of letters, he stood far above the average religious writer of his time. But his greatest mark upon his time was made by his *works* rather than his writing talent or his scholarship.

As a consequence of this difference of temperament and vocation, there was surely no "rivalry" between these two cardinals during their last years. The aged Newman, in his retreat at Birmingham, rejoiced in Manning's managerial achievements for Holy Church and for justice and truth—as much of his correspondence testifies. On the other hand, Manning, as he grew older, came to evaluate Newman's talents more and more highly.

But there was one vital question on which Newman continued to differ with Manning. This was the old Oxford question. In 1882 Pope Leo interested himself in the status of Catholic students in the English Universities. The subject was discussed with Cardinal Manning, who still adhered to the view that Catholic students should be forbidden to attend any but Catholic institutions—despite the fact that Catholic parents had so often ignored this ruling.

Newman, however, was more certain than ever that his own

view was the right one. The spread of the sceptical spirit throughout cultured circles and particularly in the Universities, where
materialism was crowding out Christian teaching, distressed him
keenly. Students should in some effective way be shielded from
these devastating influences—especially Catholic students. "When
I see a clever and thoughtful young man," he said, "I feel a kind
of awe and terror in thinking of his future. How will he be able
to stand up against the intellectual flood that is setting in against
Christianity?"

Hearing of Pope Leo's inquiries, he wrote his friend Lord
Braye in connection with this revival of the subject:

"The cardinal question at the moment is the Oxford question.
Dear Pusey has gone. [He had recently died.] Canon Liddon has
mysteriously given up his professorship. The undergraduates and
Junior Fellows are sheep without a shepherd. They are sceptics
or inquirers, quite open for religious influences. It is a moment
for the Catholic Mission in Oxford to seize an opportunity which
never may come again. . . . The Jesuits have Oxford men and
able men among them. I doubt not that they are doing (as it is)
great good there; but I suppose they dread the dislike and suspicion which any forward act of theirs would rouse. . . . But is
it not heart piercing . . . ? The Liberals are sweeping along in
triumph, without any Catholic or religious influence to stem
them now that Pusey and Liddon are gone. . . .

"The Holy Father must be put up to this fact, and must be
made to understand the state of things with us. And I think he
ought to do this:—He should send here some man of the world,
impartial enough to take in two sides of a subject,—not a politician, or one who would be thought to have anything to do with
politics. Such a person should visit . . . all parts of England, and
he should be able to talk English. . . . Next, how is the Pope to
be persuaded of this? by some Englishman in position, one or
two so much the better. They should talk French or Italian, and
remain in Rome some months. This would be the first step."

So intensely did he feel about this that he had determined to visit Rome and talk with the Holy Father himself. But his health was too poor to stand the journey. It was then that he wrote to Lord Braye, who was planning to go to Rome. Lord Braye took Newman's letter, obtained an audience with Pope Leo through Bishop Hedley. He read him an Italian translation of this letter.

The Pope was quite receptive and deeply interested in Newman's views; but when he later took up the subject with Cardinal Manning, it was side-tracked for the time being. However, Newman's effort may have influenced the Pontiff when, ten years later, after both Newman and Manning had died, he changed the ruling forbidding Catholics to send their sons to the national Universities.

It is often said that Pope Leo was frequently influenced by Cardinal Manning's ideas, a notable instance being the latter's attitude in support of the rights of labor during the 1880's. This, it is thought, brought the Pontiff's attention to the subject when, in 1891, he issued his famous encyclical *Rerum Novarum,* on the rights of labor. This may be so; but perhaps he was also equally influenced by the views of Newman when he later changed the ruling of the Church relating to the Oxford question.

3

Though Cardinal Newman's physical infirmities, which were more and more handicapping him as the decade went on, forced him to abandon all hope of ever again going to Rome—or indeed moving about very much even in England—his "passion for scribbling" was still strong. When Pope Leo issued his encyclical on the philosophy of St. Thomas Aquinas shortly after Newman was raised to the cardinalate, Newman welcomed it as an antidote to the wide prevalence and destructive influence of the modern materialistic philosophies. He expressed his interest in a personal letter to the Pontiff. It is worthy of quotation, if only because it shows how clear his mind remained despite his increasing infirmities.

"I hope it will not seem to your Holiness an intrusion upon your time," he says, "if I address to you a few lines to thank you for the very seasonable and important encyclical which you bestowed upon us. All good Catholics must feel it a first necessity that the intellectual exercises, without which the Church cannot fulfil her supernatural mission duly, should be founded upon broad as well as true principles, that the mental creations of her theologians, and of her controversialists and pastors should be grafted on the Catholic tradition of philosophy, and should not start from a novel and simply original tradition, but should be substantially one with the teaching of St. Athanasius, St. Augustine, St. Anselm and St. Thomas, as those great doctors in turn are one with each other. . . . At a time when there is so much cultivation of mind, so much intellectual excitement, so many new views, true and false, and so much temptation to overstep the old truth, we need just what your Holiness has supplied us with in your recent pastoral, and I hope my own personal gratitude for your wise and seasonable act may be taken by your Holiness as my apology, if I seem to overstep the limits of modesty and propriety in addressing this letter to your Holiness."

Old as he was, he still interested himself, not only in religious but in secular questions. Nor had he by any means lost his sense of humor in his old age. An amusing incident of his eighty-fifth year is proof of this. A very rabid anti-Catholic Anglican, Canon McNeile of Liverpool, challenged him to a debate on the subject of religion. He replied that his speaking and debating days were over but that if Dr. McNeile insisted, he would come to Liverpool, allow the Canon to open the debate with his speech, and then the Cardinal would gladly reply by playing a tune on his violin. The audience could decide which was the winner. There is no record of Canon McNeile's rejoinder to this proposal.

The Cardinal's public-speaking days—except brief efforts at his Oratory or school—were indeed now over. Not long after his return from Rome, he had made a second visit to Trinity College, Oxford, where he was given a great dinner and then spoke briefly, and on Sunday preached to an overflowing congregation in the Jesuit Church in Oxford. In Birmingham he was formally presented with a handsome portrait of himself, a portrait in oil which was the work of the famous portrait painter, Millais. At the presentation of this, he was asked for his blessing, which he gave in the following words—as beautiful as he had ever uttered:

"You ask for my blessing, and I bless you with all my heart, as I desire to be blessed myself. Each one of us has his own individuality, his separate history, his achievements and his future, his duties, his responsibilities, his solemn trial and his eternity. May God's grace, His love, His peace, rest on all of you, united as you are in the Oratory of St. Philip, on old and young, on confessors and penitents, on teachers and taught, on living and dead. Apart from that grace, that love, that peace, nothing is stable, all things have an end; but the earth will last its time, and while the earth lasts, Holy Church will last, and while the Church lasts, may the Oratory of Birmingham last also, amid the fortunes of many generations one and the same, faithful to St. Philip, strong in the protection of Our Lady and the Saints, not losing as time goes on its sympathy with the first Fathers, whatever may be the burden and interests of its day, as we in turn now stretch forth our hands with love and with awe towards those, our unborn successors, whom on earth we shall never know."

But as time went on it was more and more of a physical strain for him to speak. His days were spent in the quietude of his Oratory. Here his thoughts seemed often to go back to his early life, and he tried to get in touch with old relatives long-separated. His two brothers were still living, but not the sisters; the latter had passed away some years before. The brothers were as strangers to him still. We find him writing, "I have not met my dear brother Francis for twenty-two years." But in a letter to his cousin, Emmeline Deane, he recalls the affectionate years with his mother; and to Sister Maria Pia (who knew his family in the early days), he writes of his sister Mary, who had died so many years ago. "This is the anniversary of dear Mary's death in 1828 —an age ago; but she is as fresh in my memory and as dear to my heart as if it were yesterday; and often I cannot mention her name without tears coming into my eyes."

There is also an affectionate letter written the same year to one of his distant cousins, Eliza Fourdrinier:

"Your letter has made me very sad, especially at the thought of your solitariness, as being the only one left of your family. Thank you for writing to me. It recalls so many days and pleasant meetings of which you and I are now almost the sole living witnesses. I recollect well the last time I saw you, I think with Annie and your dear mother, who seemed to me to be looking older than when I had last seen her. If I am right, this was July 30, 1844. She died in 1850. I believe I know the days of death of all of you. . . . May God guard and protect you, and be with you now and in the future."

4

The last years of the Cardinal's life were marked by great spiritual peace. Though he left to the younger Oratorians the management of the school, and seldom ventured away from Birmingham, his lively correspondence contracted less slowly. All his life long he had been meticulous in saving letters from friends and copies of his own. In these days he busied himself with extraordinary zeal in rearranging his life correspondence in order, copying many letters which were illegible. They composed a multitude of volumes.

Father Neville has left us some interesting side-lights on the Cardinal's life during his last years. In summing up that life he says that certain words spoken by Newman at the funeral, sixty years before, of the friend and guide of his youth, Dr. Walter Mayers, exactly apply to himself. These were his words:

"His life was a life of prayer. The works and ways of God, the mercies of Christ, the real purpose and uses of this life, the unseen things of the spiritual world, were always uppermost in his mind. It pleased God to show all around him the state of his heart and spirit, not only by the graces of a meek and peaceable conversation, but also by the direct religiousness of his conversation. Not that he ever spoke for the sake of display—he was quite unaffected, and showed his deep religion quite naturally."

Certainly these words *do* apply to Newman himself, as shown in the long life we have been following in these pages.

There are many lines that are characteristic, not only of his mind, but of his genius for expressing in clear and simple language profound truths of the Faith, which may be garnered from his early writings. Here are some striking lines which convey to the world outside the Church, a simple and clear explanation of the Catholic meaning of "faith." These lines are found in a sermon delivered shortly after he entered the Catholic Church.

"Faith is a gift of God, and not a mere act of our own which we are free to exert when we will. It is quite distinct from an exercise of reason, though it follows upon it. I may feel the force of the argument for the Divine origin of the Church; I may see that I ought to believe; and yet I may be unable to believe. This is no imaginary case; there is many a man who has ground enough to believe, who wishes to believe, but who cannot believe. It is always indeed his own fault, for God gives Grace for all who ask for it, and use it, but still such is the fact, that conviction is not faith. Take a parallel case of obedience; many a man knows he ought to obey God, and does not and cannot—through his own fault, indeed—but still he cannot; for through Divine Grace only can he obey. Now, faith is not a mere conviction in reason, it is a firm assent, it is a clear certainty greater than any other certainty; and this is wrought in the mind by the Grace of God, and by that alone." [1]

Such was, in essence, his lucid answer to the sceptical world, why he, a man of extraordinary intellectual vision equal to or exceeding that of any scholar of his time, could accept with certitude the reality of the Unseen, without a shadow of turning, right up to the end of his life, while so many others of his intelligent contemporaries were floundering after the will-o'-the-wisps of the so-called "law of human progress," a totally materialistic conception. The elusive gift of Faith is a divine grace offered by God to all; but it must be *accepted*, not rejected: accepted by an act of the will.

Though his life was indeed a life of prayer in these last years, this did not prevent him from still taking interest in the various questions of the day, political and economic as well as religious. We find him writing to a friend at this time:

"I have felt the political atmosphere far more than the severe winter. I wish with all my heart that the cruel injustices which have been inflicted on the Irish people, should be utterly removed —but I don't think they go the best way to bring it about." He was still critical of Gladstone, whom he had never fully trusted even in Anglican days. He wrote to Dean Church, "How I wish that Gladstone had retired into private life, as he seems to have contemplated doing some ten years ago."

An incident which is interesting enough to record is connected with the death of General Gordon of Khartoum, which occurred about this time. General Gordon was not a Catholic, and the Cardinal had never met him; but he had always deeply

---

[1] "Faith and Doubt," in *Discourses to Mixed Congregations.*

respected him as a sincere Christian and was greatly moved by the tragedy of Gordon's death at Khartoum. General Gordon, it seems, was very fond of Newman's poem *The Dream of Gerontius,* and in the bound copy of this poem which he had taken with him to Africa, he had marked his favorite passages. Shortly before his death, he had loaned this little book to a friend, who later sent it to his sister in Ireland—a Mrs. Murphy. The latter sent it to the Cardinal for his inspection. In acknowledging its receipt he wrote to her:

"It is indeed far more than a mere compliment to have my name associated in the mind of the public with such a man—so revered, so keenly and bitterly mourned as is General Gordon." And to his friend Dean Church he wrote: "I have received a little book which takes my breath away. It is the property of a Mrs. Murphy, who received it from her brother, and was given to him by General Gordon at Khartoum. The book is *The Dream of Gerontius.* . . . What struck me so much in his use of the *Dream* was that, in St. Paul's words, he 'died daily'; he was always on his deathbed, fulfilling the common advice that we should ever pass the day as if it were our last."

And so the peaceful life went on, until the weaknesses of extreme old age (he was now in his eighty-ninth year) curtailed his activities almost to the vanishing point. His eyesight had long been failing him, and he was no longer able to read his breviary regularly. He could still get through his Rosary—which he loved —but in time that too had to be given up, due to the weakness of his fingers. Nor could he offer Mass with any regularity during the last year of his life, except with assistance of another priest. Not for a long time had he been able to offer the Holy Sacrifice at a public Mass. The last time he ventured to do this was on the Christmas day before his death, which occurred seven months later. In his private chapel, however, he still made an effort almost daily.

Yet he managed to move about and on good days ven-

tured out. In April 1890 he made a surprise visit to Bishop Ullathorne. The Bishop said of this: ". . . never did he look more
venerable, and show more feeling. . . . he was brought to my
room leaning on the arms of two priests, and we talked for an
hour, after which he left. He can no longer read, and even if he
tries to sign his name he cannot see what strokes he makes. But I
was much touched by his conversation."

Bishop Ullathorne also tells us of a touching incident which
occurred towards the Cardinal's last days. It indicates the deep
humility of this venerable Prince of the Church. In a letter to a
friend, the Bishop describes the incident:

"I have been visiting Cardinal Newman to-day. He is much
wasted, but very cheerful. Yesterday he went to London to see
an oculist. When he tries to read black specks are before his eyes.
But the oculist tells him there is nothing wrong but old age. We
had a long and cheery talk, but as I was rising to leave an action
of his caused a scene I shall never forget, for its sublime lesson
to myself. He said in low and humble accents, 'My dear Lord,
will you do me a great favour?' 'What is it?' I asked. He glided
down on his knees, bent down his venerable head, and said,
'Give me your blessing.' What could I do with him before me in
such a posture? I could not refuse without giving him great embarrassment.[1] So I laid my hand on his head and said, 'My dear
Lord Cardinal, notwithstanding all laws to the contrary, I pray
God to bless you, and that His Holy Spirit may be full in your
heart.' As I walked to the door, refusing to put on his biretta as
he went with me, he said, 'I have been indoors all my life, whilst
you have battled for the Church in the world.' I felt annihilated
in his presence. There is a saint in that man."

In these last days the Cardinal was much cheered by an affectionate letter from Cardinal Manning, which was inspired by

---

[1] A recognized rule is that the lower Dignity should kneel before the higher
one.

Newman's writing some words in strong endorsement of Pope Leo's protest against the erection in Rome of a statue to Giordano Bruno, which were read from the Oratory pulpit. "My dear Cardinal," Manning wrote, "I was rejoiced to see the other day the words you spoke in Church about Giordano Bruno. They showed the old energy of days now passed for both of us. . . . Do not forget me in your prayers; every day I remember you at the altar. Yours affectionately". An amicable exchange of letters now followed between these two elderly English cardinals, both soon to reach the end of their earthly careers.

One of the last public acts of Cardinal Newman's life, within three months of his entering his ninetieth year, was his venturing out to a factory in the neighborhood, where a number of young Catholic girls were employed by strict Protestant owners who insisted that these Catholic employes should attend daily religious instruction by Protestant instructors. The girls' parish priest had protested but was unable to accomplish anything. When the Cardinal learned of this, he had himself immediately driven to the factory to interview the employers. He succeeded in inducing them to allow the Catholic girls to have their own Catholic instructor in a separate room at the factory. When he returned to the Oratory, flushed with this success, he exclaimed,

"If I can but do work such as that, I am happy and content to live on."

It was such little acts of charity and love that dotted his days as he approached the end. There is, for instance, an affectionate letter, written shortly before he died, to a pious old Protestant whom he had known in his youth but had not seen for many a long year. It was the old Protestant's birthday—perhaps his ninetieth—and the Cardinal sent him his blessing, enclosing with his letter a slip on which was written, "My Overleaf Creed." It was his own translation of *Anima Christi,* the ancient prayer St. Ignatius Loyola had loved so much. Most American Catholics are familiar with the English rendition of this prayer. Do many

of them know that this translation from the Latin was the work
of Cardinal Newman?

> *Soul of Christ, be my sanctification:*
> *Body of Christ, be my salvation;*
> *Blood of Christ, fill all my veins;*
> *Water of Christ's side, wash out my stains;*
> *Passion of Christ, my comfort be;*
> *O good Jesus, listen to me;*
> *In Thy wounds I fain would hide,*
> *Ne'er to be parted from Thy side;*
> *Guard me, should the foe assail me;*
> *Call me when my life shall fail me;*
> *Bid me come to Thee above,*
> *With Thy saints to sing Thy love,*
>   *World without end. Amen.*

5

The summer of 1890 came and ran into August. The Cardinal
was very feeble and for weeks had been confined to his bed. But
a surprising rally took place on the ninth day of that month. That
morning, to everyone's amazement, he arose early, walked about
with an easy step and in an upright posture, performing many
duties unassisted and spending some time in the Oratory chapel,
praying and meditating before the Blessed Sacrament. All day
long his voice was strong and clear.

But the same night, after retiring, he was seized with an attack
of congestion of the lungs. The following morning he was given
the Last Sacraments. He lingered on through the day, unconscious part of the time. And now should be mentioned a little incident which Father Ryder later recorded in his reminiscences of
the Cardinal. I shall quote his own words.

"A poor indigent person, a stranger to him, had once left for him at the house door a silk handkerchief with a message of respect. This was very many years before he was a Cardinal, and when he seemed, so to speak, much set aside; at a time, too, when he was himself very poor. Both present and message were received by him as they were meant, and with a solemn gravity which checked even a smile. He kept the handkerchief as something he prized. When he went to bed expecting to die, he had it brought down to him and put on, and though the doctors said he might as well be without it, he died with it on. He had kept it quite thirty years, even more."

Thus was his last act in this world a gesture of grateful memory for one who had shown sympathy for him in the days of his great tribulations, decades before.

Death came while he was unconscious, in the evening of August 11, 1890, at about nine o'clock. The next morning his body was dressed in the full pontifical vestments and placed in the Oratory Church before the high altar. Requiem Mass was celebrated in the presence of a vast throng, with Bishop Ullathorne presiding; all the Oratorian Fathers and a host of Church dignitaries were present. The body was then removed to the chapel of St. Philip Neri and placed before the Blessed Sacrament, to await the funeral, which was to take place on August nineteenth.

His death stirred all England; the entire population laid all prejudices aside in uniting in laudation to this greatest English apostle of Christian truth of the nineteenth century; and many encomiums appeared in the public press, that of the London *Times* being the most notable.

In accordance with his own desire, he was laid to rest at Rednal, beside his dear friend and companion of many years, Father Ambrose St. John, who had died fifteen years before. The occasion has been beautifully pictured by Lewis May, in his fascinating study of Cardinal Newman. I cannot improve on this passage:

"Amid the Lickey Hills, a green space of hallowed ground, shut in by yew and oak and laurel, looks up to the sky. It is the burial ground of the Oratorian Fathers. Close to where a bed of St. John's wort flings in summer, in a riot of yellow bloom, is a grassy mound beneath which, as the simple Latin cross recalls, Father Ambrose St. John lies asleep. The St. John's wort was placed there in his memory. In this grave, beside his friend of friends, John Henry Newman, Cardinal of Saint George, was laid to rest on August 19, 1890." [1]

On the pall was inscribed the Cardinal's motto: *Cor ad cor loquitur*—"Heart Speaketh Unto Heart." And on the memorial slab, at his own wish, were engraved the words, *Ex umbris et imaginibus in veritatem*—"Coming out of the Shadows into Reality."

6

As soon as the Holy Father in Rome learned of the Cardinal's decease, he sent a message of condolence through his secretary of state to Cardinal Manning, with which, among other things, the secretary wrote to him: "His Holiness understands full well the special sorrow and grief which your Eminence must have felt in the loss of a colleague with whom you have had many events of life in common, and to whom you were bound for so many years by the closest ties of friendship. I need hardly tell you that His Holiness was also deeply grieved at the announcement of the departure of a man who, by his learning, his writings, and his singular piety, gave great splendour to the Sacred College."

Cardinal Manning did indeed grieve at the passing of his colleague. The old misunderstandings and quirks of temperament and streaks of jealousy or envy—if there were any—had long

---

[1] J. Lewis May, *Cardinal Newman: A Study.*

been left behind for both these aged men. Manning himself was now very feeble, carrying the weight of more than eighty strenuous years, and although nearly eight years younger than Newman, he would, within two years, follow him to the grave. He had not been equal to the journey for the pontifical Requiem at Birmingham or the burial at Rednal.

But a few days after the funeral, a solemn Requiem of great splendor was held at the Brompton Oratory in London; and to this the aged Cardinal was able to go. Here he delivered his famous eulogy of Cardinal Newman. It was a remarkable effort for one of his great age and enfeebled condition. In earlier years he had been a forceful preacher; but his preaching days had now long been a thing of the past.

A score or more of bishops and over two hundred priests and hundreds of nuns, besides the religious of Brompton Oratory, took part in the great procession. The Mass was sung by the Father Superior of Brompton, with Father Stanton of the Birmingham Oratory as the subdeacon. An immense company of people from far and near, with hundreds of English, American and Continental admirers of Newman were there, including a large number of Anglican clergy and laity, as well as other Protestants.

The Cardinal preached from the pulpit in good voice and with deep emotion. As this notable address, though often commended and sometimes quoted, is practically unknown to the present generation of American Catholics (as well as Protestants!) it surely is worth the space to insert the complete text here.

"We have lost our greatest witness to the Faith, and we are all poorer and lower by the loss. When these tidings came to me, my first thought was this:—In what way can I, once more, show my love and veneration for my brother and friend of more than sixty years? It was not in my power to stand beside his grave. For a time I was in doubt whether this last and solemn rite should be in my own Cathedral church, or here, as I may say, in his own home. I believe he would have wished it to be here, where the sorrow for his loss is a domestic sorrow as of sons for a father. With their filial and private grief, it is, then, most fitting that we should unite our personal and universal sorrow.

"I am not come to pronounce orations or panegyrics. I would not if I could; I could not if I would. The memories of an affectionate friendship, as I have said, of more than sixty years, and the weight of old age, put it beyond my power. Few men are living who cherish such a record of the past as I can. When I was twenty years of age and he was about twenty-eight, I remember his form and voice, and penetrating words at Evensong in the University Church at Oxford. Having once seen and heard him I never failed to be there.

"As time went on those quiet days turned into the conflict and tumult of the following years. My field of work was far away, but I knew his thoughts by letter, and when trials came I was not absent from him. Littlemore is before me now as fresh as yesterday; then came the great decision, in which the toils and prayers of so many years were fulfilled and rewarded. The next time we met was in 1848. It was in Rome. He was in the Oratorian habit, simple, humble and dead to the world. Again four years passed, and I heard once more the well-known voice, sweet as of old but strong in the absolute truth, prophesying a 'Second Spring' in the first Provincial of Westminster. Why should I go on? You have known him since then in the midst of you. My last vision of him is when, as a brother and colleague, he leaned upon my arm at the door of this church in a funeral rite well remembered by many of you, and by some of you never to be forgotten while life lasts. The last time I wrote to him some months ago, I remember saying that his length of days was a pledge of the love of God. Such is but the beginning and close of a friendship that can have no end.

"If any proof were needed of the immeasurable work that he

has wrought in England, the last week would be enough. Who could doubt that a great multitude of his personal friends in the first half of his life, and a still greater multitude of those who have been instructed, consoled and won to God by the unequalled beauty and irresistible persuasion of his writings—who could doubt that they at such a time as this, would pour out the love and gratitude of their hearts? But that the public voice of England, political and religious, in all its diversities, should for once unite in love and veneration of a man who had broken through its sacred barriers and defied its religious prejudices, who could have believed it? He had committed the hitherto unpardonable sin in England. He had rejected the whole Tudor Settlement in religion. He had become Catholic as our fathers were. And yet for no one in our memory has such a heartfelt and loving veneration been poured out. Of this, one proof is enough. Someone has said, whether Rome canonizes him or not, he will be canonized in the thoughts of pious people of many creeds in England. Nevertheless, it must be said that, towards a man who had done so much to estrange it, the will of the English people was changed, and old malevolence had passed into good will. If this is a noble testimony of a great Christian life, it is a noble proof of the justice, equity and uprightness of the English people. In venerating John Henry Newman, it has unconsciously honored itself.

"It is too soon to measure the work that has been silently wrought by the life of Cardinal Newman. No living man has so changed the religious thought of England. His withdrawal closes a chapter which stands alone in the religious life of this century. It has for the most part been wrought in silence, for the retiring habits of the man and the growing weight of age made his later utterances few. Nevertheless, his words of old were as 'the hammer that breaks the rocks in pieces and as the light which works with a sound.' It has been boldly and truly avowed that he is the founder, as we may almost say, of the Church of England as we see it. What the Church of England would have become without the Tractarian movement, we can faintly guess; and of the Tractarian movement Newman was the living soul and the inspiring genius. The sentence will be implacably resented and fiercely attacked, but it is true as the light of day. This intellectual movement was begun and sustained by one man. But for this movement Erastianism and Nationalism would by this time have reigned supreme in the national religion. The penetrating influence of this one mind has pervaded also the bodies separated from the Established Church and most opposed to it. They have been powerfully attracted, not to the Tudor Settlement, but to the Primitive Christianity. And the same sweet voice and luminous words have been working among them, all the more persuasively because he had rejected all things of this world even more than themselves. He spoke to them as a simple voice of truth, which could neither be warped by prejudice, nor bribed by silence.

"In 1861 the following words were published in a letter to Father Newman, as he then was:—'You have been a master-builder in this work, and I a witness of its growth. You remained long at Oxford, still,—with all its disfigurement—so dear to both of us, but I was removed to a distance, and had to work alone. Nevertheless, to you I owe a debt of gratitude for intellectual help and light, greater than to anyone of our time; and it gives me a sincere gratification now publicly to acknowledge, though I can in no way repay it.' I little thought in 1861 that I should have the consolation of repeating these words, as it were, over his grave. I have no heart at such a time as this to go into details. It is for others, who will hereafter give their mind to record the history of this great life and all that it has done.

"But we cannot forget that we owe to him, among other things, one singular achievement. No one who does not intend to be laughed at will henceforward say that the Catholic religion is fit only for weak intellects and unmanly brains. This superstition of pride is over. St. Thomas Aquinas is too far off and too little known to such talkers to make them hesitate. But the author of the *Grammar of Assent* may make them think twice before they so expose themselves. Again, the designer and editor of the *Library of the Fathers* has planted himself on the undivided Church of the first six centuries and he holds the field; the key of the position is lost. Moreover, his hymns are in the hearts of Englishmen, and they have a transforming power. He has taught us that beauty and truth are inseparable, that beauty resides essentially in the thought, so that nothing can make that to be beautiful which is not so in the plainest words that will convey the meaning. The English people have read these thoughts through his transparent words, and have seen the beauty of eternal truth as it is set forth in his mind.

"Thus far I have spoken of his work upon the world without; what can I, or what need I say, of his work inwardly upon the Church? You all know it, and have felt it. His writings are in your hands. But beyond the power of all books has been the example of his humble and unworldly life—always the same, in union with God, and in manifold charity to all who sought him. He was the center of innumerable souls, drawn to him as teacher, guide and comforter, through long years, and especially in the more than forty years of his Catholic life. To them he was a spring of light and strength from a supernatural source. A noble and beautiful life is the most convincing and persuasive of all preaching, and we all have felt its power. Our Holy Father, Leo XIII, knew the merits and gifts, both natural and supernatural, which were hidden in his humility; and to the joy of all he called him to the highest dignity next to his own.

"The history of our land will hereafter record the name of John Henry Newman among the greatest of her people, as a confessor for the Faith, a great teacher of men, a preacher of justice, of piety and of compassion. May we all follow him in his life, and may our end be painless and peaceful like his."

BIBLIOGRAPHY

I

NOTE: The best sources for the life of Cardinal Newman and his teachings are, of course, his own writings. All but a few of minor importance have been read and made use of in the preparation of this volume. These are listed below, in chronological order.

Arians of the Fourth Century. The first formal historical work, written in 1831 and 1832; first published in 1833.

Tracts for the Times. Newman was the sole author of Nos. 1, 2, 6, 7, 8, 10, 11, 15, 19, 20, 21, 31, 33, 34, 38, 41, 45, 47, 71, 73, 74, 75, 79, 82, 83, 85, 88 and 90; he edited or partly wrote many others.

Lyra Apostolica. A volume of verses issued in 1836. Some of those written by Newman were republished in 1868 in his *Verses on Various Occasions.*

Church of the Fathers. Essays first appearing in the *British Magazine.* Issued in book form in 1840.

Via Media of the Anglican Church. 2 volumes. Lectures delivered between 1830 and 1841 on the Prophetical Office of the Church viewed relatively to Romanism and Popular Protestantism. Reissued with annotations and an Introduction under this title in 1877.

Parochial and Plain Sermons. Delivered at Oxford and Littlemore from 1826 to 1843. Complete in 8 volumes.

Lectures on Justification. Delivered at Oxford on various occasions and published as a whole in 1838.

Sermons on Subjects of the Day. Delivered at Oxford and Littlemore between 1835 and 1843. One volume.

Oxford University Discourses. Delivered at Oxford, mainly in St. Mary's church from 1836 to 1843. One volume.

Essays on Miracles. One first written in 1827; the others near 1843; revised and reissued in one volume after 1843.

Essay on Development of Christian Doctrine. First published in 1846; revised and republished with corrections in 1878.

Loss and Gain; The Story of a Convert. First published in 1848; reissued many times in later years. Latest edition, 1935.

Discourses to Mixed Congregations. A series of lectures delivered in Birmingham in 1848. One volume.

Certain Difficulties Felt by Anglicans in Catholic Teaching. A series of lectures delivered before Anglican audiences in London in 1850.

Present Position of Catholics in England. A series of lectures delivered at the Corn Exchange in Birmingham in 1851. One volume.

Second Spring. Sermon delivered in 1852 before the First Provincial Synod at Oscott.

Idea of a University: Defined and Illustrated. Nine lectures delivered before the Catholics of Dublin; with additional discourses and essays written at the Catholic University in Dublin. 1852–1858.

Callista: A Tale of the Third Century. First published anonymously in 1856; later editions issued under Newman's name.

Sermons Preached on Various Occasions. A series of sermons delivered between 1850 and 1857. One volume.

Apologia pro Vita Sua. First edition, complete with controversial chapters, published in 1864; later revised editions 1865 and later.

An Essay in Aid of a Grammar of Assent. First edition published in 1870; revised editions in 1875 and later.

Also: *Letter to E. B. Pusey on His Eirenicon; Letter to the Duke of Norfolk; The Dream of Gerontius; Verses on Various Occasions; Select Treatises of St. Athanasius; Meditations and Devotions;* and several volumes of *Essays, Critical and Historical.*

BIBLIOGRAPHY
II

NOTE: The following books about Newman, about his religious background, about his contemporaries and about the times in which he lived, have all been read, studied or otherwise used as sources in the preparation of this volume. List arranged alphabetically *according to title,* ignoring "A" or "The" at the beginning of any title.

Analogy of Religion, Natural and Revealed, to the Constitution and Course of Nature. By Joseph Butler, Bishop of Durham. First issued in 1733. Had a profound effect on Newman's thought.

(The) Anglican Career of Cardinal Newman. By E. A. Abbot. London: 1892. A very unsympathetic life; written by a Protestant.

(The) Anglican Revival. By Yngve Brilioth. London: 1933. A modern interpretation of the Oxford movement.

Anglicanism in Transition. By Humphrey Johnson, priest of the Birmingham Oratory. An outline analysis of Anglicanism by a convert from that communion. New York: Longmans, Green & Co., 1938.

Archbishop Laud. A life of this famous Caroline divine. By A. S. Duncan Jones. This, with *Archbishop Laud and Priestly Government,* by E. Bell, is the best modern work on Laud and his teachings.

Autobiography of John Stuart Mill. Written shortly before his death in 1875. Contains an interesting explanation of his non-religious and secular beliefs.

Book of Common Prayer (including the Thirty-Nine Articles of Religion). Modern editions of the Church of England and of the Protestant Episcopal Church in the United States. Also an English edition of the 1840's, and one of the Elizabethan period.

Cardinal Manning. By Arthur Wollaston Hutton. Excellent short life by a Protestant; very sympathetic. London: Methuen & Co., 1894.

Cardinal Newman. By Richard Holt Hutton. Best written by any Protestant on Newman's Anglican years. Boston: Houghton, Mifflin & Co., 1890.

Cardinal Newman. By J. Lewis May. An excellent study of his life and achievements, particularly emphasizing his intellectual qualities. New York: Longmans, Green & Co., 1937. (First edition by Dial Press, 1927).

Cardinal Newman. By Wilfrid Meynell. A deeply sympathetic book, marked by the spiritual outlook of its author. London: 1907.

Cardinal Newman. By Bertram Newman. A biographical and literary study by a non-Catholic, treating Newman primarily as a man of letters. London: 1925.

Cardinal Newman: A Study. By Canon William Barry. A brilliant study of Cardinal Newman and his teachings, with a brief narrative of his activities. New York: Charles Scribner's Sons, 1904.

Cardinal Newman and His Influence on Religious Life and Thought. By Charles Sarolea. Interesting but superficial. London: 1908.

Cardinal Newman: His Place in Religion and Literature. By F. A. D'Cruz. Madras, India. A complete biography by an ardent admirer.

Cardinal Wiseman. By Denis Gwynn. Excellent short life of this great prelate. New York: P. J. Kenedy & Sons, 1930.

Catholic Encyclopaedia. Fifteen volumes and supplement. A mine of information on all Catholic subjects, ancient, medieval and modern. New York: The Gilmary Society.

The Catholic Pattern: By Thomas F. Woodlock. Contains a very valuable diagnosis of modern materialism. New York: Simon & Schuster, Inc., 1942.

(The) Catholic Question: 1688–1828. A Study in Political History. By Philip Hughes. Best brief account of events which affected English Catholics in the eighteenth century and which led to the Emancipation Act of 1829. New York: Benziger Brothers, 1929.

Catholicism in England: 1535–1935. By David Mathew. An outline history of Catholic culture in England during the four centuries covered. Sources used very reliable. London: Longmans, Green & Co., 1936.

(The) Church and the Liberal Society. By Emmet John Hughes. A scholarly review of the rise of Liberalism, from the sixteenth to the twentieth century, and its condemnation by the Catholic Church. Fully documented. Princeton, N. J.: Princeton University Press, 1944.

(The) Church of England. By Right Reverend Arthur Headlam, Bishop of Gloucester. A concise description of the Anglican Church by this well known Broad Church prelate. London: John Murray, 1925.

Contributions Chiefly to the Early History of the Late Cardinal Newman. By F. W. Newman. An attack on the Cardinal by his brother, after the Cardinal's death. London: 1891.

(The) Convert: Leaves from My Experience. By Orestes Brownson. Autobiography of this famous convert; written in 1857; does not cover writer's later years.

Doctrine and Doctrinal Disruption: Being an Examination of the Intellectual Position of the Church of England. By W. H. Mallock. Brilliant study of Anglican disruption. London: Adam & Charles Beck, 1900.

Dominic Barberi in England. Edited by Urban Young, O.P. London: Burns, Oates & Washbourne, Ltd., 1930.

(The) English Catholic Revival of the Nineteenth Century. By Thureau-Dangin, translated by W. Wilberforce. Well documented. London: 1915.

Great Encyclicals of Pope Leo XIII. With Preface by John J. Wynne, S.J. Thirty Encyclicals, including those on Anglican Orders, Christian Marriage, Condition of the Working Classes, Unity of the Church, Human Liberty, and so on. New York: Benziger Brothers, 1933.

Henry Edward Manning: His Life and Labours. By Shane Leslie. The most accurate and fair life of Cardinal Manning. In one volume; well documented. London: Burns, Oates & Washbourne, Ltd., 1921.

History of England in the Eighteenth Century. By W. E. H. Lecky. Best history of the period. In ten volumes, including a history of Ireland. Well documented.

History of Our Own Times. By Justin McCarthy. Covers entire period of Newman's life from 1837 (the accession of Queen Victoria).

History of the Protestant Reformation in England and Ireland. By William Cobbett. Written a century ago, it is still widely read. Though the author was a Protestant, he defends the Catholics. New edition. New York: Benziger Bros., 1930.

Historical Evolution of Modern Nationalism. By Carlton J. H. Hayes. Very valuable are the chapters on the rise of materialism. New York: Richard R. Smith, Inc., 1931.

Jeremy Bentham. By Graham Wallis. Latest and best biography of the founder of Utilitarianism. London: 1922.

John Henry Newman. By Rev. J. Elliot Ross. A short life of the Cardinal, but the Anglican years lack a full description. New York: Norton & Co., 1933.

John Henry Newman. By Newport J. D. White. Newman treated from the Anglican standpoint. London: Society for Promoting Christian Knowledge, 1925.

John Wesley and the Evolution of Protestantism. By Maximin Piette, S.T.D. Very valuable for a review of the sixteenth to eighteenth century. Fully documented. New York: Sheed & Ward, Inc., 1937.

Laws of Ecclesiastical Polity. By Richard Hooker. First issued in 1594. Modern edition edited by John Keble. (See text for brief comment on this famous work.)

Lay Sermons, Addresses and Reviews. By Thomas Henry Huxley. Best brief summary of Huxley's agnostic philosophy. New York: D. Appleton & Co., 1903.

Letters and Correspondence of John Henry Newman to 1845. Edited by Anne Mozley. A most valuable source for Newman's Anglican years. Two volumes. New York: Longmans, Green & Co., 1905.

Life and Times of Archbishop Ullathorne. By Dom Cuthbert Butler. The complete life of this great prelate. London: Burns, Oates & Washbourne, 1933.

Life and Times of Cardinal Wiseman. By Wilfrid Ward. Two volumes. The complete definitive life of the great Cardinal, with a vivid picture of his times. London: Longmans, Green & Co., 1897.

Life of Cardinal Manning. By E. S. Purcell. Complete but notably biased regarding certain events of Manning's career. Two volumes. London: Macmillan Co., 1905.

Life of Cardinal Newman. By Gaius Glenn Atkins. A readable short life, but superficial. New York: Harper & Brother, 1931.

Life of John Henry Cardinal Newman. By Wilfrid Ward. Two volumes. The definitive life of Newman; very exhaustive. Invaluable as a "source" book. New York: Longmans, Green & Co., 1912.

Life of William Ewart Gladstone. By John Morley. The definitive life of this famous statesman. London: 1905.

Literature and Dogma. By Matthew Arnold. Excellent statement of his secular views regarding religion. London: Macmillan Co., 1914.

Macaulay's Essays and Reviews. By T. B. Macaulay. Includes all his reviews and essays written between 1828 to 1850 for the *Edinburgh Review.*

(The) Mystery of Newman. By Henry Bremond. Interesting but far from convincing in some of his judgments. Paris: 1907.

(A) New History of the Book of Common Prayer, with a Rationale of its Offices. Revision of an earlier edition by Francis Proctor. By Walter Howard Frere, priest of the (Anglican) Community of the Resurrection. Very complete and well documented; but doctrines injurious to the High Church view are glossed over. London: Macmillan Co., 1923.

Newman. By Sidney Dark. A readable treatment of Newman from the Anglican standpoint. London: Great Life Series, 1904.

Newman as a Man of Letters. By Joseph J. Reilly. A splendid work of its kind; nothing to equal it has been done. New York: Macmillan Co., 1925.

Newman on the Psychology of Faith in the Individual. By Sylvester P. Juergens, S.M. A psychological study; useful, but difficult reading. New York: Macmillan Co., 1928.

(A) Newman Synthesis. Arranged by Erich Przywara, S.J. Best modern anthology of Newman's spiritual and theological writings. New York: Sheed & Ward, Inc., 1931 (reprinted 1945).

(A) Newman Treasury. Selections from the prose works of John Henry Newman. By Charles Frederick Harrold. An anthology confined largely to Newman's general rather than theological writings. New York: Longmans, Green & Co., 1942.

Newman's Apologia pro Vita Sua. The two versions of 1864 and 1865, with the Kingsley and Newman pamphlets which were left out of later editions. With an Introduction by Wilfrid Ward. New York: Oxford University Press, 1913.

Non-Catholic Denominations. By Robert Hugh Benson. A valuable analysis of Anglicanism and the Nonconformist bodies. London: Longmans, Green & Co., 1910.

Orestes Brownson: A Pilgrim's Progress. By Arthur M. Schlesinger, Jr. An excellent biography, but author lacks understanding of Catholicism. Boston: Little, Brown & Co., 1939.

Orestes Brownson: Yankee, Radical, Catholic. By Theodore Maynard. Best complete life of this famous American. New York: Macmillan Co., 1944.

(The) Oxford Movement—1833–1845. By R. W. Church, Dean of St. Paul's Cathedral and Fellow of Oriel College, Oxford. Best brief but accurate history of the movement, with brilliant appraisals of its leaders. London: Macmillan Co., 1892.

(The) Oxford Movement. By W. J. Hutchison. An Anglican version; not very exhaustive. London: Scott Library Series, 1933.

(A) Pedigree of Protestantism. By Rt. Rev. Edward Hawks. Sketches of the Protestant sects which grew out of the Reformation of the sixteenth century. By a notable convert from Anglicanism. Fully documented. Philadelphia: Peter Reilly Co., 1936.

(*A*) *Preface to Newman's Theology.* By Edmond Darvil Benard. A new analysis of Cardinal Newman's theological contributions and methods of reasoning. Very valuable. St. Louis: B. Herder Book Co., 1945.

Rationalism in Europe. By W. E. H. Lecky. Attack on superstitions and defence of scepticism of recent centuries. Also same author's *History of European Morals.* Both display superficial knowledge of Catholic Christianity. New York: D. Appleton & Co., 1903.

Religion and the Rise of Capitalism; a Historical Study. By R. H. Tawney. A standard work, fully documented. New York: Harcourt, Brace & Co., 1926.

Remains: Diary of Richard Hurrell Froude. Issued after his death in 1836 by his friends. Invaluable for study of the earlier years of the Oxford movement.

(*The*) *Rise of Liberalism;* The Philosophy of a Business Civilization. By Harold J. Laski. Very readable though uneven; strongly biased in favor of Communistic philosophy. Poorly documented. New York: Harper & Brothers, 1936.

Saint Philip Neri and the Roman Society of His Times. A good popular history of this saint and his times. By Louis Ponnelle and Louis Bordet; translated from the French by Ralph Francis Kerr of the London Oratory. London: Sheed & Ward, 1932.

Second Spring—1818–1852. By Denis Gwynn. A study of the Catholic revival in England; emphasizes the influence of the Cambridge converts from Anglicanism. London: Burns, Oates & Washbourne, Ltd., 1942.

(*The*) *Spirit of the Oxford Movement.* By Christopher Dawson. An excellent study by the well known Catholic historian, now editor of the *Dublin Review.* New York: Sheed & Ward, Inc., 1932.

(*The*) *Spiritual Legacy of Newman.* By William R. Lamm, S.M. A masterly exposition of Newman's spiritual contribution to the world. Milwaukee: Bruce Publishing Co., 1934.

(*The*) *Tractarian Movement.* By E. A. Knox. A short history of the Oxford Movement treated from the Anglican standpoint. Not equal to that written by Dean Church in 1890. London: 1933.

Turning Points in English Church History. By Rev. Edward L. Cutts. Defends the Tudor Settlement of Religion in all respects for its Protestant characteristics. Very anti-Catholic. No documentation.

William George Ward and the Catholic Revival. By Wilfrid Ward. A vivid picture of the English Catholic world during the pontificate of Pius IX. Very valuable for sources. Well documented. London: Macmillan Co., Ltd., 1893.

William George Ward and the Oxford Movement. By Wilfrid Ward. Covers the Anglican life of this eminent English Catholic convert and includes an excellent history of the Oxford awakening. Well documented. London: Macmillan Co., Ltd., 1889.

NOTE: Various shorter works on Newman and his contemporaries, including monographs and magazine articles and writings of many Anglicans during and after the period of the Tractarian movement, have been read or consulted; also Anglican reference books, Year Books and documents. In addition, the following works have been frequently made use of: *Correspondence of John Henry Newman with John Keble and Others,* edited by the Birmingham Oratory; *Reminiscences, Chiefly of Oriel College and the Oxford Movement,* by Thomas Mozley; and Father Neville's and Father Ryder's *Reminiscences,* as gathered from various sources.

INDEX